Our Idea of God

A THEOLOGY FOR ARTISANS OF A NEW HUMANITY

Volumes 1, 2, 4, & 5

The Community Called Church

Grace and the Human Condition

The Sacraments Today

Evolution and Guilt

ORBIS BOOKS

VOLUME THREE

Our Idea of God

BY JUAN LUIS SEGUNDO, S.J., IN COLLABORATION
WITH THE STAFF OF THE PETER FABER CENTER
IN MONTEVIDEO, URUGUAY
TRANSLATED BY JOHN DRURY

MARYKNOLL, NEW YORK

Abbreviations Used in This Volume

AA *Apostolicam actuositatem*. Vatican II. Decree on the Apostolate of the Laity. November 18, 1965.

Denz. Denzinger-Schönmetzer, *Enchiridion Symbolorum*. Fribourg: Herder, 1963.

GS *Gaudium et spes*. Vatican II. Pastoral Constitution on the Church in the Modern World. December 7, 1965.

LG *Lumen gentium*. Vatican II. Dogmatic Constitution on the Church. November 21, 1964.

PG *Patrologiae cursus . . . Series graeca*. Paris: Migne, 1857–1866.

PL *Patrologiae cursus . . . Series latina*. Paris: Migne, 1844–1864.

PO *Presbyterorum ordinis*. Decree on the Ministry and Life of Priests. December 7, 1965.

SC *Sacrosanctum Concilium*. Vatican II. Constitution on the Sacred Liturgy. December 4, 1963.

Biblical citations are taken from The New English Bible, with the Apocrypha (New York and London: Oxford University Press and Cambridge University Press, 1970).

Citations of conciliar documents, unless otherwise indicated, are taken from Walter M. Abbot, S.J. (ed), *The Documents of Vatican II* (New York: Guild-America-Association, 1966).

Wherever possible, other church and papal documents are cited on the basis of translations in *The Pope Speaks* Magazine (Washington, D.C.).

ORIGINALLY PUBLISHED BY EDICIONES CARLOS LOHLÉ, BUENOS AIRES © 1970

COPYRIGHT © 1974, ORBIS BOOKS, MARYKNOLL, NEW YORK 10545

LIBRARY OF CONGRESS CATALOG CARD NUMBER: 73–77358

ISBN SERIES 088344–480–1 VOLUME 088344–483–6
PAPER: SERIES 088344–486–0 VOLUME 088344–488–7

MANUFACTURED IN THE UNITED STATES OF AMERICA

VOLUME THREE

Contents

Our Idea of God

INTRODUCTION

Does God Interest Us?

What is God? How is God what he is? How does he operate? Here we have some important questions that a Christian cannot choose to sidestep. But do these questions interest anyone? Do they interest other people, or even the Christian himself? Are they really important questions to him?

It is not easy for us to answer these questions. Our religious reality is complex.

Section I

On the one hand there is no denying that certain facts point toward the importance we accord to the problem of God. For example, it has been a long and continuing tradition for Christians, when asked what is the most sublime and profound mystery of Christianity, to reply that it is the mystery of the Trinity: the one and triune God. After all, does not what God has said about himself constitute the center of divine revelation? Is it not the incomparable happening which goes on in the most sublime and perfect of realities?

Another reason, even more closely bound up with our conception of the religious sphere, points unconsciously in the same direction. We have identified the "supernatural" with what is difficult. Without even noticing it, we pass from one concept to the other—or from concept to image. Now is it quite clear that from one point of view a gift—particularly that which is essentially a gratuitous gift—is supremely difficult and, if you will, impossible. It is impossible in terms of our own capabilities, unattainably beyond our pretentions and our exigencies. But from there we take an illegitimate step. We move on to the idea—or better, the image—of something that remains "grand" for us even after it has been given as a gift, of something not cut to our human measure.

Insofar as it is a message, we picture it as a message about realities that do not belong to this world. And we feel that we will get lost among these realities if we do not resolve to learn them by rote—so grave and incomprehensible is their content.

So is it not logical, then, that the mystery of the one and triune God appears to be the core and quintessence of the supernatural, and hence of the Christian religion? If it is the most difficult thing, would it not also be the most divine, the most important, the most decisive thing?

On the other hand we run into other facts, equally convincing, that point in a different direction. They suggest that our statements above, however logical and typical they may be, conflict with a fact of life that is even more decisive: i.e., that among Christians we find a real lack of interest in the problem of God. Comparatively speaking, they are far less interested in this topic than they are in other themes of divine revelation. It is, as it were, the opposite side of the same argument used above. We are cut of such cloth that the thing which is objectively the most important, central, and decisive fails to interest us.

Let us consider a hypothetical case. Suppose someone came and told us that Vatican II had decided to replace the traditional formula, "three distinct persons in one God," with a new formula, "three Gods in one single person." Now we must admit that the vast majority of us would take careful note of the change, perhaps be intrigued or irritated by it, and then go on living our Christian life as if nothing really important had happened. Yet we have been used to saying that this is the quintessence of the Christian message!

We really cannot understand how John Q. Public, the man in the street, could have gotten so excited about Trinitarian controversies in the early centuries of church history. Why did Christians in those days talk so much about theories concerning the inner life of the deity? How could men like Theodotus the banker and Theodotus the tanner form dissident groups and enlist rabid followers over such abstruse matters?

Today the situation is quite different. Sociologically speaking, we find that interest in such questions is confined to small groups of specialists and "snobs." To be sure, we realize that the question of God's existence, and the consequences of one's answer to this question, touch upon a wide range of human problems and even affect the political realm. But once this question has been answered with a yes or a no, the rest seems to be a bit useless as far as we can see.

Why? Above all because it seems to us that there is no longer any possibility of making a *radical* mistake about God, once his existence is accepted. The question of God and our relation of dependence upon him might have been an important problem in situations where polytheism and idolatry were generalized phenomena. Identifying the *true* God was a critical and decisive issue in those days. Directing one's gaze to the truly existing and beneficent deity, rather than going off in the wrong direction and invoking an empty power, could become a matter of life and death.

But in our modern Western world today that problem seems to be basically resolved. The person who addresses God is sure—perhaps too sure—that his adoration and petition and religious worship reaches its destination. There is only one God, after all, so the message cannot be delivered to the wrong address. He, God, is the only possible addressee; so everything seems to be settled in our minds.

As a result we have ceased to concern ourselves with the task of identifying God, of knowing what he is like and how he operates. Such questions take a back seat in our preoccupations and become a matter of theoretical orthodoxy. We are irritated by the seeming uselessness of any theology that recalls the age-old controversies over the Trinity. One Latin American priest, deeply involved in the war on poverty, put it more humorously than correctly when he said: "Some day I would like to meet an Arian. I'd belt him for all the time he made the Church waste."

Section II

So we must admit that the *de facto* situation, with respect to our interest in the problem of God, is a complicated one. Credal profession and concrete reality do not seem to mesh fully at all. Were we right, then, in proclaiming that this problem is central? And if so, do we do wrong to disregard it in practice?

1. Paradoxical as it may seem, there is something positive and healthy in what we do in practice.

Take the New Testament, for example. The Word came from the inner sanctum of God to tell us about that reality (John 1:18). But what does he talk to us about? The vast majority of his statements deal with us human beings, our lives, and how to transform them. A second set of references, far less in number, deal with God; but even these passages show him operating in our lives and transforming our history. The passages which allow theologians to discourse on what God is *in himself*, independent of our life and history, can be counted on one's fingers; and it is even doubtful whether they can be separated from a context wherein God consistently reveals himself in dialogue with human existence. Would this not be odd if the center and quintessence of the Christian message were precisely the mystery of the Trinity?

Would it be too much to say that, in line with the facts, the center of divine revelation concerns man; and that God appears and shows himself on the human horizon in the process of transforming man's existence from within? Is this not the *gospel,* that is, the good news—the only news that can be truly good for us because it concerns us totally?

It might we worth pointing out here that the two New Testament texts which give promise of more directly revealing a properly divine mystery—and this amid the atmosphere of mystery religions that was pervasive in those days—do not leave the realm of the human. In fact they do not even penetrate the sphere which we would call "religious" or "sacred" within the human realm. The two texts are: "I give you a new commandment: love one another; as I have loved you, so you are to love one another" (John 13:34). And: "The kind of religion which is without stain or fault in the sight of God our Father is this: to go to the help of orphans and widows in their distress and keep oneself untarnished by the world" (James 1:27).

There is certainly no doubt that the central object of Jesus' message refers to our existence. Does this mean that he did not seek to tell us anything about what God was in himself, apart from us? Must we not admit that he *also* told us something—not much, but something—about that? Perhaps just so we would not be totally ignorant about it.

Here, as in every area of theology, we find a type of superficial solution posed. When faced with a new presentation of a problem, this superficial approach admits its validity; but it also stresses that there is the "other side" as well, that it is a matter of keeping things in proportion and not exaggerating one side. But the fact is that it is not a question of proper proportion or stress at all; it is a question of the one and only way of focusing on the totality, of gaining access to it.

The superficial approach would cause us to lose the most essential point: i.e., that if Jesus' whole message speaks to us of our existence and its transformation, it must be because through it, and only through it, we know what God is *in himself.* Even a theologian like Scheeben, who discoursed on the Trinity in very explicit and speculative terms, was nonetheless able to recognize that it is not a matter of proper balance but of the one and only access-road to true knowledge: "There is a great significance in the fact that by their common activity and mode of action the divine persons externally prolong and continue, or imitate and reproduce, their internal relations, and thereby call into being an order of things *which is an objective unfolding and revelation of the inner heart of this mystery*" (our italics).[1]

Hence we can appreciate the profound truth of the medieval statement: "Insofar as the idea of God is concerned, one's manner of living is more important than one's mode of expressing it."[2] This statement could serve as the *leitmotif* of our reflections in this volume. Saint Augustine explains why when he is discussing the Trinity. In a passage which readers of the first two volumes will find even more suggestive, he says:

> Are you contemplating what or how God will be? Everything you imagine, he is not. Everything you put together in thought, he is not. But if you wish to savor something of him, then know that God is love, the very same love with which we love . . . Let no one tell you: I do not know what it is that I am loving. Such a one need only love his fellow men, and he will love this very love itself. Because in reality one knows better the love with which he loves his brethren than the brother himself. In loving he already possesses God as known better than he does his brother man. Much better in fact, because he is nearer, more present, more certain.[3]

Hence there is no deviation involved in the fact that our Christianity seems to be centered in a love-filled dialogue with the world. For in it God is nearer, more present, and more certain than our interlocutor is.

2. But there is also something that prevents us from neglecting the problem of God, that turns any such neglect into a danger both for ourselves and others.

Above all there is the fact that our love is not perfect—not by a long shot. Commenting on Augustine's well-known phrase ("Love and do what you will"), De Lubac points out that this is true, "if you love well enough to act in accordance with your love in everything you do . . . if you know how to draw from your love, whose source is not in you, all the light that is buried within it. But do not be too quick to presume that you know what loving really is."[4]

Our love can go off the track and turn counterfeit. That is why our idea of God, more than any other idea, is a magnet for hypocrisy and deception. Worst of all, "man is afraid of God. He is afraid of getting burned by close contact, even as the ancient Israelites were afraid to touch the Ark. So man invents countless subtle ways of denying him . . . forgetting him . . . or deadening the shock. . . . All of us—nonbelievers, indifferent people, believers—compete with one another in devising ingenious ways to protect ourselves from God."[5]

Why? Because by deforming God we protect our own egotism. Our falsified and inauthentic ways of dealing with our fellow men are allied to our falsifications of the idea of God. Our unjust society and our perverted idea of God are in close and terrible alliance.

Section III

Voltaire remarked that if God had created man in his image and likeness, man had paid him back by fabricating a god of his own making.

We could say that so long as man's life on this planet did not go beyond small, interpersonal groups divided by almost insurmountable physical and cultural distances, his created handiwork, responsible in part for his notion of God, was composed of his interpersonal relationships. But as man's whole existence came to be made up of broader and more complex social relationships, the features of our *society* started to show up more and more clearly in our notion of God.

And here we run into the paradox. The society which most profoundly and decisively structures human cohabitation on this planet is indubitably that which we today call "Western society." And since it does in fact coincide with the area through which the Christian message is spread, we can say that our God is fashioned partly in the image and likeness of the social reality to which we apply two adjectives: Western and Christian.

Why do we say *partly*? Because we feel that, above and beyond any materialistic perspectives, one must acknowledge that the God of conscience is not the mere reflection of social structures and their justification.[6] Through his revelation, God unveils his countenance to us; and this countenance, which it is impossible to recognize in existing civilization, is a summons that has never ceased to ring out in our society in the most unexpected forms.

Without going to that materialist extreme, all psychologists recognize the influence of religion in the formation of what Freud called the *superego:* that is, in the adaptation of every new human creature, begun by the father, to the exigencies of real society. Now from there Herbert Marcuse, dealing specifically with the case of Christianity, formulates the following hypothesis that he regards as almost blasphemous:

> If we follow this train of thought beyond Freud, and connect it with the twofold origin of the sense of guilt, the life and death of Christ would appear as a struggle against the father—and as a triumph over the father. The message of the Son was the message of liberation: the overthrow of the Law (which is domination) by Agape (which is Eros). This would fit in with the heretical image of Jesus as the Redeemer in the flesh, the Messiah who came to save man here on earth. Then the subsequent transubstantiation

of the Messiah, the deification of the Son beside the Father, would be a betrayal of his message by his own disciples—the denial of the liberation in the flesh, the revenge on the redeemer. *Christianity would then have surrendered the gospel of Agape-Eros again to the Law.* (our italics).[7]

If we simply make a distinction, a fairly obvious one, between a mature and a puerile attitude toward the father (with a capital F or a small f), then these words of Marcuse[8] would be an almost literal echo of Saint Paul's words. Moreover, they would also take on even greater sociological and historical import: it was not betrayal by the disciples but progressive adaptation to the exigencies arising from the domination of occidental civilization that accounted for the fact that the God of the West was not the Christian God to a large extent; that the accurate embodiment of this God, even on the abstract level, continually floated outside the world in which we did and would fashion our most concrete, decisive, and motivating images. And as Marcuse points out: "This interpretation would lend added significance to Freud's statement that the Christian peoples are 'badly christened,' that 'under the thin veneer of Christianity they have remained what their ancestors were, barbarically polytheistic.' They are 'badly christened' insofar as they accept and obey the liberating gospel only in a highly sublimated form—which leaves the reality unfree as it was before."[9]

Vatican II did not regard as absurd the hypothesis that we Christians, in the most consistent reality of our lives, are relating to a God who is not the Christian God:

> Yet believers themselves frequently bear some responsibility for this situation. For, taken as a whole, atheism is not a spontaneous development but stems from a variety of causes, including a critical reaction against religious beliefs, and in some places against the Christian religion in particular. Hence believers can have more than a little to do with the birth of atheism. To the extent that they neglect their own training in the faith, or teach erroneous doctrine, or are deficient in their religious, moral, or social life, they must be said to conceal rather than reveal the authentic face of God and religion (GS 19).

Finally, we have been too quick to exclude the problem of idolatry in our society. Merely pronouncing a word will not put us in contact with the reality. Merely repeating it to the point of exhaustion in church or at church ceremonies will not suffice (*cf.* Matt. 7:21): "If I lack love or justice, then I inevitably move away from you, God, and my worship is nothing more than idolatry. To believe in you, I must believe in love and in justice; and believing in these things is a thousand times better than pronouncing your name."[10] Because they are his true name.

There is an intimate relationship between the changing fortunes of our love and our egotism on the one hand—these fortunes now being more social than ever before—and the idea we fashion of God as well as the real possibility of making contact with him on the other. For this reason we cannot cease to reflect on this theme, which is so essential to our lives. We cannot spare ourselves the continual and salutary interaction between our idea of God and real-life dialogue with human beings.

NOTES TO INTRODUCTION

1. Matthias Scheeben, *The Mysteries of Christianity,* Engl. trans. (St. Louis: B. Herder, 1961), p. 136.

2. William of Saint Thierry, *Aenigma fidei,* PL 180, 398 c.

3. St. Augustine, *De Trinitate,* PL 42, 957–958.

4. Henri de Lubac, *Por los caminos de Dios,* Spanish trans. (Buenos Aires: Carlos Lohlé, 1962), p. 129. The original is a French work, *Sur les chemins de Dieu* (Paris: Aubier, 1960). There is also an edited English translation of it, *The Discovery of God* (New York: P. J. Kenedy, 1960). An Opening Note in the English version offers this advice to the reader: "The reader who wishes to pursue any particular point might refer to the original so as to avoid the possibility of misunderstanding." Because the original is not translated in its entirety into English, some passages are missing and others are very difficult to find. For this reason, I have translated the texts as presented in Spanish by the authors of this volume, and cited their references to the Spanish translation (Translator's note).

5. *Ibid.,* pp. 227 and 133. And these words of Calvin: "Whence we may infer that the mind of man is, if I may be allowed the expression, a perpetual factory of idols. . . . The true state of the case is that the mind of man, being full of pride and temerity, dares to conceive of God according to its own standard, and, being sunk in stupidity and immersed in profound ignorance, imagines a vain and ridiculous phantom instead of God" (Jean Calvin, *The Institutes,* I, translated by J. Allen, 1936, Chapter XI, sec. VIII; cited by Langdon Gilkey, "Trends in Protestant Apologetics," *Concilium* 46, New York: Paulist Press, 1969, p. 128, note 3).

6. See Karl Marx: "Man makes religion, religion does not make man. Religion is self-awareness . . . But man is not an abstract being . . . Man is the world of man, the State, Society . . . Religion is nothing else but the unreal sun that circles around man so long as man does not circle around himself. Hence *once the beyond of truth has disappeared,* then the mission of history is to establish the truth of the here and now" (*Contribution to a Critique of Hegel's Philosophy of Right;* citation here based on French version in *Oeuvres Philosophiques,* Paris: Costes, I, 83–84).

Here we have the formulation of our problem in the framework of a materialistic thought that does not seem acceptable to us philosophically or sociologically. Moreover, speaking theologically, we can say that it is not the sun of religion that prevents man from revolving around himself (*cf*. GS 12 and later remarks in this volume). Hence we cannot accept it even when we find the reversal of priorities which Garaudy proposes: "Karl Marx showed us . . . that only the complete realization of communism *by making social relationships transparent*, would make possible the disappearance of the religious conception of the world" (cited by G. Morel, *Problèmes actuels de religion*, Paris: Aubier, 1968, p. 41).

On the other hand, we cannot help but accept this wager of Marxism: "This materialistic theory of religions has the immense advantage of presenting, for the first time in history, an experimental concept of God; and hence of subjecting it to practical verification. *If* the idea of God is the product of objective social and cultural conditions, then the modification of these conditions should modify it; and their suppression should suppress it. Once again it is a matter of dealing with history" (Michel Verret, *Les Marxistes de la religion*, cited by G. Morel, *Problèmes actuels de religion*, p. 75).

7. Herbert Marcuse, *Eros and Civilization* (New York: Vantage Books, 1962), pp. 63–64.

8. Marcuse himself calls his interpretation an "heretical image of Jesus" (*ibid*.).

9. *Ibid*.

10. De Lubac, *op. cit.*, p. 125. See note 4 above.

CLARIFICATIONS

I DOES GOD EXIST? WHAT GOD?

It may seem strange, illogical, and even anachronistic that this volume, which treats of God, does not begin by asking whether God exists and what proofs or certainty we have about this question. Our reflections begin by taking an interest in an antithesis that seems quite out of fashion, the antithesis between faith and idolatry, rather than in the seemingly more topical antithesis between faith and atheism. What is more, we leave consistency and certainty behind right at the start in tackling the faith-idolatry antithesis that we regard as more deep-rooted; for the Christian as well as the professed atheist may stand on either side of this antithesis. We feel, in other words, that human beings are divided more profoundly by the image they fashion of God than by their subsequent decision as to whether something real corresponds to this image or not. In the majority of cases, moreover, the latter decision will depend more on the former image than on specific proofs. Whether the proofs are declared valid or not does not depend so much, in this area, on the verification of their intrinsic merits as on the question whether the person who sets out on this road wants to reach its end or not. And this, once again, depends very much on how man pictures to himself this end that he is working toward in his real-life existence.

That is precisely how John formulates the problem, not as an antiquated issue but as a bedrock problem: "Here lies the test: the light has come into the world, but men preferred darkness to light because their deeds [i.e., in history] were evil" (John 3:19). In order of importance, three things enter the picture here: (1) acting uprightly in history; (2) picturing God in terms of light rather than darkness; and (3) professing whether he exists or not.

At the present time another formulation of the problem of God, which follows a different order and stems mainly from the more developed countries, seems to hold sway. It is the so-called theology of the "death of God." In the course of this volume we shall have occasion to deal with this theology. It began, without the name it now has, with such theologians as Bultmann and Bonhöffer. It was popularized by the works of such theologians as Robinson, Vahanian, Van Buren, and Altizer.

Right now we are concerned only with the point of departure for its formulation of the problem of God. Perhaps the best introduction is the classic parable that is reiterated by Van Buren:

> Once upon a time two explorers came upon a clearing in the jungle. In the clearing were growing many flowers and many weeds. One explorer says, "Some gardener must tend this plot." The other disagrees. "There is no gardener." So they pitch their tents and set a watch. No gardener is ever seen. "But perhaps he is an invisible gardener." So they set up a barbed wire fence. They electrify it. They patrol with bloodhounds. . . . But no shrieks ever suggest that some intruder has received a shock. No movement of the wire ever betrays an invisible climber. The bloodhounds never give cry. Yet still the believer is not convinced. "But there is a gardener, invisible, intangible, insensible to electric shocks, a gardener who has no scent and makes no sound, a gardener who comes secretly to look after the garden which he loves." At last the Sceptic despairs, "But what is left of your original assertion? Just how does what you call an invisible, intangible, eternally elusive gardener differ from an imaginary gardener or even no gardener at all?"[1]

Now if we substitute the word "God" for "gardener" in this parable, and particularly in the final question, then we can see the force of the problematic issue raised by the line of thought which extends from Bultmann and Bonhöffer to Van Buren and Altizer. All the proofs for the existence of God run aground on the crucial question: In what way does a world with this God really differ from a world without God?

The obvious starting point of any reply[2] is a new question that can and should be put to the two explorers: What were they expecting from the assumed gardener? If he did exist, what place would he occupy in the mental system of both? Quite obviously, he would be an indispensable component in the functioning of the total ensemble that went to make up the clearing with its flowers and weeds. It is in this context that the final question of the parable acquires its full import and meaning.

But if, in terms of the universe, the question about God represents him hypothetically as an indispensable component in the functioning of the total complex, are we not right in thinking that the problematic issue of the person who asks this question lacks certain dimensions?

Using the words of Van Buren, let us now try to sum up the effort undertaken by Bonhöffer: "*Wishing not to retreat from this new world,* Bonhöffer began what he called a 'nonreligious interpretation of biblical concepts' " (our italics).[3]

Confronted with this summary of the problem of God, we can say that Bonhöffer's effort is one of two things. Either it does not go beyond the obligation of any and every authentic theology to translate divine revelation so that it becomes an element in the solution of the problems posed by human history[4]; or else it is a contradiction in terms. For suppose that a person, in order not to flee from a world in which it is presumed that human beings ask questions about God only in a specific way, decides right from the start that God's revelation must agree with their response. Does that not presuppose that revelation does not have the duty of judging and changing the human beings who formulate the questions? And what if God, in his message, should specifically denounce this "new world" as one in which human beings formulate questions and seek answers from within a mutilated and alienated existence?

Any question which pinpoints God, and hence the supposedly ultimate reality, in the realm of the functioning of things and systems is a question typical of a world in which productive efficiency has taken on greater importance than questions about finality and ultimate meaning. For the fact is that in terms of a reason for living and exploring, the existence of a gardener in the parable cited above, however invisible and intangible he may be, is worlds apart from his nonexistence.

Now it is certainly no novel idea that industrial civilization, capitalist or not as you prefer,[5] has relegated to the background or the trash-heap questions dealing with the meaning and the *raison d'être* of things, their function, and their increase. Herbert Marcuse notes this expressly: "Thus emerges a pattern of one-dimensional thought and behavior in which ideas, aspirations, and objectives that, by their content, transcend the established universe of discourse and action are either repelled or reduced to terms of this universe. They are redefined by the rationality of the given system and of its quantitative extension."[6]

What is strange is that people uncritically accept this lack of critical perception on the part of man in industrial civilization when it comes to the problem of God,[7] the fact being that a large portion of the message from this very God consisted in denouncing the fundamental human structures that would lead to this mutilation later on.

In other words, the theologians of the "death of God" have perhaps overlooked an essential question: What is this human being seeking and doing, this human being who accepts or denies God? What is the nature of his commitment and activity in his personal and societal existence? This is the question that John begins with. And closer to us in time, it is also the question that has occupied the great thinkers who have applied the attitude of *suspicion* to the theme of man's liberation: Marx, Freud, Nietzsche, etc.[9]

For them the problem of God arises because man seeks to *do* something with God: to conceal his class interests, his immaturity vis-à-vis reality, his fragility and weakness. And the only valid refutation of these thinkers is not so much proving that God exists after all, but rather liberating ourselves from these alienations by leaning on the support of a liberator God.

This is the order we are following. And it is the order pointed out to us by the Medellín Conference.

II. MEDELLÍN AND THE LIVING GOD

The documents of the Medellín Conference have become an obligatory point of reference for Latin American Catholics. They may say more to us today than Vatican II does—not by virtue of their authority of course, but rather by virtue of their clarity, their consistency, and their proximity. Medellín represents the committed involvement of the Church, in God's name, in the "present-day transformation of Latin America."[10]

On the other hand we cannot deny that Medellín shocked people. Not only did it shock those who were making use of the Church. It may well have shocked even more those people within the Church who came to feel irritated and alienated by the themes, the interests, and the vocabulary of its declarations.

Once again we may ask ourselves a question: Is God, in the last analysis, the interest and preoccupation of the Medellín Conference? Or does it rather represent a form of demagogy, a facile surrender to themes that are more current and less abstruse, indeed, but also less transcendent and "eternal"?

In their message to the peoples of Latin America, the bishops say this: "As Christians we believe that this stage in the history of Latin America is intimately bound up with the history of salvation." They come to that belief by discovering God's activity in the signs of the time. As a result, they must "interpret the aspirations and cries of Latin America as signs that reveal the orientation of the divine plan operative in Christ's redemptive love, which grounds these aspirations in the awareness of fraternal solidarity."[11]

This grasp of God's activity impels the bishops to present "a global vision of man and the human race."[12] Once again we might well ask whether we are not dealing with an excessive preoccupation with man and a parallel indifference to the theme of God.

We find a simple, clearcut answer to this question in the Introduction to the Medellín documents: "The Church of Latin America . . . has put in the center of its attention man on this continent, who is now living through a decisive moment in the process of history. The Church has not gone 'off the track'; rather, it has turned toward man, aware of the fact that 'it is necessary to know man in order to know God.'[13] Since Christ is he in whom the mystery of man is made manifest (GS 22), the Church has attempted to comprehend this moment in the history of Latin American man, in the light of the Word that is Christ."[14]

Clearly enough, this presupposes a profound tieup between sacred history (God acting in and saving our history) and human history (human beings searching for a liberative society). That is how the bishops see it: "Without succumbing to oversimplistic confusions or identifications, we must always make clear the profound unity that exists between God's salvific plan achieved in Christ and man's aspirations; between the

Church as the People of God and temporal communities; between the revelatory activity of God and the experience of man; between supernatural gifts and charisms and human values."[15]

This principle of encountering God in man fashions an atmosphere that pervades all the documents of the Medellín Conference.

In line with this principle the bishops, when they talk about evangelization, point out to us that we must start from human experience. The transmission of the Christian message must be faithful, not only to divine revelation, but also to that "other theological *locus*"[16] which is human experience or the human situation: "Historical situations and authentically human aspirations form an indispensable part of the content of catechesis. They must be interpreted seriously within a present-day context, in the light of the living experiences of the people of Israel, Christ, and the ecclesial community."[17]

The epiphany of God in historical situations is a question posed to us. It calls for committed involvement on our part. It can take effect only within a context evincing the same commitment to liberation that pervades the documents of Medellín. One of the many texts that challenge us to involve ourselves in the liberation of Latin America:

> Let us recall once again that the present moment in the history of our peoples is characterized in the social order, and from an objective point of view, by a situation of underdevelopment. Certain phenomena point an accusing finger at it: marginal existence, alienation, and poverty. In the last analysis it is conditioned by structures of economic, political, and cultural dependence on the great industrialized metropolises, the latter enjoying a monopoly on technology and science (neocolonialism). From the subjective point of view it is characterized by a growing cognizance of this situation. In broad sectors of the Latin American population this growing cognizance provokes attitudes of protest and aspirations for liberation, development, and social justice. This complex reality forms the historical moment confronting the lay people of Latin America. It confronts them with the challenge to commit themselves to liberation and humanization.[18]

What is more, if this commitment is the proper access-road to God, then the category of *sin* (i.e., rejection of God and even idolatrous negation of him) will take on a historical and social dimension. So the bishops of the Medellín Conference call upon people to undergo a conversion; to turn away from the situation "of injustice that could be called institutionalized violence because existing structures violate fundamental rights. This situation requires urgent and global transformations that will be bold and profoundly innovative."[19]

The term *conversion* had been used greatly in an individualist sense, even as the gospel term *metanoia* quite logically was expressed in the interpersonal terms of that age. Here it acquires its authentic structural dimension, as does the term *sin* that makes it necessary: "In talking about a situation of injustice we are referring to those realities that embody a situation of sin."[20]

Thus the language of God-related issues points necessarily—not simply by adaptation but by virtue of its own intrinsic development—toward a social transformation in which we discover the "traces of God's image in man as a potent dynamism. This dynamism leads progressively toward ever greater dominion over nature, toward ever deeper personalization and fraternal solidarity, and toward an encounter with him who ratifies, purifies, and deepens the values achieved by human effort.[21]

In other words, in this historical commitment we encounter the authentic face of God. And this encounter with God in the historical mission of Latin American man is the atmosphere that pervades the Medellín documents and justifies their focus on man.

Was the Medellín Conference interested in God? The answer to that initial question is now clear. Medellín saw the "stupendous effort for rapid transformation and development" as "a clear sign of the Spirit who guides individuals and peoples to their vocation."[22] We are returning to the biblical form wherein the people of Israel recognized the presence of God in their very experience of liberation.

As one can see, the *atmosphere* of the Medellín documents, if not their logical analyses in the strict sense, does point toward a situation that is diametrically opposed to the one posed, in a different context, by the death-of-God approach.

But honesty with God is a long road to travel. Felipe Berryman makes some keen observations about Medellín in this connection:

> When we examine the conclusions formulated at Medellín, they strike us as curious. Its document on education, which bears witness to the hand of Paulo Freire, talks about the awakening of a critical sense, about an education that will free man from his cultural, social, economic, and political enslavements. . . . Compared with that document, the one on pastoral activity among the masses seems to be oddly conservative. It does not talk about the implementation of any critical sense . . . This curious contradiction is plainly a reflection of the general tendency of the bishops to prescribe much stronger medicines for society than for the Church.[23]

Suppose there is a dynamism that leads man toward "an encounter with him who ratifies, purifies, and deepens the values achieved by human effort." What happens, then, when "tradition exercises a power that is almost tyrannical," when the religious realm reveals "a utilitarian character" motivated by yearnings for security, contingency, and importance . . ."? In short: when we consider what was said above about man's liberation, what are we to think of religious expressions that "reveal spurious elements and motivations which are worldly and even egotistical"?[24]

The response of Medellín is that one should not "arbitrarily deny the character of authentic, believing adhesion" to the latter.[25] It would then be a matter of faith *in God,* even though we find here the same servile and alienating elements that are stressed in the violent and unjust structures of society. Perhaps we need not accuse Medellín of a lack of logic. But we cannot help noticing the lack of emphasis on liberation when the latter should be given an opening within the Church—and particularly, in man's relations with God.[26]

There does exist an image of God that justifies privacy, the source of individualism. Faith is linked solely to one's personal salvation and to the dictates of an individualist morality. It is the image of a God whose providence justifies passivity and resignation, of a God enshrined in devotions and sacramentals that lead to semifatalism. One says explicitly that all these things are to be avoided. But one adds: with prudence!

Apparently some attitudes, declared to be dehumanizing in the plane of history, retain a certain value when they show up within the religious realm. And those who hold them are not to be deprived of this value by imprudent tactics. But consider someone who claims that these attitudes can be useful vis-à-vis God. Is that person referring to the same God who can only be revealed in the active work of liberation?

It may well be that the documents of Medellín did fail, both theologically and pastorally, to complete their journey from God to liberation with the return trip from liberation to a liberating idea of God—to the authentic idea of the Christian God. But the very fact that it started the Church out on the road to liberation is the best augury of the necessary return trip.

NOTES

1. Reproduced by Paul Van Buren in *The Secular Meaning of the Gospel* (New York: Macmillan, 1963), p. 3.

2. This is indicated clearly by Van Buren himself in his book. But, in our opinion, his analysis of religious language does not go to the logical consequences that are already foreseeable from his starting point: i.e., the impossibility of anything that could merit the name "faith," and hence the equating of Christianity with an "existential philosophy"—the very thing he criticizes Bultmann for.

3. *Ibid.*, p. 2. This summary statement is dictated more or less by Bonhöffer's own words.

4. This appears to be the thinking of Bonhöffer (see W. H. van de Pol, *The End of Conventional Christianity*, Eng. trans., New York: Newman Press, 1968, pp. 119–122). It is not that of someone like Van Buren, for example. Wishing to go much further, his thought, like most of the death-of-God theology, would eventually end up in the snares of an affluent society that justifies the domination from which it stems through a strange amalgam of religion and a-religion. That is our opinion, at least. But while we feel obliged to make this criticism, we would not want our readers to minimize or denigrate the logic, honesty, and profundity that are embodied in these critical efforts, nor their validity in a

different context. Quite naturally this holds even more true for Bonhöffer who, in Protestant theology, represented a "conversion" akin to that which Vatican II represented in the Catholic camp. And that does not rule out his positive influence on the latter either.

5. For the moment we will not try to settle the question as to what is the determining factor in this situation. Is it the domination and repression created by the capitalist system, or is it the absence of any consideration of final causes peculiar to a technology that is spreading to every sector of existence? Today the fact is that the two are converging. But this does not mean that the political system adopted is a matter of indifference, particularly in under-developed countries. See Chapters III and IV in this volume.

6. Herbert Marcuse, *One-Dimensional Man* (Boston: Beacon, 1964), p. 12.

7. See CLARIFICATION IV of Chapter I; CLARIFICATION I of Chapter II; and CLARIFICATION I of Chapter III.

8. The passage from Marcuse cited above may make more than one reader think of the content that John's writings give to the term "world": i.e., the human structure that defends itself against the *light* coming from God. See Volume II, CLARIFICATION I of Chapter II.

9. *Cf.* Paul Ricoeur, *Freud and Philosophy: An Essay on Interpretation,* Eng. trans. (New Haven: Yale University Press, 1970), pp. 32–36.

10. *Segunda Conferencia General del Episcopado Latinoamericano: Medellín 1968,* Introduction. Hereafter the Conference documentation will be cited as *Medellín.* The documents of this conference are available in English: *The Church in the Present-Day Transformation of Latin America in the Light of the Council,* Vol. I, Position Papers and Vol. II, Conclusions (available from Latin America Bureau, USCC, Washington, D.C.).

11. *Ibid.,* "Message to the peoples of Latin America."

12. *Ibid.*

13. Paul VI, Allocution at the closing session of Vatican II, December 7, 1965.

14. *Medellín,* Introduction.

15. *Ibid.,* "Catechesis," II.

16. *Ibid.,* "Pastoral Concern for the Elites," II.

17. *Ibid.,* "Catechesis," III.

18. *Ibid.,* "Lay Movements," I.

19. *Ibid.,* "Peace," Part II, b.

20. *Ibid.,* "Peace," Part I.

21. *Ibid.,* Introduction.

22. *Ibid.*

23. Felipe Berryman, "Concientización y religiosidad popular," *Vispera,* No. 12 (1969), p. 9.

24. *Medellín,* "Pastoral Care of the Masses," I and II.

25. *Ibid.,* II. We say that it does not lack logic strictly speaking because, despite the emphasis, it does point out that "we should not be too quick to assume the existence of faith behind every seemingly Christian expression of religion" (*ibid.*).

26. See in this volume CLARIFICATION II of Chapter II and CLARIFICATION III of Chapter III.

CHAPTER ONE

God and History

Before constituting a mystery God—the Father, the Son, and the Spirit —constitutes an illumination. God is a discovery before he is a problem. What is more, he is an illumination or revelation concerning man's own existence.

The New Testament writers do not speak of three or of one.[1] They do not even locate the realities which they call Father, Son, and Spirit—or rather *the* God,[2] the Word, the Paraclete—in a distant beyond, in the "transcendent" world of the divine. What we could call the "Trinitarian formulas"[3] in the New Testament well up naturally when the new Christian ponders or evaluates the existence that has just been disclosed to him. Now his existence, activity, and history can be explained, continued, and deepened only in terms of their relationship to the Father, the Son, and the Spirit—whether the latter are three or one, one and the same divinity or distinct gods, different modes of operating, or different persons who are more or less divine.

Before these or similar problems are posed, Christian existence as a whole is conceived in relation to the Father, the Son, and the Spirit. And this holds true from the very earliest writings in the New Testament. Contrary to what we might think at first sight, these earliest writings are not the Gospels but the Epistles of Paul.

Consider, for example, the two letters he addressed to the Corinthians. In chapter 12 of his first letter to them we find this explanation of the overall existence of the Christian community with its different complementary functions: "There are varieties of gifts, but the same Spirit. There are varieties of service, but the same *Lord*. There are many forms of work, but all of them, in all men, are the work of *the* same God" (1 Cor. 12:4–6; our italics). In his second letter to them, the Trinitarian reference is of use to Paul in expressing his wish that the faithful in Corinth will enjoy the plenitude of Christian existence: "The grace of *the Lord* Jesus Christ, and the love of *God*, and fellowship in the *Holy Spirit*, be with you all" (2 Cor. 13:13; our italics).

Here, too, we find the characteristic features that we have already noted and stressed. The passage does not deal with God in his eternity, in some transcendent divine beyond. It deals with the wondrous "here and now" of Christian existence, which stands in marked contrast to their existence "before." It is here in this "now," in the "historical" end-result so to speak, that the three names appear and their being is revealed.

But what is it concretely that is revealed?

Section I

God's revelation does not begin with the New Testament. The Israel that Jesus encounters, his mass interlocutor so to speak, believed it knew God under the proper name of Yahweh. And, according to the testimony of Jesus himself, it certainly did know him to some extent or under a specific aspect. Or, to put it better, it had been in the process of getting to know him.

Thus the good news of Christianity incorporates the long history of self-revelation that Yahweh directed to his people. Addressing the Athenians, Paul divides up the two fundamental phases of God's self-revelation into that which refers to Yahweh and that which refers to Jesus:

> What you worship but do not know—this is what I now proclaim. The God who created the world and everything in it, and who is Lord of heaven and earth, does not live in shrines made by men. It is not because he lacks anything that he accepts service at men's hands, for he is himself the universal giver of life and breath and all else. He created every race of men of one stock, to inhabit the whole earth's surface. He fixed the epochs of their history and the limits of their territory. They were to seek God and, it might be, touch and find him; though indeed he is not far from each one of us, for in him we live and move, in him we exist (Acts 17:23–28).

Up to this point Paul has simply been preaching about Yahweh, the God of Abraham, Isaac, and Jacob. Or, if you prefer the terminology of Christ himself and the early Christians, he has been preaching about the Father. But he goes on, because he must make clear that there has now dawned a decisive reality relating to this God and mankind:

> As for the times of ignorance, God has overlooked them; but *now* he commands mankind, all men everywhere, to repent, because he has fixed the day on which he will have the world judged, and justly judged, by *a man of his choosing;* of this he has given assurance to all by raising him from the dead (Acts 17:30–31; our italics).

Right now let us disregard the method Paul uses to introduce the theme of Jesus in his sermon to the gentiles of Athens. What is clear is that it presumes a prior revelation, the revelation of God who is called the Father. Moreover, in Paul's summary statement we find the correct starting point for delving into the significance that this revelation of the Father had for Paul and Christians, "God before us" appears to be the formula that Paul suggests to us and that sums up the revelation of God in the Old Testament.[4]

1. It is not a question of something merely temporal, even though it does have to do with the way in which man will conceive his human, existential time. God, the Father, is the origin of any and every human destiny possible. Man can "meet God" the way the ancient patriarchs and prophets did. But when he gets to know this God better, he discovers that the encounter was in reality a process of recognition and acknowledgment. Why? Because this God in whom we live and move and exist was always there, and always there *first*.

From whatever viewpoint we look, God is the foundation we find already laid down for our destiny when we awaken to consciousness. Whatever direction we may give to our liberty, at its origin lies a world "made by him," a history started by his creative will.

2. We use the word *history* because that creation of his is destined to be somehow prolonged through man's labor. It is not merely an external framework. It is not a system, a mechanism that is finished and desired for its own sake.[5] So true is this that

> the very first chapter of Genesis teaches us that man prolongs the creative act of God through his work. The original creation is conceived and formulated in the framework of a week to inculcate the fact that man's work week re-publishes the archetypal week of creation. In the second account of creation man is pictured as fecundating the earth and making it useful (Gen.2:5 ff.); he is also pictured as its custodian (Gen 2:15). Rendering worship to God and working the land are both expressed by the same verb (Heb. *adad*; *cf.* Lat. *colere* and *cultum*). In an evolutionary context, the work acquires impressive theological volume.[6]

So it is the human being who is to "name" all the beings of creation. This expression designates man as the being destined to "possess" the earth, to gain mastery over the secret of all its components. When Paul refers to the "Lord of heaven and earth" in his sermon to the Athenians, he is not seeking to declare God "master" of the universe—not in any exclusivist sense, at least. His reference is meant to counter a polytheism in which the universe would be under the dominion of various divine beings. In Paul's discourse it is not man who threatens God's lordship.

3. This revelation involves a *history* also because the universe of the

Old Testament, unlike a cyclic system emanating from an unmoved mover, wells up from a liberty and moves through other liberties toward its end.

According to the Eloist tradition, God makes known his name when he chooses his people in history:

> Then Moses said to God, "If I go to the Israelites and tell them that the God of their forefathers has sent me to them, and they ask me his name, what shall I say?" God answered, "I AM; that is who I am. Tell them that I AM has sent you to them ... that it is ... the God of Abraham, the God of Isaac, the God of Jacob, who has sent you to them" (Exod. 3:13–15).

In Hebrew ears *Yahweh* sounds like the first person of the verb *to be, to exist.* The Greek essentialist tradition interpreted this divine self-definition as that of a being which exists by its very essence, whose essence it is to exist fully and completely.[7] Present-day exegetes, much more informed about the roots of Hebrew language and thought, and much more attentive to the overall context, see in the name which God deliberately gives to himself a rejection of what we could call man's ultimate why? in the face of his history and destiny.[8] The latter does not end up before some mechanism; it wells us from a liberty. We could translate the biblical statement as, "I'm me," alluding to the answer we give when people ask us the ultimate reasons behind our actions.

In other words, God makes himself known as person, as liberty.[9] And it is through his "history" with Abraham, Isaac, and Jacob, through his dealings with human persons, that they can come to know him even though God himself, according to the Eloist tradiiton, did not reveal his name to human beings.

Hence Yahweh will be basically "the God of the covenant." In other words, he will be the God who becomes acquainted and related through history, through the involvement of liberty with liberty, of person with person.[10]

4. This relationship is historical for another reason that we touched upon earlier. It is historical because human time and labor, joined in alliance with God, moves through countless trails in quest of a goal.[11] It is of the utmost interest to note that this goal, this utopia that founds history, is made up of the elements of history itself no matter how far it is projected into some future age. But there these elements are arranged in such a way that violence, domination by force, and external control are excluded from them:

> For behold, I create new heavens and a new earth ... There no child shall ever again die an infant, no old man fail to live out his life; every boy shall live his hundred years before he dies ... Men shall build houses and

> live to inhabit them, plant vineyards and eat their fruit; they shall not build
> for others to inhabit nor plant for others to eat...They shall not toil in
> vain or raise children for misfortune ... The wolf and the lamb shall feed
> together and the lion shall eat straw like cattle. They shall not hurt or destroy
> in all my holy mountain, says the Lord (Isa. 65:17-25).

This definitive fulfillment of man's work in history will be crowned
with the capacity to have relations with God that do not confront man's
liberty with a divine will now turned into law. That would be an even
more radical violence than the one which existed before. But now: "This
is the covenant which I will make with Israel after those days, says the
Lord; I will set my law within them and write it on their hearts; I will
become their God and they shall become my people. No longer need
they teach one another to know the Lord; all of them, high and low
alike, shall know me, says the Lord." (Jer. 31:33-34).

What is more, this goal of reconciliation will surpass the boundaries
and limits of Israel itself. It will reach all of humanity, pictured in terms
of its farthest bounds at that time:

> The Lord will make himself known to the Egyptians; on that day they shall
> acknowledge the Lord and do him service with sacrifice and grain-offering,
> make vows to him and pay them...When that day comes there shall be
> a highway between Egypt and Assyria; Assyrians shall come to Egypt and
> Egyptians to Assyria; then Egyptians shall worhsip with Assyrians. When
> that day comes Israel shall rank with Egypt and Assyria, those three, and
> shall be a blessing in the centre of the world. So the Lord of Hosts will
> bless them: A blessing be upon Egypt my people, upon Assyria the work
> of my hands, and upon Israel my possession (Isa. 19:21-25).

If a *weekly* cycle does exist, as we noted earlier, it is not meant to serve
as the repeated commencement of a circular process. It is to be the
impetus for a creation that continues on and moves toward its goal
through history. There is also the *sabbath year* and the *jubilee year,* the
latter coming after seven weeks of sabbath years (forty-nine years). The
jubilee year is the renewed and actively hastened presence of the goal
toward which history is tending: "You shall hallow the fiftieth year and
proclaim *liberation* in the land for all its inhabitants" (Lev. 25:10; our
italics).[12]

Here, in the person and work of Yahweh, the Father, we have the
first element that goes to make up human history: God before us. In
other words, human existence is always inserted in a history. The history
is a constituent of human existence according to the biblical message;
and the whole of this constituent history is permeated and sustained
by the work of the Father. It is not surprising that many Trinitarian

formulas speak of the Father as the laborer *par excellence,* or as the
very source of love who foresaw and made possible man's life and destiny
(1 Pet. 1:1–2; Eph. 2:1–14; 2 Cor. 13:13).

Section II

Jesus assumes this revelation of the Father. The figure and the very
name "Son" which he gives himself, or "Word" of God which John
the Evangelist later gave to him, clearly and primarily signify that this
revelation was assumed by Jesus.

But there is something more. It took a certain amount of time[13]
for the Christian community to advert to the fact that the coming of
Jesus confronted it with a *new* and definitive revelation of "the divine."
Undoubtedly recalling this period of time, this necessary preparation,
Paul begins to talk to the Athenians about Jesus in terms that probably
reflect very well the first sensation the disciples felt about their master:
"now he [i.e., God] commands mankind, all men everywhere, to repent,
because he has fixed the day on which he will have the world judged,
and justly judged, by a man of his choosing; of this he has given assurance
to all by raising him from the dead" (Acts. 17:30–31).

But the New Testament is already a formal statement. Through
the words of Paul and John, the Christian community bears clear witness
to its faith: encountering Jesus is encountering God with us.

1. In reality one line of Old Testament thought, which had given
rise to tension and controversy, already pointed toward this reality: that
of the prophets.

The grounding of our history by a God-before-us remained linked
to an element of ambiguity. The Father does indeed "work" and thereby
establish our history, but apparently he does so from *outside* history.
What is more, every time the Chosen People presume to impose something within this history in his name, Yahweh evades their presumption.[14]
"My thoughts are not your thoughts, and your ways are not my ways.
This is the very word of the Lord. For as the heavens are higher than
the earth, so are my ways higher than your ways and my thoughts than
your thoughts" (Isa. 55:8–9). How was man to live out this tension with
a God who invites him to history yet evades identification with any and
every human project? We are not surprised that the easy way out of
this dilemma for Israel had been the *temple.*

The temple seemed to represent heaven opening up on earth in
time and space. It represented a nonmundane precinct and a nonmundane gesture (the temple ritual) within the world itself. Thus it seemed

to be the most suitable way for the sacred to find reality and fulfillment. And if it were not the most suitable, it was at least more convenient and more adapted to human living; for it separated the sacred from the profane. The latter, by definition, was that which remained "outside the spatio-temporal precincts of the sacred." It was the realm of time and history, entrusted to man by God to occupy his energies and test him.

Another tendency, prophecy,[15] rose up in opposition to this tendency. Over against this rather domesticated presence of Yahweh in the temple, it depicted the difficult, terrifying, and yet wondrous presence of Yahweh in the *desert* where he shared the vicissitudes of his people's journey. Moses hits him with an absurd proposal: "Indeed if thou dost not go in person [i.e., with them], do not send us up from here." To this Yahweh gives an unexpected and surprising answer: "I will do this thing you have asked" (Exod. 33:15,17).

For the Israelites Yahweh does truly become, up to a certain point, *Emmanuel,* that is, "God with us." He rejects every proposal to construct altar or temple (Exod. 20:24–25; 1 Sam. 7:1–6). He wants only a tent, like that of his wayfaring people. It is not surprising, then, that the image of "Emmanuel" in the desert becomes the image that the prophets set over against temple religion when Israel is ensconced in its own home territory (Isa. 7:14; 8:10; Ps. 46:7,12; etc.). The promise of a real, definitive Emmanuel will be the messianic promise. And the Christian community believes that this promise was fulfilled in Jesus with a realism and profundity that had not been expected.

In Jesus "the Word became flesh; he came to dwell among us" (John 1:14; literally, "set up his tent among us"). He came to dwell among his people as he had in the desert, but infinitely closer. Or better: not closer but completely and definitively "within."

It is precisely when this interiorization within human history reaches its acme, in total self-giving even unto death (John 13:1:1; Matt. 27:50–51), that the veil of the temple is rent in a symbolic way. That which seemed to separate the sacred from history disappears; all that remains is history, which is simultaneously human history and divine history. Christianity does not recognize any temple in the classic, religious sense of the word.[16]

2. But what about this invasion of history by the Absolute? Does it not now become a terrifying and depersonalizing reality, a reality that turns man into a mere instrument? Faced with this God who is so terrifyingly present and powerful and decisive, must we not echo the rather irreligious sentiments of Job: "What is man that thou makest

much of him ... Wilt thou not look away from me for an instant? Wilt thou not let me be while I swallow my spittle?" (Job. 7:17,19).

It is here that the paradox of divine revelation reaches its peak. God-with-us does not invade our history. On the contrary, we can and should say that our history invades the divine realm. The Absolute enters the world of man in such a way that he does not take over possession of it; instead he places himself at the disposal of every man, and each man becomes absolute in turn. As Paul puts it: "He did not spare his own Son, but gave him up for us all; and with this gift how can he fail to lavish upon us all he has to give?" (Rom. 8:32). We could almost say that Paul does not seem to take account of the fact that his words, almost absurd for anyone who has not experienced profound love, relativize the Absolute and absolutize the relative. But it is only in such a way that we can live out history with a notion of the Absolute that does not wipe out its reality as *our* history. This is the one and only notion of God that does not alienate and benumb man.

Thus Paul admonishes us that if a person has not realized the fact that God himself has placed the universe in man's hands, then he has not grasped anything of Christianity even though he may call himself a Christian (Gal. 3, 4). If a person tiptoes through the world as if it were a stranger's house, questioning the licitness or illicitness of every possible action, then he has not comprehended the one and only divine revelation that is capable of converting human existence into a creative reality. Paul identifies this essential result of the gospel with the "mature age" of man, and rightly so. So Paul Lehmann is quite right when he says: "Salvation is maturity."[17]

3. God with us, truly with us right to the end, signifies that he freely linked his destiny to our history. Just another sharer in our humanity, he nevertheless joined in solidarity with all and became vulnerable to all by directing his love to his brothers without any trace of egotism.[18]

The gospel revelation shows him by turns angered (Mark 3:5), saddened (Luke 19:41), and moved by the things that happened to him, to his country, and to his friends. It is with good reason that Paul introduces the theme of Jesus into his discourse to the Athenians by pointing out that the time has come when God will judge men by *a man*. His divine being does not stand with one foot outside of history; he injects it into history as no one else has ever done, without any reservations or defences.

And precisely for this reason he *passes judgment* on all men, even without presuming to do it. He inaugurates "the ultimate" in history.[19] He gives it its ultimate, conscious radicalness because in it and with it the absolute wins out or is spurned: through the very projects whereby man constructs the universe and prolongs creation, or refuses to do this.

So here, in the person and work of Jesus, the Son, we have the second constitutive element of human history: God with us. In other words, the language which God uses in speaking to us acquires its totally definitive realism through the Word, the divine word turned into an historical person. It is a language that is infinitely committed and involved, and thus it bestows decisive and absolute value on man's commitment in history.

Section III

In order to share our history and be truly God-with-us, he had to shoulder the essential limits of everything historical. For that is precisely what history is: a continuing effort to give better order and arrangement to the same elements that have always existed. The gigantic work of evolution has been nothing else but that. And when man consciously shoulders this process bit by bit, it continues to be essentially the same process in his hands: i.e., the replacement of forms that are operative and then disappear with other forms that do the same thing in their turn. And progress does not consist in the fact that they do not disappear; it consists in the fact that they disappear in such a way that new and better forms are made possible.

This is what God shouldered in all seriousness. So we can see the profundity of Augustine's remark: "When the Lord deigned to be our way, he did not wish to hold us back but to let us move forward."[20] And for the very same reason, the revelation of God-with-us in history is succeeded by the revelation of God in us: i.e., by the revelation of the Spirit.

1. To be a human being is to be conditioned by the coordinates of time, space, and culture in our activity. Jesus, God-with-us, lived this condition. As the Word of God, he had a message to communicate. And he had to do it within the limitations on every message that is communicated in history. The message has to meet with the addressee. This fact has nothing to do with the quality or interest of the message. Whatever the message may be, it must expose itself to all the risks of inconvenience and meetings that do not come off. And the more important the message is, the more novelty, depth, and originality it contains, the more keenly does one suffer from the limitations imposed by the

moment and its opportuneness. Jesus makes clear and explicit reference to this experience in John's Gospel (7:6–8).

Countless elements are involved in the whole question of the "right moment," ranging from moral, cultural, and psychic factors to physical and physiological ones. The time that Jesus had for meeting human beings and giving them his message was a human time. In other words, it was a precisely defined time, limited more and more by an endpoint that was predictable by the very nature of the message. Mark comments on one occasion: "They had nothing to say; and, looking around at them with anger and sorrow at their obstinate stupidity . . ." (Mark 3:5). On another occasion, after a brief and futile attempt at dialogue, Jesus "went off and left them" (Matt. 16:4).

But what about those in whom he finds faith and the readiness to listen to his word? Here the conditioning of historical factors may well be even harsher, and the impossibility of surmounting it may be experienced in an even deeper, more radical way. If the barriers of incomprehension were to have been surmounted, the encounter would have had to take place a half hour earlier, or a century later, or in the heyday of industrial civilization.

Why? Because truth is a weighty burden. Only when it is doled out in a properly balanced dosage can man endure its weight. As Jesus points out at the Last Supper: "There is still much that I could say to you, but the burden would be too great for you now. However, when he comes who is the Spirit of truth, he will guide you into all the truth" (John 16:12–13). Thus the parting words of Jesus, God-with-us, could be summarized and expressed this way: "With my word and my life I have formulated for you the truth about the whole of history. But I cannot communicate this total truth to you in such a way that it would be truth in you, precisely because I am formulating it from within history—from within my history. The world would have to undergo a transformation for you to be able to understand many aspects of this truth, this truth which I am. And you yourselves would have to move on further; because if you stick where you are now as human beings, you will only be capable of opposing this world and not understanding it. If that happened, then those who came to follow my path and yours would not be able to *hear* my word. They would not be able to have an encounter with me because I, being the real human being that I am, will truly and irreversibly belong to the past."

Precisely for this reason Jesus departs. And it is good for the disciples that he does (cf. John 16:7) because the Spirit, from within the interior of the human realm, is God *attuned to the rhythm of history.* In the face of each new juncture in history, he will make the good news sound out anew—ever the same (the message of Jesus) but ever different. Like Jesus at one moment in history, he too is the helper and consoler and advocate. He leads men to the total truth by recalling the message of Jesus *at the right time* (John 16:13–14).[21]

2. God-in-us, attuned to the rhythm of history, ensures the continuing presence of Jesus' word in a creative way. And, as we have already seen, this word is the thing that reveals the less visible value and import of human history.

The Spirit enables us to reiterate the statement of Paul: "We . . . possess the mind of Christ" (1 Cor. 2:16). Thus he ensures that the function of Jesus in history will maintain its creative continuity. It will continue to reveal man to himself (GS 22) to the extent that this revelation is made possible and necessary by history. It is his presence that allowed Jesus to make this promise to his disciples on the eve of his departure: "I am going away and *coming back to you*" (John 14:28; our italics). Or, as Matthew's Gospel puts it: "I am with you always, to the end of time" (Matt. 28:20).

So the heterogeneousness of history is overcome by the truth that "recapitulates": i.e., the truth that gives meaning, one and the same meaning but in a gradually developing way, to that which changes. In like manner, as the historical figure of Christ inevitably succumbs to faulty portrayals and is fixed in an era, a language, and a culture that belongs to the past, we continue to encounter the word that wells up suggestively within us. It is in this word that he would today communicate his good news about our history in order to give it full meaning. It is a better presence indeed, but do we really believe it as such?

Faced with the new perspectives opened up by God's presence in us, Paul remarks that if he had once known Christ in terms of history (i.e., "according to the flesh" or "worldly standards"), such a measuring rod no longer counts in his evaluation (2 Cor. 5:16). We, however, do not tend to think that way. Almost automatically we cling vainly to some letter of ours, to some past figure who is no less in contradiction to the revelation of Christ and the outpouring of his Spirit for being the very figure of Christ.

3. Clearly this happens because we do not conceive Christianity as a responsibility oriented toward the construction of human history. Insofar as we turn it into a privilege, we orientate God's revelation toward the individual, despite the fact that the Spirit shows himself to us precisely as the unifier *par excellence*.

Because the Spirit is the penetration of Christ's mentality into us, he overcomes all our external differences (1 Cor. 12:4; Eph. 4:3–16). As we shall see in the texts cited in the next chapter, the great unifier of history is also the creator of our community "we": i.e., the community that is proper to those who bear within themselves the word of God addressed to history.[22]

Thus, in the Trinitarian formulas of the New Testament, the Spirit is the factor of *communion*. This does not prevent the Eucharistic body and blood of Christ from being the same thing, since the Spirit's work is not physical but rather spiritual. In other words, it is a process of discernment (*cf.* 1 Cor. 11:28–32).

So here we have the third element constitutive of human history: God in us, *God within us*. Or, to put it another way: it is the word of God made our word, the word of God tranformed into a creating, communitarian word that reveals our history because it follows its rhythm. It is the rhythm of the signs of the time which we must pay heed to.

Precisely because the revelation of the Christian God brings us face to face with history, God willed to dole it out by degrees as history made it feasible and necessary. Saint Gregory Nazianzen describes the unfolding development of this revelation in these terms: "The real situation is this. The Old Testament spoke openly of the Father, and more obscurely of the Son. The New Testament pointed plainly and clearly to the Son, and obscurely to the divinity of the Spirit. Now the Spirit himself dwells with us and presents himself more openly to us."[23] In and through history he leads us toward the full truth.

NOTES TO CHAPTER ONE

1. In some editions of the Bible we find this statement in 1 John 5:7: "For there are three that bear witness in heaven—the Father, the Word, and the Holy Spirit—and these three are one" But this phrase is an interpolation of the Latin Vulgate Bible.

2. Differing from the Latin translation of the Bible and later translations, the original Greek text clearly distinguishes the Father specifically from the divinity in general (if we might use that phrase). It does so through its use of the definite article (*ho, he, to*). The deity is *theos*. The Father is *ho theós* (literally, "the God") So in John 1:1 we find literally: "The Word was before the face of *the* God [pròs tòn theón], and the Word was God [kai *theós* en ho lógos]." In other words, the Word possessed divinity without being the Father.

3. See CLARIFICATION V in this Chapter.

4. See Appendix II in this volume. The similarity between the gradually progessing revelation of the Old Testament and attitudes existing among people who call themselves Christians today can be seen in my book (done in collaboration with J. P. Sanchis), *As Etapas Pré-cristâs da descoberta de Deus: Una chave para a análise do cristianismo (latinoamericano)* (Petrópolis; Vozes, 1968).

5. In the words of Vatican II, "all that creation which God made on man's account" (GS 39).

6. J. Croatto, "La creación en la Kerigmática actual," *Salvación y construcción del mundo* (Barcelona: Dilapsa-Nova Terra, 1968), p. 100. Done in collaboration with G. Guitérrez, J. L. Segundo, B. Catao, and J. Comblin.

7. "Thus, since existence is the very essence of God and this is not true of any other being, it is clear that, of all names, this is the name most proper to God" (Thomas Aquinas, S.T., I, q.3, a.11).

8. Commenting on the thinking of Ian Ramsey, Paul Van Buren writes: "The text of the revelation of the divine name in chapter 3 of Exodus is, moreover, an example of the final form of the language of loyalty. The last answer to why I have acted as I have, after all the partial explanations, is the statement, 'I'm I.'" Van Buren, *The Secular Meaning of the Gospel* (New York: Macmillan, 1963), p. 88.

9. "Should we understand Yahweh's words to Moses to mean: 'I am he who is'; or 'I am who I am'? Do we hear the Absolute proclaiming himself or the hidden God remaining silent? . . . The first interpretation is, perhaps, difficult to justify as it stands, gramatically and historically; and at first sight the second interpretation may sound a little thin considering the solemnity of the occasion. But although they may seem to be opposed, are they not at bottom very close to one another? The first formula is full of grandeur . . . The second formula is no less precious. It suggests a concrete personality which escapes us. 'I am that which it pleases me to be.'" (Henri de Lubac, Eng. trans., *The Discovery of God*. New York: P. J. Kenedy, 1960, pp. 137–138). Current exegesis leans more to the second hypothesis, to the connotations of personal, salvific presence and guidance of the chosen people. See the article on "God" in *Vocabulaire Biblique*, 3rd ed. (Neuchâtel: Delachaux and Niestle. 1964), p. 69.

10. In the Prologue of John's Gospel the revelation of the Father, of whom his only Son is the image and word, is summed up in the phrase "full of grace and truth" (John 1:14). In the context of the whole Old Testament, this phrase could well be reformulated as "full of gratuitous generosity and fidelity."

11. But it is not a clear, untrammelled line. Seeking solutions that will offer an easy way out, Israel is led to a religion of temple and cultic worship (see Section II above), to an abstract universalism and an elusive "beyond" (see Appendix II).

12. "In this year of jubilee you shall return, every one of you, to his patrimony" (Lev. 25:13). "No land shall be sold outright, because the land is mine . . . it shall remain in the hands of the purchaser till the year of jubilee. It shall then revert to the original owner, and he shall return to his patrimony" (Lev. 25:23, 28. "When your brother is reduced to poverty and sells himself to you, you shall not use him to work for you as a slave. His status shall be that of a hired man or a stranger lodging with you; he shall work for you until the year of jubilee. He shall then leave your service, with his children, and go back to his family and to his ancestral property . . . You shall not drive him with ruthless severity, but you shall fear your God" (Lev. 25:39–43). "The same law shall apply both to the native-born and to the alien who is living among you" (Exod. 12:49).

In the context of that era, the line of history clearly passes through these texts.

13. We must not exaggerate this indisputable length of time, either in one direction or in the other. Certainly the term "son of God" from the Synoptic texts is not synonymous with the second person of the Trinity. What is more the Synoptic writers, who have some respect for the time that separates the redaction of their texts from the time when the events took place—even though they bear witness to the faith of the community, clearly do not express the divinity of Jesus in explicit form. It is tacitly or virtually implied in many of their passages, but the virtualness is awaiting further reflection, as it were.

On the other hand, we do not have to wait for John's Prologue or his Gospel. Paul, whose Epistles must have preceded the final redaction of the Synoptic Gospels, explicitly drew the ultimate conclusions; see, for example, Phil. 2:6–11.

14. See Appendix II.

15. On the turbulent and ambiguous biblical history of the import and value of the temple and its rites, see Volume IV, Appendix II, of this series.

16. The definitive kingdom, which is already present in our history (GS 39) but which will be manifested fully in the new heaven and earth, is the transfigured continuation of this situation, established by the very revelation of God itself: "So in the Spirit he carried me away . . . and showed me the holy city of Jerusalem coming down out of heaven from God. It shone with the glory of God . . . I saw no temple in the city; for its temple was the sovereign Lord God and the Lamb" (Rev. 21:10,22). "I heard a loud voice proclaiming from the throne: 'Now at last God has his dwelling among men! He will dwell among them . . .'" (Rev. 21:3). This text alludes to Exodus and to John 1:14.

17. See in this series, Volume II, Chapter IV, CLARIFICATION I.

18. "Without noticing it, we have witnessed the introduction of a morality . . . that cast aspersions on man. This morality seeks to explain why the individual must be sacrificed to the community. But only by tricks and artifices of languages will it ever be able to explain . . . why it is fair that a thousand should die to free one single person from prison or injustice. I understand the origin of human beings' respect for each other. The wise man owes respect to the cobbler because . . . he respects God, whose ambassador is the cobbler as well . . . I understand, finally, why the love of God has made human beings responsible for each other . . . In making each one an ambassador of the same God, it placed the salvation of all in the hands of each" (Antoine de Saint-Exupéry, *Pilote de guerre*, 18th ed. Paris: Gallimard, 1949, pp. 232, 224–27).

19. With Christ, the ultimate age has arrived in history. Fully agreeing with both Catholic and Protestant theology, we are right in the midst of the eschatological age. But it is here that the differences start. We do not agree with Jean Daniélou that history, since the time of Christ, is simply waiting for its final hour. The mission of history is to realize and fulfill the total presence of Christ, to build up his body. Christ is the ultimate reality, indeed. But, as the New Testament suggests. Christ forms a unique and progressive reality with his body and his work.

20. PL, 34, 33. Cited by Henri de Lubac in his *Catholicisme*.

21. "The action of the Spirit is precisely to *call to mind* all that Jesus said. But it is not simply a matter of recalling to memory a teaching that may have been forgotten. His real work is to make one understand the words of Jesus from the inside, to lay hold of them in the light of faith and discover all their historical potentialities and all their richness . . . Through the secret activity of the Paraclete, then, the message of Jesus ceases to be exterior to us. He makes it something interior to us." (Ignace de la Potterie, "El Paráclito," in *La Vida según el Espíritu,* in collaboration with Stanislas Lyonnet; this is the Spanish translation of a work originally in French; it is now available in English, but the latter translation was not consulted by the translator of this volume; see *The Christian Lives by the Spirit,* New York: Alba House, 1971).

22. See in this series, Volume I, Chapter III.

23. Theological Discourse V.

CLARIFICATIONS

I. LATIN AMERICA: HISTORICAL AND THEOLOGICAL LOCUS

In the Introduction to this volume we spoke of the *occidental* image of God. We were referring to the conditionings which the structure of human relations in societal life impose on our image of God. And since the West has been the "milieu" for the expansion of Christianity, our image of God quite logically reflects the conditionings of Western civilization.

Would we be out of line in suggesting that Latin America has its own special destiny today? Would we be wrong to suggest that it is meant to give voice to the crisis which foreshadows and proclaims a new understanding of the history that has passed for occidental civilization, and that formulated the idea of God in its own categories?

Let us make one point clear before we go into this notion. The relationship between the West and Christianity is a very complex one. It entails more than the mere conditioning of the latter by the former. The fact is that some authors see the West as something more than merely one civilization among others. They see it as a human venture and adventure, as a general direction of existence which, through a series of converging lines, became the principal axis of anthropogenesis (i.e., of the gradual, progressive buildup and flowering of man in society).[1]

In this adventure the Judeo-Christian ferment had a decisive role. Not only did it make some explicit contributions: e.g., the notion of person, which was clarified through the Trinitarian and Christological controversies.[2] It was responsible also for other attitudes that were generated out of elements belonging more or less explicitly to the Christian message. It is no accident, for example, that the milieu of Christian expansion has been the creative focal point of two attitudes basic to the process of liberating man from his enslavement to nature: i.e., the scientific outlook and the technological outlook. The fact is that the seed of secularization contained in Christianity led to a positive and higher valuation of the world; and such a valuation is a prerequisite to any exploration into nature's rationality or to its control by man.[3]

It matters little that these seeds germinated outside the institutional Church. Even scattered abroad in the world, they cannot deny their Christian origin.

Nor is it accidental that it was in the West that there emerged historical consciousness: i.e., man's capacity to see historical happening as a process with a meaning, that meaning being the progressive fulfillment of man in a process where he himself is the decisive actor.

Thus, through a process of reciprocal influence, occidental civilization and Christainity became so closely united and identified that it was hard to distinguish the elements specific to each. Yet the present moment in history is characterized by a questioning of this identity. This questioning starts from a Christian awareness. It confronts the problem of occidental society with a critical eye, insofar as it sees in this society obstacles to the complete fulfillment of man. Such critical questioning, however, cannot logically avoid creating a crisis for the image of God as well.

What happened in the Occident—and more concretely, in Latin America—to make such a rupture possible? If we examine the ongoing process of occidental society, we note a twofold feature. On the one hand the growing complexity of social structures—labor relations, commercial transactions, class relationships, power structures, etc.—is betokened by a continual reinforcement of the domination of minorities over majorities. On the other hand, the more these structures of domination are perfected and seemingly made more subtle, the more clearly is their inhuman character revealed.

No one today doubts that the transition from feudal society to modern society represented a forward step in the positive valuation of the individual and his rights. Consider, for example, the problem of the distribution of the social product, which is always inferior to real-life needs. It is obvious that in the feudal period "certain classes had the power to appropriate the best of the social product for themselves, and to assign to other classes the heavier and dirtier work and a smaller share of the product."[4] In a market economy, by contrast, this unequal distribution shows up, not as something imposed by force, but as something regulated by the mechanisms of the market wherein individual liberty seems to be safeguarded better. No one is constrained by force to enter into a work contract.[5]

Yet, for all that, the market economy introduces such a competition-dynamic that, even though it may prompt social mobility to a degree never known in feudalism, it simultaneously shatters any and every schema of human solidarity. In the struggle for the best part of the social product, which is theoretically open to all, only a few people occupy the best places.

The exploitation is thus made more subtle, but at the same time more inhuman. Referring to the paternalistic system of feudalism, Fromm indicates why: "In feudal society the lord was supposed to have the divine right to demand services and things from those subject to his domination, but at the same time he was bound by custom and was obligated to be responsible for his subjects, to protect them, and to provide them with at least the minimum—the traditional standard of living. Feudal exploitation took place in a system of mutual human obligations, and thus was governed by certain restrictions."[6]

This feature of mutual obligation within a domination-relationship was gradually lost as the market economy took over. Labor became a product that was to be bought and used without restrictions.[7] The employer-master became anonymous and impersonal. As a result, the domination acquired a dynamic thrust toward cold calculation and pitiless injustice.

There is no doubt that an accelerated pace of development in the metropolitan centers of colonialism throughout the twentieth century produced a greater distribution of wealth. This fact enabled people to forget the essential crux of the problem: the use of man by man. But in Latin America, a dependent continent, we have not taken that step. Hence the domination, with its less subtle and impersonal mechanisms, *faces a crisis* when it is confronted hostilely by people's conscious advertence to the growing dehumanization. They evince a critical awareness vis-à-vis the structures that impede human fulfillment, and a growing awareness of the new possibilities that would be opened up to man by a new societal schema.

This is the context within which the rupture of identity between Occident and Christianity is taking place. It is easy enough to see the tension produced by this situation in Christian consciousness, particularly with respect to the image of God. On the one hand, once the capitalist system has revealed the full dimensions of its inhuman domination in the course of its development, the Christian finds no element in his concrete societal existence that would help him to ponder the God who revealed himself in Jesus Christ. What is more, his indictment of the social system necessarily leads him to criticize a notion of God which is the projection of the false image created by an ideology of domination. In this sense we can say that never before has it been so difficult to conceive the Christian God in real-life terms.

At the same time, however, we see dawning on the horizon the possibility of a new organization of societal life that will overcome the dominator-versus-dominated dialectic. This fact bespeaks the dawning of a new, more profound, more authentic image of God. So we can also say that never before, even in the West, have we been so close to discovering the true face of God.

Latin America is *on the periphery* of occidental civilization. At this moment in history, when historical sensitivity and ecclesial flexibility are converging in Latin America as never before, this continent can be the fermenting-ground of a new conception of history, not only for itself but for Christianity. This new conception would start out from the Occident and a new idea of God that is closer to Christian revelation. And the two tasks may well be one.

II. HISTORY OF SALVATION OR SALVATION OF HISTORY?

Throughout this first chapter we have seen that God's progressive revelation pointed toward what we could call *the salvation of history*. When we understand what the Christian God is, then history is saved from any and all victimization by frustration (see Rom. 8:19), from any definitive "corruption," from any and all destructive, desparing urgency (see 1 Cor. 15:50–55).

But if this revelation of God, this salvation of history, has been gradual, progressive, and spaced out over the unfolding development of mankind—as we have seen it has—then we should also call it *the history of salvation*.

In recent times attention has been called to the inescapable relationship of the Christian message to history: firstly to the history of man's beginnings, then to the history of Israel, and finally to the history which culminates with the death and resurrection of Jesus and announces his second coming.

Without any doubt that is the theme of Holy Scripture. And pastoral effort can only gain by shifting from a static, legalistic presentation (i.e., the conditions surrounding salvation) to the dynamic biblical presentation (i.e., the history of salvation).

Yet, for all that, history itself can be, and remain, radically static. It is not enough to teach history to a human being during childhood, adolescence, and early adulthood, if it simply means the accumulation of more and more precise data. History becomes a dynamic thing only when it gradually shifts from the narration of alien events to the interpretation of historical happenings and one's own personal existence.

We could say that a presentation of Christianity is adequate only when it moves from the history of salvation to the salvation of history in man[8]: i.e., to the buildup of history by man, whom God has prepared and commissioned for this task.

This pastoral approach, which seems unavoidable to us, presupposes three attitudes that are intimately and dynamically tied together; (1) one must move from a particularist history of salvation to the total history of humanity (i.e., to the process of humanization); (2) one must gradually give priority to interpretation and its unfolding development over a mere recounting of events; and (3) within the ecclesial community one must continually reinterpret this history in the face of problems confronting man's liberation.

1. At the start of the humanization process, history is given to man readymade. He does not interpret it; he simply reacts to its immediate challenges. His control of events is limited to small-scale operations. When confronted with decisive, critical events, he realizes that his life depends wholly on them and that he can do nothing but accept them.

One of the characters in *The Children of Sanchez,* a superb biographical and sociological work, puts it this way:

> To me one's destiny is controlled by a mysterious hand that moves all things. Only for the select, do things turn out as planned; to those of us who are born to be *tamale*-eaters, heaven sends only *tamales*. We plan and plan and some little thing happens to wash it all away. Like once, I decided to try to save and I said to Paula, "Old girl, put away this money so that some day we'll have a little pile." When we had ninety *pesos* laid away, *pum*! my father got sick and I had to give all to him for doctors and medicines. It was the only time I had tried to save. I said to Paula, "There you are! why should we save if someone gets sick and we have to spend it all!" Sometimes I even think that saving brings on illness! That's why I firmly believe that some of us are born to be poor and remain that way no matter how hard we struggle and pull this way and that. God gives us just enough to go on vegetating, no?[9]

At this stage of existence, history seems to be a series of irrelevant, profane, day-to-day events that are interrupted by decisive happenings. Even though these happenings may be small in themselves, they are considered divine precisely because of their decisive nature. So we have a sacred, decisive history alongside a profane, irrelevant history.

In this vein the Bible shifts significantly from the origins of humanity (divine history) to Abraham, the origin of the people wherein divine history will continue on. Moses, David, and the Exile are other key moments in that sacred history. What the people of Israel saw expresssed in these happenings was not an interpretation of the overall human reality but interventions by God. God had determined these happenings and brought people to the reality in which they were now living. The New Testament is also viewed and frequently interpreted in this same manner.

This is the first and most primitive stage of the history of salvation. It deals with the series of events that have been decisive in leading us to the privileged position we now find ourselves in with regard to salvation. But the perspective of evolution, when applied to the human species, give us a very different outlook even as it explains the preceding fact.

It has been said of man that he becomes evolution when this process is shouldered and directed by him. Man is indeed a product of evolution. But in man evolution reaches the point where it is handed over to the initiative, energy, and free, conscious orientation of this being who proceeds from it. And man prepares himself for the task of taking hold of his own evolution by distinguishing the critical points which, at first glance, are responsible for the reality that is his.

But at that early point in reflection there could be no difference between a "miracle" and a decisive event. Both escape man's capacity for decision. The two are comprehended under the same category. Both are decisive events which occur because God intervenes. We are anachronistic when we suggest that people with this mentality see a miracle as a suspension of some natural law. The very notion of a law of nature belongs to a different stage of thinking.

At bottom, then, the events which mark the "history of salvation" in this stage are decisive events which, through the interpretation suggested by God, will help man to take charge of history as a whole (not just a limited sacred history) by interpreting it.[10]

2. Arriving at the stage where interpretation became dominant and liberative was the aim and end of the whole "sacred history of Israel." For Paul, the same holds true for the revelation that goes to make up Christian life. If the Paschal Mystery is not to be in vain (Gal. 5:1-6), then history must shift from the hands of natural evolution to the hands of mature human beings who are fully prepared to shoulder this task.

Knowing what we do today, we can and must translate[11] what Paul says in terms of his own day, when he speaks to us of the transition from law to liberty, through proper comprehension of the the paschal event and its import.[12] In Paul's thought the *law*, which Christ gained mastery over after being born under its yoke (Gal. 4:4-5), comprises all the impersonal factors that condition man. And they range from those things which appear to determine man in themselves, such as race and sex, to religion with its sacraments, laws, and personages (see, for example, Rom. 14:14; Gal. 3:28; 1 Cor. 2:15; 1 Cor. 3:21-23). Everything must cease to dominate man, both *de jure* Gal. 4:1-7) and *de facto* (1 Cor. 6:12), so that man may use these factors to build up the total body of Christ, to fashion the complete image of man in history.

In the domain of time, then, salvation is a "political" maturity. It is the maturity of the "political being" that every human being is. It will entail putting all the elements of the universe in the service of the humanization process. It will mean gradually stripping them of their determinant, compulsive character (in both the physical and moral sense), so that they can be put in the service of liberty. In this way history will be saved for man, even though its forward march will not cease to be ambiguous, hesitant, and fraught with lapses.

The primary condition and first result[13] of this creative transformation is a shift of stress and emphasis. In a compulsory evolution, a history that pushed man from behind, the most important thing was the unforeseeable, determining factors, the mighty forces unleashed over man or by certain men. In each and every case people saw the divine in action. There were extraordinary happenings inseparable from the miraculous, and extraordinary beings representing the divinity and its powers (note David in 2 Sam. 14:17). Now however, the most important thing is to shift one's attention, to some extent, from the material aspect of those persons and events in order to discover the real determining conditions behind them. And the aim is not to deify or submit to these underlying conditions; it is to take hold of them and direct them.

Thus the message contained in the event takes over first place. On the cognitive level it is above the event itself and its magnitude. We thus come to realize that humanity's most real history has not proceeded from happening to happaning, but rather from interpretation to interpretation.

Obviously the latter is not contradictory to the objective truth of the events being interpreted. It is the liberating and liberated way of knowing both historical and legendary events. This point is simple enough to understand in practice, but a concrete example may help. A young pupil growing up in a Latin American country will learn the history of his nation as a great deed centered around the decisive destiny of the nation's liberator. But the more creative the pupil's mind and spirit is, the more he will gradually come to realize that there is another history far more gripping than any anecdotal account of the life of the national hero. This other history is the history of the various interpretations that have been formulated about the hero's life and work. Moving from one interpretation to the next, without necessarily denying the facts he knew at the start, the pupil will frame the hero's life within a web of sociopolitical forces that are much more profound and decisive. These forces explain the past, and enable one to decipher and perhaps control the present.

Returning to our topic in the light of this example, we will not find it accidental that at the precise stage of humanization in which we are beginning to comprehend history as a task, we are also beginning to grasp something more than a mere succession of events in Scripture. We are beginning to see a succession of interpretations of these events.[14] It is more than a history of salvation; it is the gripping history of the different interpretations of that history, these interpretations having been suggested by God the Savior himself. And we come to realize that the authentic process of divine education and the salvation of history was his work of inducing his people to move from one interpretation to the next.

3. Obviously enough the primacy of interpretation over event produces a coefficient of relativity—not relativism—which is part and parcel of maturity and hence a wellspring of creativity and liberty. For it is not just a matter of one interpretation, but of successive interpretations. Even within the Bible itself we note that there are different ideas about the "creation" event. The Yahwist writer makes one thing of it. During the exile, the priestly source and Deutero-Isaiah make something else of it. The Book of Wisdom, too, has its own interpretation. With respect to the figure of Abraham, some people would have reacted strongly against Paul's interpretation of him. If one were accustomed to view him in terms of the convenant issuing from the sacrifice of Isaac, then Paul's emphasis on his faith as the source of his justification could seem to be a dangerous relativization (cf. James 2:20 ff; and, perhaps related, 2 Pet. 3:16).

Thus demythologizing, as we understand it, does not entail arbitrary denial of the historicity of any and every narrative that pictures God intervening in this world, just because one wants to be a man of today.[15] It consists in not choosing to ground our grasp of the word of God on some literal, immobile comprehension of the events narrated.

But this simple step of moving from an immobile account to the flexibility of its various possible interpretations as suggested by the problems of history is not so easy. It causes us discomfort and insecurity, and faces us with a crisis. If we proceed from interpretation to interpretation, then are we not moving away from any and every sure criterion? Will we not end up not knowing where to stop and hold on?

W. H. van de Pol has some keen remarks to make about this crisis, which is nothing else but the price we must pay for maturity. He points out that three attitudes are possible:

> The one extreme point of view is that of the Holy Office: as far as doctrine and theology, piety and morality are concerned, conventional Christianity must be preserved and protected at any cost against undermining of whatever nature and from whatever side.
>
> The other extreme position is that of an ever-growing number of believers: it is apparent that Christianity has in so many respects and so many ways become undermined that it is no longer possible to accept it. Therefore it is better to leave it behind altogether, either with regret or with definite aversion.
>
> Between these two extremes is the middle of the road which the Second Vatican Council and the synods and world conferences of the non-Roman Catholic Churches try to take. This position makes a sharp distinction between the essence and the formulation of the Christian faith, between what is essential and what is accidental in the practice of the church and the personal living of the faith, between authority and the personal conscience, between charity and justice, between the human and the divine aspect—in short between the immutable core and the changeable, partially antiquated exterior of conventional Christianity.[16]

But this *via media* runs into a serious problem if it tries to be something more than a facile and superficial balance: "This is the problem of what norm must be used to establish—without falling into error—where the borderline lies between the unchangeable core and the changeable exterior."[17]

Posed in those terms, however, the question does not and cannot have an answer; for any such answer would run counter to the maturity with which man, be he Christian or not, must face up to the ever new problems of history through trial and error. If we could recognize "one norm" which would enable us to determine "without errors" the "exact" borderline between the unchangeable core and the changeable exterior, then we would be the slaves of history rather than its creators. And we Christians would still lack the most liberating elements of our faith: i.e., those which the Trinitarian Creed attributes to the activity of the Holy Spirit, as we saw in the main article of this chapter.

The fact is that it is he who begins the work of interpreting the material history of salvation, he "who spoke through the prophets." It is he who enlivens and guides the prophetic community known as the Church. It is he who makes the Church worthy of faith, so that in the Church our continuing interpretation of the very same salvific events will lead us "into all the truth" (John 16:13). That is why we do not say, "We believe that the Church is one . . ." but rather, "We believe in the Church . . ."[18]

It is Christ himself who promised his "spiritual" presence, not to each individual Christian but to those who gather together in his name, so that the necessary succession of interpretations dealing with salvation right up to the end of time would not end up in relativism or error, but rather in the truth that saves human history step by step.[19]

III. PRAYER, PROVIDENCE, COMMITMENT

The intimate relationship between the revelation of the Christian God and the value of history can be attractive to Christians who feel separated from the worries of their fellow men by the very fact of their faith itself. But it can just as well shock those who feel that the possibility of *praying*, of asking "things" from God, is the one and only religious recourse in their lives. How can they ask things from a God who is "the salvation of history"?

1. The crisis here usually does not come from any transformation in the idea of God. It comes from facts and events themselves, from what we might call history's refutation of prayer. Three different responses to an inquiry may serve as examples here:

"For a whole year I prayed desperately for the health of my father, who was being eaten away by cancer. But he died in the bloom of life. God does not exist. Or if he does exist, he takes no interest in me." (22-year-old laborer)

"Once upon a time I asked God to help me pass my exams. Then I decided to go on a diet so that I would lose weight. I did lose weight, and it was not due to God but due to my will power in giving up sweets and other fattening foods. I suddenly realized that the same thing was true about exams, and I gradually gave up praying. I no longer found any meaning in prayer." (15-year-old student)

"From the age of twelve on, I used to run in and out of confession with sins of a sexual nature. My sex life was in disorder. But for the past three months, the 'good example' of an atheist companion has helped me and made confession superfluous. This friend's sexual conduct is much more ordered than mine because he has learned to discipline himself. I suddenly realized that the recitation of countless Our Fathers meant little. If I am to shape up, I must will to do it. *It depends on me.*" (16-year-old student)

Countless statements along these lines could be added here.

The image of God that lies behind many of our prayers is that of a God who is a better technician than our human technicians, a better doctor than our doctors. In other words, it is the image of a God who occupies a place in our lives that has not yet been reached by human knowledge and effectiveness.

Logically, however, the notions of supplement and competency go hand in hand. The more we become accustomed to asking from science and technology, the less we ask of God. Or, to put it better: the more familiar we become with scientific and technological effort, the more we assume the responsibility of finding in them the solution to man's suffering and misery, so much the more does the attitude of asking these things from God seem to us to be a diminution of man and a crime against humanity.

In this context God loses what man gains, and vice versa. And the most important and improbable thing is that God himself, in this same context, is more interested in losing than we are!

2. The fact is that maintaining this sort of "faith" may be far worse than losing it. After all, what is the image of God lurking behind prayers that are "answered"? To put it another way: What would happen if God should heed the pleas of some? What would happen if he were to heed the petitions of all?

We have already seen[20] that Jesus' miraculous deeds, or what were taken as such by those who saw them at the time, were not manifestations of preternatural capabilities designed to force recognition of his divine status. In liberating the people of his day from many different bonds, Jesus revealed that God is not absent from the world wherein sickness, death, paralysis, and wretchedness enslave man; that God does not want human beings to be alienated people, riddled with blindness, paralysis, and diabolic possession. Jesus reveals God revealing to us that everything that wounds man wounds him equally. We could say that in human history we discover God's tangible point.

This summons to responsibility in history would have been totally annulled if Jesus' "power" could have been used as a cure-all. But it would have been even more radically annulled if Jesus could have been used only by the few who had access to him. In this world that was his, millions and millions of sick people were not cured miraculously. Millions upon millions of people were not nourished by miraculous deeds with loaves and fishes. The sorrow of infant mortality, which bypassed the house of Jairus, continued to visit the houses of his neighbors; it may even have returned to his house later, after it had been expelled accidentally and for the moment. The chains of enslavement were not burst asunder for the vast majority of people living under the exploitation of the Roman Empire.

A God who heard everyone's prayer would have been a God of *children*. A God who heard the prayers of his closest followers, of those whom he himself had given a faith "capable of moving mountains," would have been a God of the *privileged few*. These few would have

found a way to get the better of the rest of mankind in the use and
enjoyment of the world; they would operate religiously, through God.

Here we have another reason why it was good for them that Jesus
go. It is as if Jesus had said something like this: "Through my resurrection
and the sending of the Spirit, I have replaced proclamation with reality.
Henceforth I shall never calm the storm again as I once did. But my
Spirit will calm the storm when you have mastered the technique of
constructing ships strong enough to ride out its waves. I shall never
again return to feed a multitude in the desert, but I shall do it when
my creative Spirit in you has led them to improve the earth's soil and
distribute its fruit better. And if you suffer in these love-inspired tasks,
I cannot help it. Because now I am no longer 'in your midst' and rather
'within you': as the source of the love, the creativity, and the persistence
that leads men to love each other more effectively and fraternally. Indeed
it is I in each of you that suffers from the stormy sea, the arid soil,
the misery of poverty and alienation. Like you and with you I suffer
too. I have not shipped you off on a voyage without knowing whether
the port of arrival is worth the trip. The great guarantee, the only
guarantee, that I can give you is that I have shipped out with you in
a committed and definitive way."

3. Within this framework of reference we can see that *divine providence,* in the Christian view, is not and cannot be a doctrine propounding
some sort of divine interference that dislocates man's affairs and efforts.
Nor can it be the inaccessible start of a world that goes on from there
to operate under its own laws without any personal reference.[21]

In the concrete, temporal history of his love for us, God gives us
a world that functions in accord with its own proper laws (GS 36). But
he does not give it to us as some sort of alien and inert material. He
fashions this world into a system of signs (revelation, which culminates
with its total insertion into this world; see GS 22), through which he
leads us to shoulder the task of freeing all its dynamisms for the service
of love and the construction of the world. In its definitive form, this
world will be not only the *new earth* of man but also the *new heaven*
of God. "Providentialism" and "passivity," which were so often tied
together in customary usage, [22] are contradictory in reality.

In a previous CLARIFICATION we saw that the signs of the times varied
their mode of signification insofar as man shouldered them. Well, in
the case of Christians, reflection is presupposed if they are to lay hold
of the signs of the times and advance toward new horizons, new operational uses, more proximate and practicable utopias. In short, it presupposes that some period of time has been rescued from the press of
everyday life and the efficiency that is already known and practiced.

This period of time does not take us out of the world. But it does
relate us explicitly to God, since it consists in lending a more attentive
ear to his word that is transmitted by what happens in time. It is a
time of interpretation which makes us less and less inclined to be dis-

tracted from small things by great things, to lose sight of conscious realities in the face of basic, infrastructural things (GS 38).

This activity of reflection and interpretation is *prayer*. In the deepest sense it is the encounter of two words, of two languages. And there is no Christian living at all without such prayer, whether it takes the form of a petition or not.

4. But precisely here, in connection with this notion of prayer, we are again confronted with the same question that we asked at the start: Does it still make sense to ask "things" from a God who connects his salvation with us through history?

If we look at the Gospel, we find that it not only makes sense but is also expressly suggested by Jesus when he teaches his disciples to pray: "Give us today our daily bread . . ." (Matt. 6:11). "Ask, and you will receive; seek, and you will find; knock, and the door will be opened. For everyone who asks receives, he who seeks finds, and to him who knocks, the door will be opened . . . If you, then, bad as you are, know how to give your children what is good for them, how much more will your heavenly Father give good things to those who ask him!" (Matt. 7:7–11). "Ask and you will receive," like Paul's "I am free to do anything," represents an opening up and out that shatters the contradiction. To give them an intelligible content we must situate both within the framework of what we might call "the Christian project": i.e., the fashioning of love in history; or, what comes down to the same thing, the liberation of the universe from all the enslavements that weigh down upon it, until our creative work is revealed for what it is—the work of God's children, us (Rom. 8:19). For this purpose we have within us the Spirit of the Son; that is, the Spirit "of sons," the Spirit of creativity and liberation. To sin against the Spirit is precisely to refuse to accompany Jesus in his work of liberation.[23]

In Matthew's Gospel, Jesus promises that God, being our Father, will give "good things" to those who ask them of him. Luke is more theological, and he spells this out more precisely: God will give "the Holy Spirit to those who ask him" (Luke 11:13).

Thus we see that the infallibility of prayer is tied up with the salvation of history. At first reading, the text of Matthew seems to promise us help in our most difficult undertakings, while the text of Luke goes much deeper in its interpretation. It suggests that God's help, his reply to our petitions, does not consist in a "helping hand" but in his gift of himself, of his Spirit, who is the fountainhead of creativity and the guarantee of incorruptibility for our love in history.

We could say that revelation establishes the fact that no love is lost. And to be more specific, that no love is lost when limitations, which do not come from ourselves but from things themselves, step in between us and the carrying out of our love. There where our powers end, the heart can still go much further. The limitations that do not come from our own egotism, be it conscious or unconscious, are not limits.

The construction of the future earth does not take place solely within the limits of the means, and forces, and influence at our disposal. The poor, the sick, the marginal people do construct the future earth, if they expend their forces to the limit in the work of liberating love. We all experience this limit. If we are sincere, it becomes a point of anxiety for us. If we are Christians, this anxiety turns into hope, and the hope into words: i.e., into *prayer*.

There is no reason why our hope, now turned into spoken word, should be abstract. If our love is faced with the illness of a loved one, it is only logical that it find expression in a petition for that person's health. To ask for this is not to ask for miracles. We are simply voicing the limit confronted by our love, and the victory of our hope over that limit. And there is no limitation on *that petition* except that imposed by our own commitment. Total commitment, with forces no more powerful than that of a mustard seed, will move mountains. Because, to repeat it once again, in the history we share with God no love is lost.

IV. DEMYTHOLOGIZING: THE SEARCH FOR WHAT IS LEFT

If the reader has followed our exposition in this chapter, an exposition that is much closer to the language of the Bible, he will have already noted, or can readily note, that this "self-revelation" of God has certain special characteristics.

The first characteristic can be summed up concretely in the phrase that the Acts of the Apostles uses to describe the preaching of Jesus: "In the first part of my work, Theophilus, I wrote of all that Jesus did and taught from the beginning until the day when . . . he was taken up to heaven" (Acts 1:1-2). God's revelation as a whole is the full conjugation of these two verbs. The Father does and teaches through the prophets. The Son does and teaches in person. The Spirit does and teaches through the very life of the Church in the world.

What is more, what God does is precisely the thing that reveals him: "God is love . . . It is by this that we know what love is: that Christ laid down his life for us" (1 John 4:8 and 3:16). What we call the miracles of Jesus were in fact, as the Gospel tells us, signs: i.e., acts signifying something, acts that spoke in themselves and revealed who was doing them.

The prophets of Israel were not men who saw into the future—except on rare occasions and in a very secondary sense. They were men with double vision, so to speak. In things that happened they saw signs of the one who was responsible for them. Through the prophets, the historical event revealed him who was acting in history.

In these two examples, which are clearer than any that can be offered to us by the activity of the Spirit in the Church, we see that it is God's activity that reveals God. There is no grounding statement or teaching about God on the abstract plane of essences. God reveals himself in and through his activity.

By the same token, however, the mere fact of God's activity does not reveal him if the "signification" of this activity is not comprehended. Jesus must teach people what his activity signifies. Narrative without interpretation is not enough to reveal God to us. Those who crucified Christ saw the same things as the apostles. But the former did not interpret these events and did not recognize the God who was revealing himself in them (1 Cor. 1:22; 2:8, 14).

So we can say that God's revelation is necessarily made up of two inseparable elements: a narrative and an interpretation. The first element presents a fact: God's activity in the world of men. The second element interprets this event for precisely what it is: an activity that reveals God and illuminates our existence at the same time.

And it is here that a problem comes up, concerning specifically the truth of the narrative. Are we really dealing with facts and events like those which a historian investigates? Are we dealing with "historical events," in the scholarly and current sense of the term? Can they be verified by the current methodology of historical science, independent of an interpretation of them as manifestations of God?

Insofar as certain narratives of the Bible are concerned, we can give a categorical "no" to the questions just raised. Take the narrative about a flood that covered the whole earth and its mountains, for example. It is a legend taken over by the biblical writers from narratives that already existed in the pagan Semitic world. What is more, it was altered precisely to teach something directly contrary to what those other legends taught about God's activity. The biblical story sought to teach that man could cultivate the earth and build upon it without fear that divine caprice would destroy his work at a moment's notice.[24]

So then the question is: Must we extend this judgment to cover all the actions of God that are narrated and interpreted by Scripture? Bultmann was the first theologian in our day to answer this question with a "yes." We can sum up his thought on this point by using the words of Paul Van Buren: "Myth, as Bultmann uses the word, is the presentation of the transcendent in terms of this world . . . Divine action is conceived as an intervention in this world by heavenly, transcendent powers. But men today can no longer give credence to such a way of thinking. The scientific revolution, with its resulting technological and industrial development, has given us another, empirical way of thinking and of seeing the world."[25]

Demythologizing, then, consists in declaring that all the narratives about divine interventions in history are *myths*. In other words, if God does reveal himself, he does not reveal himself acting directly.

Does that mean that any and every narrative about divine action in history would be devoid of truth, according to Bultmann? By no means. A fable, for example, is not devoid of truth by virtue of the fact that it narrates an event which never actually took place. Precisely insofar as we recognize it to be a fable, our attention moves on from the accidental and unessential to the authentic aspect: that is, interpreting the intention of the fable-teller, the truth of his message that comes through the fable.

So now we can come back to our problem. We said that God's self-revelation always involves a combination of action and interpretation. For Bultmann, no activity of God is acceptable as literal truth; it is acceptable only as literary truth. So there remains interpretation. By interpreting this account we recognize the message that God is directing to our existence, the lesson that he is teaching us about our life and history.

Two things ought to be accepted in Bultmann's formulation. The first is something we have already said. It is that many of the divine interventions narrated in the Bible, in accordance with their literary genre, are accounts designed to be interpreted; they are not accounts to be kept as an objective description of how things happened.

The second, and the more important, is the primacy of interpretation over narrative. It is certain that nothing in God's message is given as a topic of mere information. The fact of knowing something objectively does not contain any power for salvation. God's message is a personal dialogue with us. It relates to us, to the import and orientation of our existence. It is highly significant and noteworthy that the first writings of the New Testament that we have, not only are not "histories" of Jesus (and not even the Gospels are that in the strict sense), but actually relate practically nothing about his life. All the Epistles of Paul are an uninterrupted "interpretation" of God's activity in Christ.

It is also certain, as Bultmann says, that this interpretation presupposes some knowledge of ourselves and opens up this knowledge to wider and deeper dimensions. That is what we have tried to do concretely in the main section of this chapter, and we shall continue to do this throughout the remaining chapters.

But there are also two things in Bultmann's view that are unacceptable, as we see it. They are unacceptable, not only because they do not accord with Catholic doctrine, but also because they do not accord with his own logic.

The first thing is something we adverted to in the CLARIFICATION of the Introduction to this volume. It is the approach of taking what "modern man" accepts in fact as the outer limit of what is acceptable—as if modern man were not the product of a liberty and a society that are to a large extent alienated.[26] Even though he may be too quick to take it for granted, Bultmann may be right in saying that a certain empirical "man of the present day" does not accept representations of the transcendent world in terms of this world. But we are perfectly justified in asking why, for concrete experience certainly cannot indicate how the transcendent is to be represented.

And if "empirical" here means that modern man does not accept anything transcendent, then this stance does not come from experience but from an *attitude*. And it is in fact an attitude for which any sort of revelation would lack meaning. So this modern man is opposed to accepting the transcendent, not because of his modernity, but because of an attitude that is as old as the world itself.[27]

The second thing we cannot accept in Bultmann's formulation of the question, for the sake of logic itself, is something that Van Buren himself points up to some extent. If there is no divine intervention in history, not only is the biblical account mythical, but the interpretation of it is merely human. Accepting it has nothing to do with faith.

We are in fact faced with two alternativers. Either the prophets—or Christ himself—transmit an interpretation that God is sending to us; in that case the message itself is a divine intervention in history, of the same order as any in the biblical account. Or else they are transmitting their own thoughts about our existence; and in that case I accept them or not, as I choose, just I as would those of a Socrates, a Nietzsche, or a Heidegger. And that certainly has nothing to do with the attitude of faith.[28]

What is more, if that is the case then we must agree with Van Buren in saying that the very use of the word *God* in that context is counterproductive. For then God does not intervene in real-life events, nor is he the source or subject of their interpretation.[29] In such a case the word *God* is a cause of confusion. It should be translated systematically by some other term, such as "what I desire my existence to be."

In conclusion we would say that we are here confronted with one of the most significant phenomena in the occidental world. Jean Paul Sartre has criticized the comfortable bourgeois morality of the "upright" man, which has tried to go on being the same as it was even after God had been eliminated from the picture.[30] We could just as well say that the religion of the industrialized capitalist world has tried illogically to keep using gestures and words that are totally devoid of meaning in the life-style that is generally its own.

Hence Latin America, in its struggle for liberation, is not confronted with the "death of God" but rather with the task of ensuring the "death of the idols" that hold it in bondage and that are too often confused with God.

V. THE EARLY CHURCH INVOKES THE TRINITY

If the reader is used to the simplicity, perhaps more apparent than real, of the Gospel narratives, he or she may well ask whether the profundity of the Trinitarian mystery does not signify a *later* construct quite alien to the message of the New Testament.

Father, Son, Holy Spirit: three divine persons, one God. This is the traditional, age-old formulation of the divine Trinity in Christian theology. But despite its antiquity, we shall see in the following chapters that the Church took a long time to arrive at this formula. The revelation of the Trinitarian God first went through more simple and less precise stages.

The very term *Trinity* itself suggests a certain equivalence and equality among the three that make it up. So it is not surprising that we do not find the word *Trinity* in the earliest testimonies. The first dogmatic formulas, the symbols of faith or creeds (as we call them today), date from the end of the second century after Christ. They present the three persons as objects of faith, that is as part of the content of divine revelation, along with the resurrection and the Church: "I believe in God the Father almighty, and in his only-begotten Son, Jesus Christ our Lord, and in the Holy Spirit . . ." (Denz. 1). Even our use of the word *persons* is anachronistic here, because they had not yet been characterized as such.

Since these creeds do not affirm anything essential about the Son and the Spirit, we can only conclude from them that the Christians of that time united the Lord Jesus and the Holy Spirit with the revelation of God the almighty Father at the very heart of their faith.

But we have another similar testimony which is even more ancient and more directly related to Christian praxis. And it enables us to glimpse the fact that Christian life was only conceived in relation to "the three," who are objects of faith. This testimony is the baptismal formula. From the very beginnings of the Church it was employed in its full form without distinciton. And, what is even more important, it was used even by those who maintained doctrinal differences. Three times, once for each divine person, the catechumen is asked whether he or she believes: Do you believe in the Father? Do you believe in the Son? Do you believe in the Holy Spirit? And immersion in water followed each "yes" response.

It cannot be denied that this triple parallelism and its intimate relationship with the Christian life constitutes first-class testimony to the fact that the Son and the Spirit were considered in practice as constituent elements of the revealed divine mystery.

What is more, this is the baptismal formula familiar to Matthew's Gospel (28:19): "Go forth therefore and make all nations my disciples; baptize men everywhere in the name of the Father and the Son and the Holy Spirit."

We said that this testimony is of first-class importance because it puts Father, Son, and Holy Spirit on the same level of divine revelation, even when it does not mention the word *Trinity* or even the number "three." In the New Testament, as a matter of fact, we do find an explicit reference to "three witnesses" in the Vulgate: "There are three witnesses in heaven, the Father, the Word, and the Spirit, and these three are one" (Vulgate, 1 John 5:7–8). But it is the unanimous opinion of exegetes that this explicitly Trinitarian reference is a much later interpolation.

In this connection, even the baptismal formula of Matthew's Gospel is late when compared with that of Acts. The latter consisted in baptizing the neophyte "in the name of Jesus Christ" (Acts 10:48) or "into the name of the Lord Jesus" (Acts 8:16).

The fact is that in reality the Synoptic Gospels were written when the Church was already a structured community of faith, even though to some extent they re-create the atmosphere of the disciples' first contact with Jesus. Thus the Synoptic Gospels represent an attempt to fix and perpetuate the principal sayings and most significant deeds of Jesus Christ, particularly his passion and resurrection, with a view to the work of evangelization.

Their very intention undoubtedly makes them the most direct books in the New Testament, those which least of all have been passed through the sieve of the author's conceptual elaboration. We say "least of all" because they too reflect a "recollection" of Jesus that has been reflected on in the light of faith. This notwithstanding, the Gospel of Matthew does not contain the thinking of Matthew in the sense tht one of Paul's Epistles represents an expression of Paul's reflection.

The direct focusing of the Synoptic Gospels on the deeds and sayings of Jesus could give the reader a false impression: that they are the first and earliest writings after Jesus. But the fact is that the block of Pauline Epistles antedates the extant redaction of the first three Gospels. And in them we see how much the Church had already pondered the revelation of Father, Son, and Spirit.

The fact is that in Paul's writings we often find passages that mention the three divine persons. Let us take, for example, the Epistle that in all probability constitutes the oldest document in the New Testament. It is the Epistle to the Galatians, in which we read the following: "To prove that you are sons, God [ho theos] has sent into our hearts the Spirit of his son, crying 'Abba! Father!' " (Gal. 4:6). As the reader can see, Paul associates the combined effort of God (the Father), the Son, and the Spirit with the reality of the Christian vocation.[31]

Let us take another example, this time from the first letter to the Corinthians. Here again the three names appear within one phrase: "Such were some of you. But you have been through the purifying waters; you have been dedicated to God and justified through the name of the Lord Jesus and the Spirit of our God" (1 Cor. 6:11). Again we note a characteristic that we have already encountered and stressed: the phrase does not have to do with God alone in his eternity; instead it describes the wondrous "now" of Christian existence as opposed to the "before" of their lives as pagans. And in the work that brought about this "now" we see the Lord Jesus, the Spirit, and the Father converging for a joint effort.

Apart from this Epistle, we find a similar example in the letter addressed to the Romans: "From Paul, servant of Christ Jesus, apostle by God's call, set apart for the service of the Gospel. This gospel God announced beforehand in sacred scriptures through his prophets. It is about his Son: on the human level he was born of David's stock, but on the level of the spirit—the Holy Spirit—he was declared Son of God by a mighty act in that he rose from the dead" (Rom. 1:14).[32]

But there is more. In the examples cited so far it was important to point out how the three names were invariably associated with the essential totality of the Christian vocation. From this we could and should conclude that this vocation would be comprehensible only in a *triple* relationship. But in these examples the phrase pointed toward one of the three names and tended to bring in the other names in its wake. Thus these passages do not testify to the identity of the three persons so clearly as does, for example, the baptismal formula.

But it is interesting to note that we do find, in New Testament documents dating back to the earliest period, formulas that we could call *strictly* Trinitarian formulas: i.e., formulas designed to show the convergence of the three divine names in the creation of Christian existence.

We find a rough approximation to such formulas in passages like this one: "You have been through the purifying waters; you have been dedicated to God and justified through the name of the Lord Jesus and the Spirit of our God" (1 Cor. 6:11). We find it difficult not to see a threefold, parallel relationship between the three verbs, which put their mark on the rhythm of the phrase, and the three names that end it. What is more, we have here themes that are common in Paul's corpus: ablution in the name of Christ, sanctification by virtue of the participation of the Spirit, and the active justice of God that makes just those whom he chooses.

The rhythm of a triple parallelism shows up equally in another description of the Christian vocation: "There is one body and one Spirit, as there is also one hope held out in God's call to you; one Lord, one faith, one baptism; one God and Father of all, who is over all and through all and in all" (Eph. 4:4–6).[33]

Finally, there are Trinitarian formulas that are so clear and so explicit that we are amazed to see how the Church, barely recovering from the impact of the happenings themselves, has managed to grasp the message about the three persons in the framework of one divine reality directed toward man. In addition to the two formulas cited in the main section of this chapter,[34] we can offer this exhortation of Paul to the Christians of Philippi: "If then our common life in Christ yields anything to stir the heart, any loving consideration, any sharing of the Spirit, any warmth of affection or compassion, fill up my cup of happiness by thinking and feeling alike, with the same love for one another, the same turn of mind, and a common care for unity" (Phil. 2:1–2).

Hence we can conclude that what the Church formulated dogmatically much later on was nothing else but the explication of what the early Church believed and lived about the three witnesses in heaven who are one.[35]

NOTES

1. "At this point of our investigation, we would be allowing sentiment to falsify the facts if we failed to recognize that during historic time the principal axis of anthropogenesis has passed through the West. It is in this ardent zone of growth and universal recasting that all that goes to make man today has been discovered, or at any rate *must have been rediscovered*. For even that which had long been known elsewhere only took on its definitive human value in becoming incorporated in the system of European ideas and activities" (Teilhard de Chardin, *The Phenomenon of Man*, Eng. trans. New York Harper & Row, 1959, p. 212).

2. In *Die Gnosis des Christentums,* G. Koepgen asserts that the personality of man in the West came to light under the influence of the dogma of the Trinity. Koepgen is cited by C.G. Jung in *Psychology and Religion: East and West,* English translation of his collected works, (New York: Bollingen Series XX, 1958), pp. 189–90, footnotes 45 and 46.

3. For a more detailed development of Christianity's contribution to the phenomenon of the Occident, we refer the reader to Denis de Rougement, *L'Aventure occidental de l'homme* (Paris: Albin Michel, 1957. However questionable his portrait of the future of this adventure may be, he offers very suggestive analyses of the relationship between Christianity and culture in the past.

4. Eric Fromm, *The Sane Society* (New York: Holt, Rinehart 1955), p. 87.

5. *Ibid.,* p. 88.

6. *Ibid.,* p. 92.

7. Fromm takes note of this loss of reciprocity: "Since it [i.e., the worker's labor] had been bought for its proper price on the labor market, there was no sense of reciprocity, or of any obligation on the part of the owner of capital, beyond that of paying the wages" (*ibid*).

8. This is far more than a mere play on words. To begin with, it is obvious that there is a danger of salvation history's being turned into nothing more than a narrow, unacceptable "sacred history for adults."

9. Oscar Lewis, *The Children of Sanchez* (New York: Random House, 1961) p. 171: Part II, "Manuel."

10. *Cf.* André Scrima: "I tell myself now and again that the notion 'history of salvation,' traced out on its fullest horizon which is that defined by the relationship between *oikonomia* ('economy' in the sense of 'plan' or 'dispensation') and *theologia,* differs markedly from the 'local' and restricted use that is made of it by a certain occidental theology which is too greatly stamped with a specific cultural problematic (now somewhat out of date). The *oikonomia* does not lend itself to ready identification with the merely 'historical' aspect, as the latter is understood by those who maintain this line of thought. What I would like to see in the not too distant future is the cosmological emphasis gaining the upper hand, within a total Christological perspective, over the historicism that now dominates." In *Mito e Fede,* a collaborative effort by Castelli, Panikkar, Ott, et al., Archivo di Filosofia, Padua: Cedam, 1966. p. 311.

11. *Cf.* Volume I, Chapter V.

12. Christ's death and resurrection point specifically toward a transition from the blind weight of an evolution that must be borne to the liberty of a creation that shoulders and directs it. Thus, if the resurrection establishes Jesus as Son (Rom. 1:4), the revelation of our own quality of sonship is presupposed if all the dynamisms of the universe are to be crowned with meaningfulness (Rom. 8:12).

13. Even with Paul himself, as we shall see.

14. Hence, for example, the importance of Abraham for the New Testament, and for Paul especially, does not reside in the fact that he, by leaving Ur and becoming a nomad, set in motion a series of events which, through the creation of the people of Israel, made possible the Christ event. Abraham, illuminated by the interpretation which proceeds from Christ, allows Paul to interpret anew the religion of Israel, to appropriate its most liberating message, and to free himself from the rest of it (cf. Gal. 3–4; Rom. 4:9–11).

15. Karl Rahner feels this way: "This is not to say that it is, in general, particularly profitable for theology to take as the explicit starting point of a critical consideration of the average Christology current today, any characteristic features of just that spiritual situation which has been imposed upon us, in so far as they are apprehended *reflexively*. Such a method is seldom successful, if only because these reflexively apprehended characteristics of the time are probably signatures of a time which is on the way out . . . For it is quite meaningless to want to be modern on purpose" (*Theological Investigations* I, Engl. trans., Baltimore: Helicon Press, 1961, p. 153: Chapter 5, "Current Problems in Christology"). The admonition also holds good for a modern theologian like Rahner if it fits. In connection with our theme, see Chapter III, CLARIFICATION III.

16. W. H. van de Pol, *The End of Conventional Christianity*, Eng. trans. (New York: Newman Press, 1968), p. 74.

17. *Ibid.* It is not surprising that this problem does not have a solution for Van de Pol as yet, since at certain points in his book he too seems to turn the mentality of "the man of today" into an absolute: "If by the force of circumstances we follow the way of symbolization because we accept the achievements of science, philosophy, and cultural development just as we accept the content of the Christian faith, we must realize that while we do know where we begin, we do not know where we shall finish" (*ibid.,* p. 76). There is nothing to indicate that the author does not include himself in the "we" of this passage.

18. For that very reason we do not consider tradition as a "second font," from which we get things that do not exist in the biblical history of salvation. Rather, we regard it as the hermeneutical continuity which unites the Christian community, through the epochs of history, in its work of interpreting divine revelation. This continuity is the living work of the Spirit, not our fidelity to the letter. And since one cannot find a *norm,* as it is defined by Van de Pol, one commonly resorts to a position in which everything or almost everything takes on the same essential character. Van de Pol identifies this position with the "Holy Office." Undoubtedly there does exist in ecclesiastical circles a certain amount of anxiety over the task posed by maturity, which is not successfully mastered by faith in the activity of the Holy Spirit.

19. Our comments in this chapter have a specific pastoral application in the area of liturgy. Under its cover of signs, the liturgy really manifests the Lord present in the history of the salvation of humanity. Without undermining our intention to treat this topic in the next volume, we could say here that

any plan for liturgical renewal must pass through the stages that mark the transition from "history of salvation" to "salvation of history." It must pass from the history lived in the liturgical sign to history as a whole. It must gradually give priority to the interpretation of the liturgical sign rather than to the quantity, invariability, and validity of the commemmorative rite. It must continually reinterpret the happening, which is alluded to by the sign, in the light of the "signs of the times," i.e., of the current problems posed in connection with man's liberation.

20. See the previous CLARIFICATION; also Chapter IV, CLARIFICATION I.

21. A God *too near* is unacceptable. We are thinking of *The Plague* by Camus. There is also a passage in which J. M. Le Blondel sums up, and perhaps oversimplifies, the thinking of Merleau-Ponty on this point: "God is incompatible with the existence of human science and activity . . .In effect he [i.e., Merleau-Ponty] feels that if the history of human thought and action unfolds according to some pre-established plan, if the whole of it has already been thought out—not to say 'written out'—by God, then it loses its human import. It then loses the meaningfulness that man desires to give it and does in fact give it—for which reason man is irreplaceable" (*Études*, 1953, p. 353).

A God *too far away* is equally inadmissible. We are thinking of the finale of Kafka's *The Trial*, wherein a strange, fragile apparition appears, weak and delicate, at a great distance away.

22. A recent draft-document, prepared for the Latin American Confederation of Religious, specifically criticizes any and all "providentialist passivity."

23. *Cf.* Chapter IV, CLARIFICATION I.

24. *Cf.* Gustave Lambert, "Il n'ya aura plus jamais de déluge (Gen. 11:11)," *Nouvelle Revue Théologique* (1955), pp. 581–601; 693–724. It was Pius XII's encyclical *Divino afflante Spirtu* that set Catholic exegesis squarely on this path. It asked that in each case study be devoted to the intention of the author and the literary genre of which he made use to express his truth, which was God's truth as well.

25. Paul Van Buren, *The Secular Meaning of the Gospel* (New York: Macmillan, 1966), p. 5.

26. It is here, and not in its attack on the "precomprehension" required for grasping the message, that Barth's attack on Bultmann retains its full value—especially if it is given its rightful social dimension.

27. In the twofold sense of the term *world*: i.e., its current sense and its theological sense.

28. Through the course of this volume and especially in some sections (such as in CLARIFICATION II of this chapter), we do more justice to Bultmann's enormous contribution to theology than we do in this section devoted to demythologizing. We agree with W. H. van de Pol when he writes: "The actual problem which Bultmann—in my opinion quite *ad rem*—has raised is whether and how far the translation from one form into another influences, affects, and possibly even undermines the *kerygma* itself. This is the actual and inevitable problem. No theologian can or may withdraw himself from reflection on this problem, particularly because of pastoral reasons. This does not necessarily mean that a person must and can agree with Bultmann on all points. Numerous questions have arisen which are either directly or indirectly connected with Bultmann's demythologizing. These are not questions which proceed from unbelief. Nor are they artificial, arbitrary, and unnecessary questions. They simply are questions with which any Christian who is not playing hide-and-seek is necessarily faced

because of the many different causes dealt with in the preceding chapter, and which have in various respects undermined conventional Christianity" (*op. cit.* p. 109.)

29. *Cf.* Paul Van Buren, *op. cit.,* Part I, Chapter IV.

30. *Cf.* Jean Paul Sartre, *Existentialism Is a Humanism,* English translation in (e.g.) Walter Kaufmann (ed.), *Existentialism from Dostoevsky to Sartre* (New York: Meridian Books, 1956).

31. Strictly speaking, one can debate whether the term "spirit," as used by Paul in opposition to the term "flesh," does or does not designate the Holy Spirit in his writings. Our opinion is that it does, both in general and principally in our text here. Even back in the Old Testament "spirit" designated God in an indefinite, undefined sense that the Christian message personalized. The fact is that the Epistle to the Romans, after opposing the flesh to the Spirit of justification, goes on to say: "Moreover, if the Spirit of him who raised Jesus from the dead dwells in you, then the God who raised Christ Jesus from the dead will also give life to your mortal bodies through his indwelling Spirit" (Rom. 8:11).

32. Identical characteristics are provided by many other examples. "Through him [Christ] we both alike have access to the Father in the one Spirit" (Eph. 2:18–19). "God [*ho theos*] not only raised our Lord from the dead; he will also raise us by his power" (1 Cor. 6:14). That this power is synonymous with the Holy Spirit, and therefore might well be capitalized, is clear from the formula just cited in the text.

The evangelization praxis of the primitive Church also used these texts in which the three persons came together for the work of proclaiming the good news of Christianity: "You know about Jesus of Nazareth, how God [*ho theos*] anointed him with the Holy Spirit and with power. He went about doing good and healing all who were oppressed by the devil, for God was with him" (Acts 10:38). See also Eph. 3:14–17; Titus 3:4–7. Outside of Paul's epistles, see Heb. 9:13–14; 1 Pet. 3:18–19; John 4:2; Acts 20: 28; etc.

33. See also 2 Cor. 1:20.

34. See pages 20–21.

35. We could carry this analysis much further, going beyond the mere existence of Trinitarian formulas. We could show, for example, that the early Church attributes such divine operations as that of "creating" to the Son and the Spirit as well as to the Father, albeit with distinct shadings. On the Father see Heb. 3:4–6. On the Son see Col. 1:16; John 1:3,10. On the Spirit (in relationship to Gen. 1:2; Ps. 104:30; Judg. 16:14) see John 3:3–8; Titus 3:5.

CHAPTER TWO

God and Society

There is no suggestion of different essences in the three names that successively occupy the center of divine "revelation" in the broad sense:[1] i.e., the revelation that takes in the Old Testament, the gospel message, and the life of the Church (guided by the Spirit through the course of history). On the contrary, the names suggest the unity of an effort that comes from God and fills all the dimensions of man's existence.

Each one of the names is associated with the same divine work, realized on a different level, so to speak, but yet converging toward one and the same goal: i.e., that the God who is Love be all in all (1 Cor. 15:28), and that man be fully man as a result (Eph. 4:13).

In other words, when we look at revelation and its message, we do not find ourselves with the bases of a theological tract on the supramundane and the transcendent. Instead we find ourselves being enlightened about what Paul Lehmann calls "the politics of God" to "make and to keep human life *human* in the world."[2] We are confronted with each and every one of the elements which will bring humanity toward the full measure of man during the course of history (*cf.* Eph. 4:13; GS 11).

When we contemplate a force, a profundity, a being that transcends everything else, it is quite possible that we are not contemplating the Christian God at all. On the other hand, when we or other people dedicate our effort and our lives to the work of fostering mutual respect and love and unity among men, the end product of all the justice, love, and solidarity created by our world relates us infallibly to the Christian God[3] whether we are aware of it or not. In his *El Evangelio Criollo*, Amado Anzi begins and ends his poetic effort by conjuring up the whole of reality with the "name of the Father and of the Son and of the Holy Spirit."[4] The whole history of man seems to rise up and move on toward its Omega Point: "May they all be one; as thou, Father, art in me, and I in thee, so also may they be in us" (John 17:21).

The Scriptures, then, do not give essential definitions nor enter into

57

theological explanations. They limit themselves to revealing the existence and activity of Father, Son, and Holy Spirit in giving value to our history and transforming it. That is what was really important, to God and to us.

But that does not mean that a certain number of very understandable questions are not left still unanswered. For example: How can God be Father, Son, and Holy Spirit at one and the same time? How can we say that there is only one God while at the same time we talk about three? Three what? Three distinct gods? But then what would it mean to assert that there is one and only one God?

Clearly highlighted here is something that is *one* and something that is *three*. But how are we to name or define one or the other of these things? In its day-to-day life the primitive Church did not pose this question to itself on the level of logic. The first Christians were monotheists as the Jews were, and they saw themselves as people who would continue to be monotheists. By the same token they spoke readily and familiarly of the three, relating them to the new existence that had been disclosed to them.

In this and the following two chapters we shall follow the course that the Christian Church took over the span of three centuries, as it moved from this familiar awareness that Father, Son, and Holy Spirit constituted one single divine reality toward the correct, rational formulation of what is one and what is three in God.

But here again, that is only the start of our theme. It is our suspicion that it is not just a question of an intellectual attempt, that something more is involved in this whole process. It is our feeling that something much closer and more vital to our life and our society is at stake here, hidden under the guise of a mere "theological" controversy.

Section I

If we start off with the New Testament, we find it only logical that it would be Christ—his humanity, his person, his divinity—that obliged Christians to decide how they were going to express God in accordance with the message they had received. Christ does indeed continue the molds wherein monotheism had been expressed earlier. At the same time, to all outward appearances at least, he also breaks these molds—not only the molds of Greek culture but also those of Old Testament revelation.[5]

To be perfectly logical, we must say that the Spirit, the one sent to the faithful by the Father and the Son after Jesus' departure, could have posed the same problem. The undeniable fact, however, is that the closeness of the first Christians to Jesus' human life made it almost inevitable that it would be the focus of their questions and their formulation of the problem.

What are the fundamental facts and data in each of the two cases here?

1. Jesus never claims to be God (*ho theos*); rather, he calls God his Father.The presence of the definite article (*ho*) before the word *God* (*theos*) has great importance in the Greek text of the New Testament. We must not forget that *God*, in itself, is a common noun even though it is accepted that it refers to a unique reality.

Long before the time of Christ, the Old Testament had ceased to employ the proper name of God, more than likely *Yahweh*. It simply used the common name together with the definite article to designate the one and only, truly existing God.

Well the point here is that Jesus calls this God (*ho theos*) his Father. To use the word *Father* is to say, for all practical purposes, that it is God (*ho theos*) who has sent him. To be "son" is to "proceed from" (*cf*. John 7:27–29; 8:24; 13:3; 16:27–28; 3:16; etc.). What the Son transmits is what he "has seen and heard" of him whom the Jews have learned to call their God (John 8:54; also 8:36–42).

The use of the word *Son* in connection with the word *Father* suggests continuity more than difference—to such an extent, in fact, that it alarms the adversaries of Jesus rather than calming them down. True enough, they cannot be unaware of the fact that he is not claiming to be *the* God (*ho theos*). But they attack him nevertheless because an identity between him and God gradually crystallizes in his insistence and barefaced use of the "Son" and "Father" concepts. Quite soon they must have come to realize that his use of these terms posed anew the problem of divinity at least, if not of *the* God: "You, a mere man, claim to be a god" (*theos* without accompanying article; John 10:33).[6]

Jesus responds to this accusation with an ambiguity that is a common feature in the fourth Gospel, serving the same function that is attributed to the use of parables by the Synoptic writers. It sets the listeners off into two groups: those who are content with the surface meaning of what is said, and those who are stimulated by the ambiguity to search deeper. When we read his answer, we must remember that Jesus is narrating what he has seen and heard as the Word within the godhead itself. Here is his response: "Is it not written in your own Law, 'I said: You are gods'? Those are called gods to whom the word of God was delivered—and Scripture cannot be set aside. Then why do you charge me with blasphemy because I, consecrated and sent into the world by the Father, said, 'I am God's son'?" (John 10:34–36)

Attuned to this procedure used by John the Evangelist, the Christian community quickly came to realize that the word *Son*, which Jesus attributed to himself in this ambiguous form, was destined to lead the understanding of the disciples bit by bit toward a realization, not of what distinguished the Son from the Father, but of what united them in the same divinity, the same work, and the same being and life. This realization is fixed firmly in the highly precise language of John 1:1, which speaks of the *Word*: "When all things began, the Word already was. The Word dwelt with God, and what God was, the Word was." If the rules of capitalization in this matter were not so firmly fixed, and if we could use the definite article as Greek does, we could bring out the fact that the first God here refers to the Father, while the second refers to godness as a common attribute of a subject: "The Word dwelt with *The God* (i.e., The Father), and the Word was god."[7]

Even before the time of the passage we have just cited, Paul had said that Jesus had the form of god (*morphē theou*, no article with *theos*) and could claim equality with god (*theos*, again without the article). To this statement in the Epistle to the Philippians (2:6), the Epistle to the Colossians adds that he is the (visible) "image of the invisible God" (Col. 1:15), referring even more concretely to the Father; and that in him "the complete being of the Godhead dwells embodied" (Col. 2:9).

Something else must be added here. We must note that the New Testament applies equally to Christ the functions and operations that it attributes to the Father. It does not take them away from the Father, and it also applies to him functions and operations that are attributed to Christ. If the different names were specifically intended to designate a distinction between them, we would expect certain functions to be the private preserve of each; but that is not how they are presented. This holds true for such functions as creation (John 1:3, 10; Heb. 1:4; Col. 1:16), election (compare John 15:16 with John 17:6–11; 1 Cor. 1:27; Rom. 8:29; Eph. 1:4), protective guardianship (compare John 17:12 with John 17:15), and love (compare John 15:12 with John 16:27). And it holds true for others too.

But it is not just the identity of their work that is underlined by the use of the names; it is their total identity of being. So true is this that Philip's request to see the Father is absurd, because he would see *nothing* distinct from what he can already see: "Anyone who has seen me has seen the Father" (John 14:8). As the Church understands it, if Christ is "the stamp of God's very being" (Heb. 1:3) with respect to

the Father, then he is not only the unique access-road to the Father
(*cf.* Luke 10:22; John 8:25–28; 8:54–55; 10:15; 10:38; 12:40–50;
13:20; 14:23–24; 16:15; 16:26–27) but also the very end point of all
knowledge of God: "My Father and I are *one*" (John 10:30; our italics).

The same observations can rightfully be made about the Spirit who
will be sent, even though there is a smaller foundation of biblical data
in this case.

When Christ promises the sending of the Spirit, he presents it as
his own return after his death: "I am going away, and coming back to
you" (John 14:28; compare with 14:18–20; 16:19–25). So true is this
that when he speaks of the Spirit, he is not announcing another reality
but his own presence, the presence of his Spirit. Hence the Epistles
of Paul will refer with frequency to the Holy Spirit as "the Spirit of
Jesus" (Phil. 1:19; Col. 4:6; Eph. 3:16). What is more, they will also
refer to him as the "Spirit of the Father" or "of God" (*ho theos*). See,
for example, 1 Cor. 6:11 and Eph. 4:30.

It is equally interesting to observe that the same reciprocal functions
are attributed to the Father, the Son, and the Spirit. Take, for example,
the function of leading or introducing: the Spirit introduces us to the
Father (Eph. 2:18; but John the Evangelist tells us that the Son introduces
us to the Father (John 14:6), and that the Father leads us to the Son
(John 6:44) and sends us the Spirit (John 14:26).

The work of the Spirit, then, is identical with that of Christ in these
terms. We are led to another passage which resembles Jesus' response
to Philip cited earlier. This time the apostles are sad over the thought
that they will be left here without Jesus. Jesus' response is: "It is for
your good that I am leaving you. If I do not go, your Advocate will
not come, whereas if I go, I will send him to you" (John 16:7; compare
John 14:7). If their being and function were not identical, divine, then
there would be a contradiction in his use of the term "for your good."
The statement implies something that Jesus could have said explicitly
about the Spirit, even as he did say it about the Father: "The Spirit
and I are *one*."

We can sum up what we have said in this section by stressing the
main point once again. In the difference of names we cannot possibly
look for an indication of any difference that might be attributed in
itself to the being or to the activity of the Father, Son, and Spirit.

2. Let us stop for a moment, now, to consider a precise and specific
phrase in John's Gospel: "My Father and I are one" (John 10:30). We
might well say that the shadings of this phrase, like those of the Johannine
prologue treated earlier, indicate quite precisely how to express the
reality of the Christian God.

The original Greek of this passage uses the neuter of the adjective or number "one" here, rather than the masculine. It uses *hen* rather than *heis*. When it is used like this with reference to personal subjects, the neuter indicates the content of a concept: essence, property, distinctive attribute. So we could translate this phrase more accurately as: "My Father and I are *one and the same thing*." In other words, the person who sees the Son sees *no other thing* but the Father; and the person who contemplates the Son contemplates *no other object* but the Father.

By the same token, Christ's phrase can be broken down another way. Since he was talking about the Father in the preceding verses, he could have simplified the phrase even further and said: "*He and I* are the same thing." We are thus ushered into the peculiar realm of language that is represented by the personal pronouns. *He and I* make up the *we* embodied in the verb of this passage. For literally it says: "My Father and I, *we are* one." Identity of object quality does not indicate an identity of subjects. Jesus can say: "My Father and I, we are one and the same thing." But he cannot say: "My Father and I, we are one and the same *subject*."

So when Jesus employs the Father-Son relationship, he does not do so to explicate the properties that differentiate God in himself or his work. At the same time, however, it is evident that there does exist a clear and earnest I-Thou relationship between the two. The Son orientates himself to the Father as one person to another. With the same earnestness he evinces toward our human nature, he makes use of our personal pronouns to indicate that which relates him to his Father.

What is more, this is no illusory use of language. So true is this that it costs Jesus sweat and blood to put himself in agreement with this common work: "Abba, Father . . . all things are possible to thee; take this cup away from me. Yet not what *I* will, but what *thou* wilt" (Mark 14:36, our italics; *cf.* Luke 22:42–44). Only at the cost of such effort and anguish, which is far from being illusory, can Jesus make this statement at his leave-taking: "all that is mine is thine . . . May they all be *one* (again the neuter, meaning "one and the same thing"); as thou, Father, art in me, and I in thee, so also may they be in *us*" (John 17:10–21; our italics).

In like manner the identity of Jesus with his Spirit is spelled out in another succinct Joannine formula: "The Father . . . will give you *another* to be your Advocate" (John 14:16; our italics). Paraclete, Advocate, Helpmate: all these words translate the Greek term *paraklētos*. Christ, in his own way, was all these things; the Spirit, in his own way, will be all these things too.

Here again Jesus in a way is telling us: "The Spirit and I are *one and the same thing.*" But here again he cannot say: "The Spirit and I are *one and the same subject.*" Nor can he say: "I am the Spirit." In fact the difference in subjects is so serious that Jesus must draw the ultimate, heartrending conclusion: "It is for your good that *I am leaving you.* If I do not go, your Advocate will not come" (John 16:7). And it certainly costs him effort to say: "I shall not talk much longer with you . . . There is still much that I could say to you . . . However, when he comes who is the spirit of truth, *he* will guide you into all the truth (John 14:30 and 16:12–13; our italics).

Once again we have a difficult "we," earnestly willed by Jesus for our sake in his self-giving and sacrifice.

The message of the New Testament about Father, Son, and Spirit presents us with the example of the most intimate and magnificent collaboration in history. That is the way, the only way, that the God who is Love presents himself to us. Apart from this we know nothing else about his divine inner life.[9] God opened up the mystery of his being to us in order to show us a total and intimate collaboration in a history of love that is our own history.

Section II

If we rely on the conceptual tools of modern thought, it may seem easy enough to give expression to these two highwater-marks of the New Testament, when it is a matter of what is one and what is three in God.

It seems obvious that fidelity to the biblical text obliges us to speak of one single and unique *objective* content, common to the Father, Son, and Spirit; let us call it "nature," "essence," "being," and the attributes that flow from it. It seems equally obvious that the second biblical highwater-mark should be translated in terms of three "subjects" or "persons." We simply cannot forget the fact that it is the (realist) use of the personal pronouns which allows us, in the last analysis, to speak of plurality in the divine mystery.

We might also point out that while all this was part and parcel of the Church's everyday life for centuries, it took about three hundred years to explicate it with precision. We shall soon have occasion to see that different "convenient" solutions tended to oversimplify the revealed data unduly. These deviations were further abetted by the deficiencies inherent in the terminology of Greek philosophy.[10] Once these deficiencies were overcome, the traditional formula was arrived at: *one sole substance and three divine persons.*

Here we have the formulation that the Church hit upon, and that is undoubtedly a faithful expression of what she already possessed in a living way. It expresses the data in a language that is capable of avoiding fundamental misunderstandings and deviations.

Like any formula, however, it paid a price for the requisite precision. It lost something in suggestive power and existential coloring. Such formulas are useful, and even necessary. But they cease to speak to man's existence and history if they do not go back to the living language of Scripture, or if they are not translated into the language of concrete human experience.

The formula known as "The Merciful Trinity" formula can be characterized as an attempt at the latter approach. Its author and date are uncertain, but it appeared in France about A.D. 500. In part it is a precise and logical formulation. But it goes well beyond mere dogmatic precision, especially toward the end, to enter the realm of suggestive images and to offer us a Trinitarian message that is an authentic "find," even after the richness of the biblical data. The formula says this:

> The merciful Trinity is one sole divinity . . . The Father God, and the Son God, and the Holy Spirit God. We do not say they are three gods; in all piety we profess that they are only one. Because in naming three *persons*, we profess with catholic and apostolic voice that they are one single *substance* . . . Three neither confused nor divided; as united in their distinction as they are distinct in their unitedness . . . equal in divinity, co-similar in majesty, concordant by virtue of trinity, sharing in resplendent clarity. One single thing in such a way that we do not doubt that they are three as well. Three in such a way that we profess they cannot be separated from each other. Hence there is no doubt that injury to one is affront to all, because praise of one touches upon the glory of all (Denz. 17).

Before we delve into this formula, we would like to make a few parenthetical remarks. If the language in which God speaks to us of himself is to have meaning and add something to our knowledge, then it will do so by showing God in relationship to the real-life experiences of our human existence. So, for example, when John wants to express in a word the content which the inner life of God, as revealed in his Word, has for him, he looks over the various human experiences that are capable of being named. And he stops at one of them: love. He chooses it because it is in reality that which best expresses the content of God's self-revelation. And should someone be appalled at his colossal presumption of using a human experience, and go on to ask him what love is when it is predicated of God, John would simply refer that person back to experience. He would not refer him to some notion defined from above, nor to a concept stripped of most of its empirical content (*cf.* 1 John 4:8). As Saint Augustine puts it: "God is love, *the very same love with which we love.*"[11] And Saint Bernard, seeing that holiness is nothing else but love realized in action, draws the proper conclusion: "The saints comprehend (God). How? you ask. If you are holy, *you already know*. If you are not, try it *and you will know*."[12]

So here we are confronted with a self-revelation of God which passes from Scripture to the dogmatic formula and seeks to be comprehended in the same way. Let us first recall a few passages in the formula: "three neither confused nor divided"; "concordant by virtue of trinity"; "injury to one is affront to all, because praise of one touches upon the glory of all." Now let us try to describe the concrete human experience toward which these phrases point.

Of course the reference to the human experience of love appears in each one of the terms of the formula. But there is more. Our natural and all too facile tendency would be to attribute the concordance or harmony of the three persons to the oneness of being that underlies the three. That which is one cannot help but be "concordant." But the text we are considering (and the Scripture which serves as its foundation[13]) does not see it that way. It says: "concordant by virtue of trinity."

We would have said: concordant *in spite of* their trinity, i.e., in spite of the fact that they constitute three persons. The formula, by contrast, presents the unity of being and the unity of action as results of the love among the three, three who decide from all eternity to hold everything in common, to be one for all and all for one in an unlimited way, indeed to the point where "injury to one is affront to all" and "praise of one touches upon the glory of all." Jesus did not say: How can I not love the Father, if we are the same thing? He said: How can we not be the same thing if we love each other without limits? And he affirmed the same thing about the "we" formed by himself, the Father, and the human beings to whom they offer their love.

What is more, the unity thus acquired is not only not brought about by a diminution of their distinction and personal originality. Rather, the latter elements constitute a positive and essential element in their union: "neither confused nor divided."

These last words bring two opposed biblical images to mind. One stands at the start of human history: i.e., the tower of Babel. The other stands in the fullness of time: i.e., the coming of the Spirit to the multitude of believers. The import of the biblical symbolism seems to be obvious. The first seems to embody God's "no" to an attempt to build the city of man on a foundation of undifferentiated unity. The second seems to embody his "yes" to the idea of constructing the human community on the foundation of the "different languages" (*cf.* Acts 2:1–11) that contribute to humanity all the needs and riches of each and every individual, each and every human grouping, each and every human community.[14]

The society of the future, toward which man has been journeying with painful, hesitant steps ever since history began, could be expressed in terms of the symbols used here for the Omega Point of its journey: "concordant by virtue of community, neither confused nor divided, in such a way that the good of one is the good of all, because the needs and hope of one touch upon the needs and hopes of all."

In other words, we have arrived at the experience we were looking for in order to put a name on that which the Trinitarian formulas suggested. That experience, still a hope and an unfulfilled thing, is the concrete experience of *society*.

God, the Christian God, is love. But not simply or not so much a love that unites two people and separates them from the world and time; that would be a false love. Rather, the love that fashions human society in history. The love which, ever since the first stages in the evolution of matter, has systematically broken up and broken through every simplistic synthesis in its quest for more costly but more total syntheses in which originality would be fully freed and a "We," such as all our "We's" on earth struggle and would like to be. Despite all our twisted and distorted images, the God that Jesus revealed to us is a *God who is a society*.

Section III

Why have we evinced such persistence in fashioning an image of God for ourselves that is not the one we get from our faith? That is not the one which he himself has given of himself?

We could underline various speculative influences that were alien to the biblical message, and many indeed have done this before us. But we suspect that there must be something deeper and more decisive at work here, because these speculative influences were already around when the Church was elaborating the correct and clearcut formulation about a *God who is a society*.

Let us recognize certain significant facts. In the society we are familiar with, the human ideal consists in the emergence of a realm that is identified with "the private"; it is presumed that this ideal fits in with the blossoming of the individual.

This is not just something that the rich man defends. According to the first statements of Catholic social doctrine, it is something that the worker was claiming as his right or certainly should claim as such. In *Rerum novarum* Leo XIII says: "The intrinsic reason for the work that a man takes on . . . the immediate end toward which the laborer tends, is the attainment of a good as his own, private right. Because if he places his labor and industry at the disposal of another, he obviously does this for no other end than to provide for his own maintenance and the necessities of life. From his labor he expects not only the right to a salary but also a rigorous and strict right to use it as he wishes."[16]

In this conception, presented within the framework of capitalist society, work is the price man pays in order to live a human life. In consequence, the latter is something that is separated and withdrawn from activity that is more bound up with society. Man lives his leisure hours, his private life, thanks to the work he performs for society's advancement.

Even at the risk of presenting a caricature, we must allude briefly to the imaginative context of "the private realm" as the realm in which the human person finds fulfillment. Everyone knows how much the middle class is lured on by the dream of its own "little plot of earth." The most important thing on it is the private fence, be it a physical or a legal one. For, as *Rerum novarum* points out, the human person must be able to use his goods as he sees fit within this private orbit. And this presupposes, first and foremost, that these goods are taken out of the critical and physical reach of the rest of society.

No one feels truly free if he cannot have his own place, where he can plant tomatoes or roses as he chooses. That is his *private domain*, where he can do what he wants. Logically enough, he accepts in principle the fact that this privatization of goods and their use has certain limits, these limits being imposed by the need to preserve "the private realm" of others. And the best society seems to be the one in which the scope of the private realm is as great as possible for each individual.

This situation is not just a socioeconomic one. It is found everywhere in a world where repression and domination are prevalent.[17] The slave's inner world is his own private realm; the political subject still has private control over his own moral principles.

Now in this setup God is much more the guarantor of this moral privatization than its possessor or beneficiary. A saint, such as Rose of Lima, fashions her solitude in order to contemplate and serve God alone. She thus frees her life from the enticements of society, a society that may indeed be frivolous but that is also a potential field for love, liberation, and revolution.

So we have a society which regards someone as alienated if he or she must shoulder the weight of activities that are more immersed in the societal realm. And it is not surprising that such a society would

fashion an image of God in which he was the "private," independent
being *par excellence*.

Traces of this conception, learned of course in the process of growing
up in a traditional Christianity of the wrong kind, led an author like
Mario Benedetti to describe the sea—a vast, private space—in terms
that allude to God: "The sea is a kind of eternity . . . A moving presence,
but lifeless. A presence of dark, *unfeeling* waves. A witness to history,
but a *useless witness because it knows nothing of history*. And what if the
sea were God?"[18] To talk about love in connection with this God is,
for Benedetti, "a harmless little expression that improves on *the monoton-
ous love of God*."[19] God, for him, is a distant and solitary thing to whom
we never do or will have access. We stand on his shore, alien and distant,
for he does not hate or love us.[20] God and we are like retired old men,
shut off within the boundaries of their own private estates, kept apart
by their fences and by their own conception of what is due them.

Christians evince a persistent tendency to reject, in practice, the
notion of an incarnate God; and to reduce it to the notion of an inaccessible God who is perfectly happy *in se*. This tendency is nothing but the
most blatant kind of anthropomorphism: it shifts onto God the features
wherewith the individual feels he can find self-fulfillment in a society
based on domination.

And, by the same token, the growing interest of the Church in forms
of society where personal fulfillment is achieved in societal work itself
rather than in a private realm cut off from it constitutes the best way
of preparing Christianity to deepen its theology of an incarnate God:
i.e., to solidify its theology of a divine person who "worked with human
hands . . . thought with a human mind, acted by human choice, and
loved with a human heart" (GS 22).

As far back as 1946, Pius XII offered his own different and distinct
conception of the relationship between the personal fulfillment of the
individual and his work within the network of social relationships. Speaking to Italian farm workers, he presented his ideal: "You form a great
community of labor . . . This is the authentic Catholic conception of work.
It brings human beings together in common service to the needs of
the people."[21]

Hence the human person does not find fulfillment outside his work,
in the "private realm." His work itself, his societal task, is to be "the
task of his personal life."[22] This notion finds its fullest expression in
the social thought of John XXIII, as embodied in *Mater et Magistra*:
"Justice is to be observed not only in the distribution of wealth, but
also in regard to the conditions in which men are engaged in producing

this wealth. Every man has, of his very nature, a need to express himself in his work and thereby to perfect his own being" (n. 82).

As John XXIII observes accurately, it is only a "need" at present. But the convergence of this critical, creative, social awareness with a more adequate theology will be one more positive factor for the future. It will point toward and look for concrete embodiments that offer more promise of such human relationships. And these relationships in turn will be the best foundation for further purification of our notion of God.[23]

NOTES TO CHAPTER TWO

1. In the strict sense divine revelation terminates with the apostolic age. In other words, in order to reveal himself to human beings henceforth, God will not use new "words," new documents, new "scriptures." Instead the Spirit will lead the Church to a better comprehension of this same content: "When he comes who is the Spirit of truth, he will guide you into all the truth; for he will not speak on his own authority . . . for everything that he makes known to you he will draw from what is mine" (John 16:13–14).

2. Paul L. Lehmann, *Ethics in a Christian Context* (New York: Harper & Row, 1963), p. 85 and *passim*.

3. See in this series Volume I, Chapter III, main section; and Volume I. Chapter II, CLARIFICATION III.

4. Amado Anzi, S.J., *El Evangelio Criollo* (Buenos Aires: Agape, 1964).

5. Paul Van Buren exaggerates when he states: "The assimilation of the idea of the Logos into Christian doctrine was christological, not just theological" (*The Secular Meaning of the Gospel*, New York: Macmillan, 1966, pp. 25–26). Here Van Buren is trying to indicate that the identity of Jesus with the divine Logos was not introduced as God's self-revelation (theology) but as an explication of Jesus' person (christology). He goes on: "The Logos idea was not first used to solve a problem about God and his relationship to the world, but to justify the worship of Jesus of Nazareth" (*ibid.*, p. 26).

Throughout the Gospel of John and his first Epistle—not to mention Paul who, though he does not use the term "Logos," is greatly concerned with God's relationship to the world—the theological problem occupies a central place, as we explained in the Introduction.

6. It matters little whether one accepts the textual historicity of these words or not. If one does, then they would be a direct expression of the preoccupations of Jesus' Jewish interlocutors. If one does not, then they would be part of John's theological problematic and, at the same time, the norm and expression of the Church's faith.

7. It cannot be unintentional that John makes note (John 8:24–28; 13:19) of Jesus' use of the expression, "I AM" (without specifying who or what). This expression takes us right back to the definition of the deity in Exodus: "I AM has sent me to you." See the preceding chapter, main section, page 23.

8. Another difficult passage of the same Gospel remains to be explained: "If you loved me, you would have been glad to hear that I was going to the Father; for the Father is greater than I" (John 14:28). Theology has always encountered difficulty in interpreting this text. It seems evident that it cannot be in opposition, quite obvious opposition at that, with his reply to Philip a few verses earlier: "Anyone who has seen me has seen the Father" (John 14:10). It seems that the context of John 14:28 is seeking to compare not so much the two persons as the state in which they find themselves. Jesus is returning to the Father. He points out that this fact should be a cause for joy among his friends because it is an advantageous thing for himself. His return to the Father is the opposite of the *kenosis*, the "self-emptying," that Paul mentions (Phil. 2:7). In more veiled terms Jesus refers to the same *kenosis* repeatedly in his farewell discourse at the Last Supper (*cf*. John 13:32; 14:1–3; 16:28; 17:6).

9. Speculative theology has tried to "trace out" the Trinitarian relationships, as it were, seeking to distinguish them on the basis of the names as indicators of essential differences *ab aeterno* (*cf*. M. J. Scheeben, *The Mysteries of Christianity*, Eng. trans., St. Louis: B. Herder Company, 1961, Chapters 2 and 3). Thus the Son is said to be the (intellectual) image of the Father, an image so perfect that he constitutes a person who is equally as divine as the Father. And the Holy Spirit is said to be the (volitional) mutual love that issues forth from the first two persons.

The trouble with this theological reflection is not so much intellectual. It is the fact that it endeavors to introduce us into a world that is alien to our own. It is highly doubtful that divine revelation seeks to inform us about such a world and to interest us in it. Moreover, even though this theological speculation does not point to temporal differences, it is difficult to evade the idea of a God who at the start must be conceived as being *one alone*.

The final remarks of this chapter, we feel, will show how important it is for Christian thought to begin with the God who has revealed himself as a society of love. The latter feature is not a property of the first two persons or, if you will, of the three. It is the very origin of the Trinity in the knowledge we have of it.

10. Van Buren (*The Secular Meaning of the Gospel, op cit.*, p. 34) cites these remarks of William Temple in his article, "The Divinity of Christ" (published in *Foundations*, B.H. Streeter ed., London: Macmillan, 1912, pp. 230 ff.): "The Fathers had done the best that could be done with the intellectual apparatus at their disposal. . . . The whole of Greek theology, noble as it is, suffers from a latent materialism; its doctrine of substance is in essence materialistic."

The judgment is just. Without it one can hardly understand the long and intricate history of the controversies. The key word in the Trinitarian discussion, *hypostasis* (the Greek equivalent of Latin *substantia*), arose from a reflection on things. Now a substance brings together two notions: the notion of "nature" and the notion of "individual." And we could very well say that when the word is employed, one of these two notions is being stressed. Sometimes it means "an individual thing considered in terms of its nature"; other times it means "a nature considered in terms of an individual thing." Hence ambiguity results. It would appear that one must look for the individuality (and hence the personality) in a component of the substance. This holds true right up to Saint Thomas. Only a more spiritualist type of philosophy would separate the order of the (spiritual) individual, that is, the order of the personal and the subjective, from the components of objective nature.

Thus the Church Fathers had to struggle with the aforementioned ambiguity until bit by bit they managed to set up a contrast between the oneness of the *ousia* (Lat. *essentia* or *substantia,* in the sense of "individual subject"). But the word *substantia* was not used here, so as to avoid the ambiguity. The Latin formula then was: *one substance or nature, and three persons.* The oneness of the *ousia* ("nature") was defined at the First Ecumenical Council (Nicea, 325; Denz. 54). The expression about three persons (or *hypostasis*) appears at the Rome Council of 382 (Denz. 79), following the Second Ecumenical Council at Constantinople.

11. *De Trinitate*, I.VIII, c.VIII, n.12 (PL 42, 957–58). As we shall see, that does not cover everything. The empirical concept (of love) is *true* when applied to God, but the reality is much greater. It is not more incomprehensible for that reason; on the contrary, it is more comprehensible. Augustine himself, commenting on the prologue to John's Gospel, notes something that holds true for all of Scripture: "Perhaps not even John spoke about the reality as it was, but simply as best he could. For he was speaking of God, and he was only a human being—inspired by God to be sure, but a human being after all. Because he was inspired by God, he was able to say something . . . "

12. *De Consideratione,* l.V, c.XIV, n.30 (PL 182,805).

13. What Robert Guelluy says of God in the Old Testament could and should be applied to the Trinity and the New Testament as well: "The Old Testmant speaks of God, not in terms of *metaphysics* (i.e., of essences) but in terms of *action.* It does not ratiocinate about the essence of the divinity as the philosophers do. Instead it describes what the Creator of heaven and earth, the God of Abraham, Isaac, and Jacob, has in his own unique way in terms of power and demands . . . (cited by De Lubac, *Por los caminos de Dios,* p. 271; see Note 4 in the Introduction about this book).

In the New Testament, the Trinitarian God is not presented to us as the fulfilled embodiment of an essence (if we can put it that way), but as the result of an action. If we want to understand it, we are summoned to review this action in our history as best we can.

14. Confer the contribution of E. Castelli in the work cited earlier, p. 54, Note 10, *Mito e Fede* (p. 15), which reproduces the papers and discussions of the VI International Colloquium on demytholigization.

15. Speaking about this love that goes about building ever more complex and interdependent social syntheses, *Gaudium et spes* says not only that it is "the basic law of human perfection" but also, in life with an evolutionary perspective, that it is "the basic law . . . of *the world's* transformation" (GS 38; our italics).

Three texts culled from a work by Teilhard de Chardin (*Le Phénomène humain*) will bolster this latter affirmation of Vatican II with the broader vision of a look back at physical, biological, and historical data:

> Life advances by mass effects, by dint of multitudes flung into action without apparent plan. Milliards of germs and millions of adults jostling, shoving and devouring one another, fight for elbow room and for the best and largest living space. Despite all the waste and ferocity, all the mystery and scandal it involves, there is, as we must be fair and admit, a great deal of biological efficiency in the struggle for life . . . "Survival of the fittest by natural selection" is not a meaningless expression, provided it is not taken

to imply either a final ideal or a final explanation. (*The Phenomenon of Man*, Eng. trans., New York: Harper & Row, 1959, p. 109)

And now we have arrived, *ipso facto*, at the solution of the problem posed for us. We are seeking a qualitative law of development that from sphere to sphere should be capable of explaining, first of all the invisibility, then the appearance, and then the gradual dominance of the *within* in comparison to the *without* of things. The law reveals itself once the universe is thought of as passing from State *A*, characterized by a very large number of very simple material elements (that is to say, with a very poor *within*), to State *B* defined by a smaller number of very complex groupings (that is to say, a much richer *within*). In State A, the centres of consciousness, because they are extremely numerous and extremely loose at the same time, only reveal themselves by overall effects which are subject to the laws of statistics. In State B, on the other hand, these less numerous and at the same time more highly individualized elements gradually escape from the slavery of large numbers. They allow their basic non-measurable spontaneity to break through and reveal itself. We can begin to see them and follow them one by one, and in so doing we have access to the world of biology. (*Ibid.*, p. 61)

In trying to separate itself as much as possible from others, the element individualizes itself; but in doing so it becomes retrograde and seeks to drag the world backwards towards plurality and into matter. In fact it diminishes itself and loses itself. To be fully ourselves it is in the opposite direction, in the direction of convergence with all the rest, that we must advance—towards the 'other' . . . There is, however, an obvious and essential proviso to be made. For the human particles to become really personalized under the creative influence of union—according to the preceding analyses—not every kind of union will do. Since it is a question of achieving a synthesis of centres, it is centre to centre that they must make contact and *not otherwise*. Thus, among the various forms of psychic interactivity animating the noosphere, the energies we must identify, harness and develop before all others are those of an 'intercentric' nature, if we want to give effective help to the progress of evolution in ourselves. (*Ibid.*, pp. 263–64)

16. *Cf.* J.Y. Calvez and H. Perrin, *Eglise et societé economique* (Paris: Aubier, 1959), pp. 307–308.

17. Consider these remarks of Herbert Marcuse in his article, "The Affirmative Character of Culture," reproduced as Chapter III (pp. 88–133) of *Negations: Essays in Cultural Theory* (Boston: Beacon, 1968):

By affirmative culture is meant that culture of the bourgeois epoch which led in the course of its own development to the segregation from civilization of the mental and spiritual world as an independent realm of value that is also considered superior to civilization. Its decisive characteristic is the assertion of a universally obligatory, eternally better and more valuable world that must be unconditionally affirmed: a world essentially different from the factual world of the daily struggle for existence, yet realizable by every individual for himself "from within," without any transformation of the state of fact. (P. 95)

All human laws and forms of government are to have the exclusive purpose of 'enabling man, free from attack by others, to exercise his powers and acquire a more beautiful and freer enjoyment of life' (Herder). The highest point which man can attain is a community of free and rational persons in which each has the same opportunity to unfold and fulfill all of his powers. (P. 101)

Culture means not so much a better world as a nobler one: a world to be brought about not through the overthrow of the material order of life but through events in the individual soul. (P. 103)

The liberation of the individual was effected in a society based not on solidarity but on conflict of interests among individuals. The individual has the character of an independent, self-sufficient monad. (P. 111)

Also, in this society, poverty is a condition of profit and power, yet dependence takes place in the medium of abstract freedom. The sale of labor power is supposed to occur due to the poor man's own decision. He labors in the service of his employer, while he may keep for himself and cultivate as a sacred preserve the abstraction that is his person-in-itself, separated from its socially valuable functions. He is supposed to keep it pure. (P. 116)

18. *La Tregua* (Montevideo: Alfa), pp. 112 ff.

19. *Ibid.*, p. 166.

20. *Ibid.*, p. 172.

21. *Cf.* Calvez-Perrin, *op. cit.*, p. 304.

22. *Ibid.*, p. 305.

23. De Lubac (*Por los caminos de Dios, op. cit.*, p. 270) cites this remark of Benjamin Constant in his work, *De la religión*: "The isolation in which the fetishes lived ceases to be conceivable to the gods of tribes living in societies . . . They place their gods in common. And this reunion of the gods follows of necessity from the reunion of human beings."

Overlooking the kind of latent determinism in this phrase, we can say that it points toward a tieup that is central in Christian theology. J.B. Metz points up this tieup in a fine article, "The Church's Social Function in the Light of a 'Political Theology.'" *Concilium* (New York: Paulist Press, 1968), Volume 36, *Faith and the World of Politics*, pp. 4–6):

The present prevailing forms of transcendental, existential and personalist theology seem to have one thing in common: concentration on what is private. . . . We seem, therefore, to be in need of a new critical approach in order to reverse the basically individualistic tendencies in the very foundation of our theology. . . . *The reversal of this "privatizing" tendency is the primary critical task of political theology.* Here we discover the positive task of political theology: it aims at reassessing the relation between religion and society, between the Church and public society, between eschatological faith and social life, not in a pre-critical sense . . . but in a post-critical sense, the sense of "second thoughts." As political, theology is forced to go in for these "second thoughts" if it wants to formulate the eschatological message in the condition and circumstances of modern society.

The only complaint we would have with Metz is that he does not point up the fact that all theology, even when it is concerned with the Trinity, is political. And doubly so when it does not seek to be political.

CLARIFICATIONS

I. BETWEEN SECULARIZATION AND THE "DEATH OF GOD"

We often hear people talk about "death of God" theology and secularization carried to its ultimate conclusions, as if the two were synonymous for all practical purposes.[1]

However, our working hypothesis here is that in pastoral terms we find such phenomena as the "death of God" precisely when the Church refuses to embark sincerely and totally on the road of *secularization*.

1. To prove this hypothesis we must, first and foremost, explore the meaning of the term "secularization," or its homonym "desacralization." Now the secular (or, the profane) and the sacred constitute the two possible poles of reality. Secularization (or, desacralization), then, represents a shift of realities from what we might call "the realm of the sacred" to the realm of the secular or the profane.

But what would have shifted from one realm to the other? Strange as it may sound: everything! At least in theological terms. Even though in terms of sociological reality this process, visualized in the relationships between the Church and public institutions, may still be far from having reached its end.

Secularization is a central postulate of the Christian message.[2] As Paul tells the Corinthians: "For though everything belongs to you—Paul, Apollos, and Cephas, the world, life, and death, the present and the future,[3] all of them belong to you—yet you belong to Christ, and Christ to God" (1 Cor. 3:22–23). This outlook radically alters the traditional religious schema of man, sacred things, and God. Now everything is under man's dominion. And above man there is only Christ; that is, the whole Christ, the Christ who is affected by what happens in each of his brothers, the Christ who recapitulates all humanity. It is there that we encounter God. If a person does not lay hold of this full measure and maturity, then he comes to Christianity in vain (*cf.* Gal. 2:21; 3:4; 4:1–7; 4:11; 5:6).

We have already considered this point in some detail at other places in this series.[4] So here we choose to express the same line of thought by quoting the comments and conclusions of another author. In *Cristianismo y nueva ideología*, Conrado Eggers Lan has this to say:

74

In the Greek New Testament *to hieron* signifies both "the temple" and "the sacred." But it does not refer to any temple built of stones or any place set apart; it refers to the whole world, the whole of history, that is still to be constructed. Still to be constructed is *the body of Christ*, in which we shall achieve the full measure of manhood (Eph. 4:12–13). Still to be constructed is the temple of God which, as St. Paul tells the Corinthians, is "you yourselves" (1 Cor. 3:16–17): i.e., *everybody*.

Now this does not keep us from admitting the need for what we might call the little temple—as counterpoint to the big temple—to which Jesus gives the name, house of prayer, from which he expels the buyers and sellers, and in which he teaches the good news to the people (Luke 19:46—20:1). And this little temple need not necessarily be of stone and cement, as we are assured by the Sermon on the Mount and many other passages in the Gospel. It is wherever two or three gather together in the name of Christ (Matt. 18:20), that is, in the name of the one who declares that he has come to fulfill the prophecy about the liberation of the oppressed (Luke 4:18–21). There we have the cement or cornerstone (Rom. 15:20; 1 Cor. 3:10–12; Eph. 2:20; 1 Pet. 2:5–7; etc.) of the big temple that is to be constructed . . .

From all this we can formulate two tentative conclusions. 1. The sacred is in the entire edifice, in the big temple that we are to construct in history, and not just in the cement that is the little temple. 2. Just as our experience of love requires a moment of setting ourselves apart from the rest of people, the construction of the big temple requires the momentary segregation of the little temple; but this must be done in such a way that it truly forms a cement and a leaven, rather than turning into a conventional formalism wherein the would-be salt loses its savor.[5]

So we can make a statement that seems paradoxical. Secularization, far from signifying an abandonment of the profane to its profaneness, is a recognition of the sacred that it contains within its very dynamism. It is the authentic *consecration* of the profane. Why? Because if everything in the little temple is supposed to be in the service of humanity and its tasks, then the latter are recognized to be sacred, to be the site of the encounter between God and human beings, to be the big temple.

2. In pastoral terms, however, this synthesis is not only far from being realized; it is also far from being a coherent schema of thinking and evaluating.

There is no doubt that the major texts of Vatican II recognize and acknowledge it, even though we must also admit the presence of a contrary current in lesser documents, in the cautious tones of some language, and even in whole sections of such documents as *Gaudium et spes*.[6]

Nor is there any doubt that the long praxis of the so-called "Constantinian era" militates against the acceptance of secularization. This period was characterized at first by "administrative" sacralization, and later by a "separation of planes" which was no less opposed to the aforementioned schema even though it modified the first stance.

Now a superficial glance might suggest that the Church of Latin America is much more "Constantinian" than that of Europe. It is more united with political regimes, more deeply involved in the public sphere, more "religious" in its preoccupations, and more inclined to foster and monopolize popular piety. In a word, the general cast it presents is that of a reality which is much less secularized than that of Europe or the United States.

Yet if we look more closely at various phenomena, we find a paradoxical situation. Consider, for example, the statements of the Latin American bishops at Medellín on the one hand, and the famous Dutch Catechism approved by the bishops of Holland on the other.[7] One would have to say that Medellín represents a much more advanced degree of secularization than the famous and controversial catechism.

Perhaps we should say that there are two tendencies at work in the Latin American Church. While one part of it remains fixed in a reality that is quite Constantinian and sacral, another part of the Latin American Church is being pushed forward by a keen awareness of exploitation and human suffering. The latter part is rapidly mounting the steps toward full secularization, seeing the Church as a whole in terms of the task of liberating man from "any and every servitude."

In the developed countries, by contrast, the Church may have stopped at a convenient and comfortable "separation of planes." As a result it goes only so far as a certain measure of secularization which, in fact, represents an erosion of the religious rather than a frank and open stance supporting the value of the temporal and the profane. It is the "death of God" more than it is secularization. Or, if you will, it is defective secularization, devoid of "signs of the times" or of any sensitivity to them.

How could they be perceived within the system that exists in an affluent society! According to the teaching of Jesus in John's Gospel, the "world" has a tendency to form a system that is closed in upon itself, and to fill up any crevice that might allow rays of newness and disturbing light to filter through. It hears what it has always heard, it loves what it has always loved; a system of needs and rewards functions almost automatically. The relatives of Jesus epitomize this "world" and want to force him into its mechanism. They do not have an "hour" of their own, and neither does this "world" of theirs. In terms of the aim it pursues, every moment of time in this world is the same. There are no signs of the times. There is no measure of distance, where one can stand back and question the purpose of what one is doing, and thus introduce the moment of *crisis*, of judgment (*cf.* John 7:4–8).

Now there is a striking agreement between these evangelical viewpoints and the following description of the affluent society by Marcuse. And this society, needless to say, has an influence on the Church:

> In this process, the "inner" dimension of the mind in which opposition to the status quo can take root is whittled down. The loss of this dimension, in which the power of negative thinking—the critical power of Reason—is

at home, is the ideological counterpart to the very material process in which advanced industrial society silences and reconciles the opposition.[8]

The fortune of the Latin American Church is that it is situated on the periphery, the suffering and exploited periphery, of the industrialized world. There, despite isolated patches of affluence, or perhaps precisely because of them, the opposition cannot be silenced or reconciled. There the crevices open a pathway for the signs of the times, for signs that send out a summons simultaneously to society and to the Church.

In the affluent societies by contrast, a *modus vivendi* holds sway to a large extent; and it leads ever so slowly to the "death of God." The very slowness of the process is misleading. It allows room for the Church to occupy herself with her own internal reform, and for people to engage in a nonconformity that does not call the overall totality into question:

> The reign of such a one-dimensional reality does not mean that materialism rules, and that the spiritual, metaphysical, and bohemian occupations are petering out. On the contrary, there is a great deal of "Worship together this week," "Why not try God," Zen, existentialism, and beat ways of life, etc. But such modes of protest and transcendence are no longer contradictory to the status quo and no longer negative. They are rather the ceremonial part of practical behaviorism, its harmless negation, and are quickly digested by the status quo as part of its healthy diet.[9]

3. Now it is time to take a closer and more careful look at this perhaps exaggerated description of the Church's activity in an affluent society. We must try to see what element of truth and, above all, what pastoral import it contains.

For the moment, secularization and the "death of God" go their separate ways in their concrete way of looking at the Church. Despite the change brought about by the Council, we cannot deny the fact that we have one conciliar Constitution that deals with the mystery of the Church in itself (*Lumen gentium*), and another that relates the Church to the contemporary world (*Gaudium et spes*). Secularization would mean working to see to it "that *Lumen gentium* and *Gaudium et spes* are not separated from each other, but rather united in one integral reflection on the Church that is a reflection on the world as well."[10]

And we have something else that is the prolongation of this divorce, and that is much more evident and emphatic in the European and North American Church: i.e., the attempt to begin with an *internal* renewal of the Church. Sooner or later this leads to the "death of God":

> The Church, like man himself, is a being-in-the-world. And if we are trying to reorganize the Church for the sake of the world, we cannot put the world in parentheses. Such an *epochē*, applied to the fundamental features of today's historical reality that are not *outside* but *inside* the Church itself, closes us up in a solipsistic circle. And we cannot get out of it by building

some sort of imaginary bridge to the outside world after we have straightened up our own house from inside. We cannot act as if the outside world is not there in the house to begin with. We cannot destroy the dialectical unity that exists between a Church in the world and a world in the Church, in order to lay hold of the Church all by itself or, what is worse, of those features that are of historical institution. Such an approach is an illegitimate abstraction . . . We cannot entertain the naive idea that we will do a better job of shouldering the common human task *after we have overcome* the Church's internal tensions, as if we could overcome these tensions *beforehand*. The tensions existing between man and man today constitute an essential part of the Church's own tensions.[11]

At bottom secularization means that everything in the Church, absolutely everything, must be translated from "religious" terms into man's tasks in history. On the whole, that is how Medellín saw the problem. And the guidelines and conclusions of the International Catechetical Convention, which took place at Medellín shortly before the episcopal conference to which we are referring, framed the difficult problem of "popular religion" in Latin America in much the same terms.

Aldo J. Büntig felt that he could deny the value of these conclusions with these words of criticism: "We sincerely feel that this decidedly pejorative evaluation, even though it does take into account aspects of the real situation that cannot be denied, starts off from a one-sided conceptualization of popular religious practice and is loaded with a good dose of 'ideology.' "[12]

Now the "one-sidedness" which Büntig sees in the conclusions of that catechetical conference springs from the very fact that the conference refused to accept any "religious" evaluation *as such*; that it sought to translate it in terms of the historical task of liberating man on the Latin American continent. And the "ideology" perceived by Büntig derives from the same fact.[13]

In general we can say that the Latin American Church, far more than the European Church, does not regard the world of religion and religious realities as the necessary or real-life introduction to the message of Christ. In this respect it differs sharply from the Dutch Catechism.[14]

A third point follows from this. There arises the practical problem of figuring out to what extent, or better, at what pace, a Church should go about the task of self-renewal if it is willing to accept the challenge of secularization.

Suppose that the Church has concrete means at its disposal, a determined corps of ministers, and a formative influence that is measurable in sociological terms. What choice is it to make when it finds important Christian groups putting up resistance to the process of transformation? It is our feeling that the very wealth of their resources in men and materiel has allowed the Churches in the affluent society to hedge on this option. They straddled the fence, leaning at times one way or the other.

When this is not possible, when the demands of social liberation

are so urgent that they compel a decision, then it may well be that
Latin America will have its own specific role to play. It may be obliged
to study the option for secularization in both theological and practical
terms; and, even more specifically, to consider the whole matter of pace.

For the moment this option is held off by the tendency to maintain
"the unity of Christians." In other words, the only acceptable pace is
one that keeps all those united in the same faith and sacramental practice
who have been so united up to now. But more and more groups of
Christians are beginning to see clearly that a profoundly antisecular
option is at work here under the guise of practical reasons. This is
not to look for the right pace at all, because the death of God is an
accomplished fact long before Christian transformation is brought to
completion. And this "death of God" can co-exist for a long time with
continuing sacramental practice on a mass scale.

In Latin America one cannot help but be impressed by the defence
of "church tradition" and "popular religion" which is undertaken by
people who represent an established order in which the "death of God"
is already an accomplished fact. And these same people act as if they
were unaware of the desertion of those who are seeking man's liberation;
the latter, weary of waiting for a transformation that never comes, leave
the church community altogether or simply use it politically as a pressure
group.[15]

Here, where pastoral effort, practical reality, and theology meet at
the crossroads, our image of God will be decisive.

II. THE CHURCH: RELIGION, SECT, OR COMMUNITY?

If what we said in the previous CLARIFICATION is true, a secularized
Church would be far from being a phantom Church. On the contrary,
secularization and meaningfulness necessarily go hand in hand.

Now if the Church is to be the sign of man's fashioning of history
in freedom, then it must go within itself and tackle the problem posed
by the notion of God that inspires and judges it. But it must not operate
on the assumption that once it has gone through this inner work of
purification and renewal, it can then go on to decide how it will make
a contribution to man and the world. Its exploration of its own inner
life and inner structures must be inspired and motivated by the latter
goal from the very start.[16]

These inner structures do exist. And though it is true that they
are conditioned by society as a whole, and that they must be considered
in terms of this society, they nevertheless are something more than a
mere component of this society that can be understood solely in terms
of the sociopolitical structures of the latter.[17]

1. In reality it is not easy to decide what kind of human grouping
should be formed by those who desire to follow Christ. This is particularly
true when we start off with the reality of a supposedly "Christian" continent.

Not every sort of association is the right kind for carrying out a mission which entails being a sign of the liberative salvation (GS 41) that God offers to the whole community of mankind (LG 9).

With this premise in mind, and with one eye on the disturbing impact of popular religion on the problem of liberating Latin American society, we can examine the two options or alternatives posed by the Medellín episcopal conference in its statement on pastoral care of the masses:

> Given this type of religious sense among the masses, the Church is faced with the dilemma of either continuing to be a universal Church or, if it fails to attract and vitally incorporate such groups, of becoming a sect. Because she is a Church rather than a sect, she must offer her message of salvation to all men, running the risk that not all will accept it in the same manner or with the same degree of understanding and maturity (n. 3).

Now if we ask what this document means by "sect," the answer seems to be clear in sociological terms. It means privileged groups that feel they already possess both the qualities and the means required for participating in the divine kingdom. In addition to this, and as a logical result of it, they are characterized by a cohesiveness that is all the greater when the required quality is envisioned as a privilege that separates them from others, rather than as a creative responsibility toward others.

On the other hand, if we ask what this document means by "universal Church," we find that the term is ambiguous. This ambiguity inclines us to look at the overall context and the conclusions. Taking all this into account, however, we have no hesitation in saying that this term can be defined in terms of the definition that Büntig gives of "popular Catholicism": "The normal result of the process of institutionalization and acculturation, which are part and parcel of *every universal religion*, is that the religion becomes a connatural part of a specific sociocultural world."[18]

Thus the universality to which our document alludes is that of participating in a universal religion on an almost infinite number of different degrees and levels: "There will always be elite groups who will shoulder the message of a universal religion in a more profound way. There will always be masses, educated or uneducated, who will shoulder it in more limited and imperfect ways."[19]

We can readily see that Medellín's term "universal Church" is really equivalent to the more precise term used by Büntig, i.e., "universal religion." What comes into account in this term is various degrees and levels of religious adherence. No consideration is paid to the function of the group vis-à-vis the rest of the human community—which influence could be more or less universal, independent of or even in opposition to this religious adherence on a mass scale. For, as Büntig says pointedly, this adherence presupposes becoming "a *connatural* part of a specific sociocultural world."[20]

2. The Church of Latin America wishes to avoid the Scylla of a

"universal religion" that would entail the loss of Christianity's universal *liberative* signification; and also the Charybdis of a "sect" that would lead to the same loss by a different route. In the process of forming a group, the Church seeks to embody the quality of being "neither confused nor divided" that is the essential feature of the Christian God.

In this connection we would do well to analyze some of the protest documents that have been composed by various groups of Latin American Catholics. One such anthology of documents was published recently by Father Juan José Rossi under the title, *Iglesia latinoamericana: ¿Protesta o profecía?*. These documents pass judgment on the whole web of the Church's internal relationships, and they do so from the proper critical impulse. In other words, they are motivated by the same critical impulse that compels the Christian conscience to denounce the existing social order in the name of the God of revelation.

To appreciate this criticism, we must be clear about the context in which it shows up. It surfaces in a period of transition when the Church is turning a critical eye on the internal reality implied by her status as a universal religion now transformed into a "connatural part" of the established society.

The first implication was that she saw herself as a carbon copy, in the "spiritual realm," of a society that had its own dimensions and subjects. So she defined herself in *juridical* terms, indeed in the same terms as society as a whole. In *Immortale Dei* Leo XIII described the Church as a "supernatural and spiritual society . . . complete in its own order and juridically perfect" (n. 9).

Paradoxically enough, this definition of the Church as a society runs directly counter to the Trinitarian definition of God as a society. For the former is a carbon copy of existing society while the latter is an impetus to implement new and more humane social initiatives that go far beyond the existing order.

We would say that "society" is not the term that the Church should use today to designate the reality she wishes to be. The term she should use is *community*. It is this term that sums up the contribution she wishes to make toward fashioning a society on earth that will mirror the divine reality of the Trinity. Thus Vatican II talks about the Church as "the community of faith, hope and charity" (LG 8).

It is not just a mere change in vocabulary that is at stake here. What is entailed is a wholly different conception of the Church's existence and function. The Church is to loosen her ties with the civilization of which she has been a "connatural part" in the past—so much a part that her "establishment" shared the characteristics of the larger social order. Now she is to convert herself into a community that will join with the rest of mankind in trying to fashion a new society; and she herself is *already* a preview and proclamation of this new society (GS 40; LG 8 and 9).

This is the general context on the level of theological formulations.

Such formulations are important, but in themselves they are not enough to bring about the required transformations. For if the Church as community is to be fleshed out in reality, there must be a change in the internal relationships existing between her members and a re-definition of their roles, in terms of equality, whatever position they may occupy in the community: i.e., whether they be clergy or laity. And it is at this point that conflict arises between the vanguard of perceptive people and the Church-society that resists tranformation. The former see more clearly what the implications of this transformation are. The latter may indeed have changed its language, but it remains wedded to its old pattern of relationships that are based on domination.

Here we will present some of the statements that have been put forward by the former group. And the first thing we would point out is its more or less explicit awareness of the fact that the ideology of society interferes with the internal climate of the Church, producing tension and disorientation:

> There is evidence of deep tension and definite disorientation in the ecclesial community, and it shows up in a lack of coordination between its members. We also see a certain lack of the human capacity to establish contact and initiate dialogue on an adult level. The almost unanimous impression is that any reflection or pastoral action seeking to fashion a new image of the Church is left orphaned and without support. The consequent feeling is one of great loneliness. This situation produces problems on the personal level and an atomistic pastoral effort. This effort is suffused with signs of individualism, group factionalism, etc. Within the community we see strong residues of clericalism and authoritarianism, which prevent lay people from assuming their proper role and responsibility as members of the Church in the world.[21]

A second point brought out by these documents is that the description of the Church in juridical terms is an anachronistic barrier to proper comprehension and exercise of the Church's true role:

> The juridical framework, which was elaborated and crystallized in a past age, does not allow the personality of the man of today to manifest itself . . . People are crushed by the absence of flexibility, and by the failure to change structures that are not in line with the new dimensions and pace of today's world: universality, cosmic vision, technology, equality, etc. Law has meaning when it supports man and the community in their constructive, real-life efforts. Otherwise it simply restricts the development of the individual person and the community.[22]

A third point is that the transformation of the Church into a community presupposes a change in the way that authority is exercised. But here again ideological conditionings tend to maintain a vertical exercise of authority that is of the ruler-subject sort for the most part. A group of Ecuadorian priests puts it this way:

> Christians have received diverse gifts and functions from the Holy Spirit (LG 7). Bishops and priests exercise the function of representing Christ

the head in the community of believers. But there is real equality among all the members of the Church with respect to their dignity and their common task of building up Christ's body (LG 32). This rediscovery of the Church as community obliges all to participate in her life and its external expression with co-responsibility.[23]

As we can see, the text makes a clear distinction between diversity of functions, among which it recognizes authority, and a new way of exercising the latter. The new way of exercising authority is called for by the new sociological reality of community. Theological elements must be distinguished from sociological ones, as one writer brings out quite pointedly:

> We believe that bishops and theologians[24] are wrong if they think that the theological order can be translated into social structures which are entrusted with the task of safeguarding these elements of the Christian priesthood: relationship with the bishop, episcopal authority over the government and mission of the Church, etc. To take one example: Who can say for sure that union with the bishop and respect for his pastoral, teaching, and missionary authority must take the present-day form of filial dependence? Behind the theological concepts we can see the clear outlines of sociological and psychological models that have been inherited from the structures of a bygone day rather than from the gospel.[25]

A group of Salvadorean lay people sketch the positive features of an authority exercised in a way that would accord with the Church as community:

> Within the Church we must look for a system of exercising authority which, while respecting the basic principles of the gospel, fits in with the processes of maturation and democratization that the Catholic world is now going through. We feel obliged to fight for the "rightful participation of all in the decision-making process by authority." The axiom, *Roma locta, causa finita* (i.e., "Rome has spoken, the case is closed"), is not valid in a Catholic world which is growing more and more aware of its obligations and rights.[26]

A group of Venezuelan Christians express their own similar view:

> When Jesus spoke to his apostles about exercising authority, he said: "Among you, whoever wants to be great must be your servant; and whoever wants to be first must be the willing slave of all" (Mark 10:43–44. So the authority of which he speaks here is a *service* performed by some who are called to it. They listen, reflect in common, and make decisions that are in line with the truth and look to the greater good of all human beings. In like manner we believe that the obedience and respect owed to superiors should be a cooperation that is properly coordinated and that is based on reason as well as on the person and word of Christ. Listening is involved, of course . . . so that our collaboration is human, adult, and responsible. It cannot be blind, irrational submission, for that would hurt all concerned.[27]

These sample texts clearly prove that people cannot overlook the web of internal relationships operative in the Church, once they have begun the process of liberation within their overall social awareness. By that very fact they show that they are directly opposed to a sect-oriented outlook. But they also show their rejection of a brand of authority that is tied up with a universal religion which has become a connatural part of a given culture. They will have nothing to do with a religion that has become a carbon copy of the surrounding culture, where ties of domination look to religious authority for support and serve as the model for the latter.

The dilemma of universal religion versus sect must be overcome in a Church that sees itself as a community. Such a Church can acquire solidity only by standing firmly between the two poles that should serve as its compass points: i.e., the Trinitarian idea of God on the one hand, and the new aims and projects of human society on the other.

III. THE ROLE OF "NO" IN OUR KNOWLEDGE OF GOD

As we saw in the main section of this chapter, the Christian revelation of Father, Son, and Holy Spirit is presented in such a way that we are gradually forced to look for words in our own language that will best express the ultimate result of this revelation.

Now the question is: What happens when we say "God is love," or "God is a society"? What sort of knowledge do we claim to arrive at in the process of comprehending such statements? Do we claim to know God?

The suspicion that all this never takes us out of the human realm goes way back in our culture. We use human words and human faculties of cognition. So is it not logical that we improperly attribute human features and characteristics to God? Do we not fall into *anthropomorphisms*?

This concern to avoid anthropomorphisms is quite understandable in one sense, but it is very odd in another sense. After all, are we not dealing with a God whose inner life was revealed to us by a Son who became incarnate in history, who was made man and dwelt among men? Why are we so anxious to avoid anthropomorphisms when the Gospel records Jesus' critical response to Philip: "Anyone who has seen me has seen the Father" (John 14:9)? When, for the apostles, the proclamation of the "good news that makes our joy complete" consists in transmitting what they have seen and heard and touched with their hands (*cf.* 1 John 1:1)?[8]

Yet, all this notwithstanding, the suspicion has been a constant feature of Western culture. It shows up especially in a feature that betrays its indebtedness to Greek thought: i.e., the tendency to offer a heavily negative criticism of the procedures wherewith our mind seeks to go beyond the human realm and know God.

1. It is logical that this tendency started out by distrusting the power of our *imagination*. This faculty or capacity in man starts off from images and goes on to compose images. Hence it makes the incorporeal show up as something corporeal, and makes the transcendent appear as some-

thing in this world. Much more confidence was placed in the ability of reason to bring us to a knowledge of God because it functioned in a more incorporeal and less time-bound way.

But Greek philosophy soon went on to suspect the functioning of reason too with respect to the domain of the divine and the revealed. And it did so, we believe, not *in spite of* its rationalist character but precisely because of it.

It was Neo-Platonism, as mediated to us by Plotinus in particular, that influenced Christian theology here. The point of its precautions and reservations was quite clear. Even if our reason can operate beyond the strictures of the body and time, it is always burdened with the weight of its starting point: i.e., concrete things. To conceive the infinite, for example, it simply conceives the finite and adds a negating prefix *in-*. To reach the absolute simplicity of the divine, reason builds a series of mental steps to form a stairway. But as Plotinus sees it, these steps really should be kept together as a unified whole. For him, therefore, the work of reason is merely preparatory and simplifies the process. After reason has done its work, the mind must divest itself of the results obtained, empty itself completely, and allow itself to be filled by the One.

This was the starting point for the development of a "negative theology" within Christianity. The trend was given great impetus by the writings of Pseudo-Dionysius.[29] This *apophatic* (i.e., no-saying) theology was based on the judgment that it was radically impossible for finite, created reason to lay hold of anything divine.[30] And despite its more positive aspects, the way of "analogy" used by Thomas Aquinas is basically and truly a negative theology. In it reason arrives at God by becoming cognizant of its finitude when it moves on from created values to uncreated values. And for all the positive overtones in his poems,[31] we find the same emphasis on the *via negativa* in Saint John of the Cross.[32]

2. But it was Kant who introduced an even deeper motive for restricting the use of reason in the realm of divine things. According to Kant, the normal scope of *pure reason* is the world of concrete things, of phenomena; it can bring order and system into the world of natural phenomena. But it is *practical reason* that leads man to use his rational processes beyond their normal range. Man is deceiving himself if he thinks that some desire to know reality is what leads him beyond the world of phenomena. What happens is that man's *will* needs God, and reason is drawn in to serve this intention.

Thus another suspicion becomes operative from the time of Kant on. Man begins to wonder about the practical intentions that lie buried behind reason's attempt to go beyond the visible and know God. What does man need God for? On the one hand, this suspicion leads us toward the wellsprings of atheism. On the other hand, however, it leads us back toward an outlook that is presented, paradoxically enough, in the first Epistle of Saint John: "If a man says, 'I love God,' while hating his brother, he is a liar. If he does not love the brother whom he has seen, it cannot be that he loves God whom he has not seen" (1 John 4:20).

But there is no doubt that the two great modern exemplars of suspicion toward reason, especially toward the idea of God fabricated by it, have been Marx and Freud. Here is not the place to consider the thought of these two great critics in depth. Let us simply say that, in general, their suspicion as such is well founded even though we may not agree with their conclusions. We cannot go along with the idea that reason is totally dominated by practical interests. Nor can we agree that the idea of God is merely the projection of some more or less hidden intention of the individual or society. But their suspicion helps us to realize that while the idea of God can be liberative, it may also be the source of much hypocrisy. As Henri de Lubac says: "The coating of hypocrisy is never so great as round the idea of God."[33]

The point is that we often use reason to justify and protect what we are doing or what we want to do. It becomes a defense for our fears and limitations and questionable commitments.

And there is something more to be added here. In all his works, Martin Buber has pointed out that what constitutes a human being as such is the *I-Thou* relationship, the interpersonal relationship that culminates in a "we." Buber, along with other thinkers such as Marcel and Berdyaev,[34] quite rightly insists on two points. Firstly, God reveals himself as a Thou vis-à-vis man, not as some vague dimension or transcendence. It is this Thou that serves as the foundation for all I-Thou relationships between human beings. God is not the "depth" or "ground" of man. He is a personal reality who summons us to a dialogue between his liberty and our own.

Secondly, human reason has a basic tendency to reduce every *Thou* to an *it*. Whether it be a human being or God, human reason tends to turn the other reality into a thing that can be manipulated. Human reason is the great systematizer that tries to manipulate and de-absolutize beings. Left to its own devices, it would carry this tendency too far, reifying human beings and God. It is an even more radical source of "anthropomorphisms" than is man's imagination or emotions. Our reason entices us to apply the same reifying tendency to our knowledge of God.

Thus a negative, apophatic theology—a theology that says "no" to reifying language and cognition—is a necessary complement to what Berdyaev has aptly labelled "apophatic sociology."[35]

What is really anthropomorphism is the desire to know some God outside the world, using the same cognitive procedures that apply to the inert things which compose the universe. God reveals himself to us within the world. He reveals himself as the one who gives meaning and value to our lives through a personal realtionship with us. Every search for some physical or metaphysical reality (*ens in se*, etc.) ends up where it begins. For all such things *transcend* what our cognitive faculties are capable of reaching. A concrete, personal encounter within the world is more decisive than all this transcendence. It is our encounter with a person who summons us *absolutely*. The only thing is that it is not *one* person but a *society* of three persons which sends out the summons to us. These three persons are absolutely free, but essentially united in one being.

If interpersonal relationships are an "anthropomorphism," then such anthropomorphism is the means chosen by God to reveal himself to us. In that case "anthropology" is not a level inferior to that of "theology" (like the mundane vis-à-vis the extramundane, the immanent vis-à-vis the transcendent); it is the one and only place where God and man encounter each other.

Sometimes Christians are cautioned about the danger of ending up in "tritheism." It is pointed out that the concept of "person," as we use it today, means a subject endowed with self-awareness and liberty; while in God there is only one self-awareness and one free will.[36]

This argument is deceptive insofar as it is grounded on the ancient practice of identifying the will with being, and liberty with the will (Denz. 294). While the men of another day may have used language in that way, that does not mean that *the language of today* can say there is only one liberty in the Trinity. Jesus' words, "Not my will but thine be done," would be a mere play on words if they did not proceed from a liberty that was distinct from the one which formulated the Father's plan. If the Trinity has only one will and one being, it is because these three persons have freely chosen to surrender themselves that completely (Denz. 296).

The Church does not face danger from "tritheism," which is heterodox. It faces danger from "monotheism," which is orthodox. Why? Because there is a mode of thinking that starts from the end instead of from the beginning. The unity or oneness of God is not the first thing, from which we go on to explore how three could spring from there. The Christian message shows us *three*, loving each other in such a way that they constitute *one*: "The Father God, the Son God, the Holy Spirit God; we do not say they are three gods, but one" (Denz. 17). This is the proper order. We cannot start with one single God all alone (*cf*. Denz. 15), without falling into the most blatant and deforming anthropomorphisms.[37]

IV. IS THERE A MIDDLE TERM BETWEEN ATHEISM AND FAITH?

In his well-known book, *Honest to God*, Bishop Robinson poses a set of questions:

Suppose belief in God does not, indeed cannot, mean being persuaded of the "existence" of some entity, even a supreme entity, which might or might not be there, like life on Mars? Suppose the atheists are right—but that this is no more the end or denial of Christianity than the discrediting of the God "up there," which must in its time have seemed the contradiction of all that the Bible said? Suppose that all such atheism does is to destroy an idol, and that we can and must get on without God "out there" at all?

What prompts these questions? The very title of Robinson's book suggests an answer to us. They are prompted by a desire to be honest and sincere, specifically in our *use of language*.[38]

1. It is obvious that when we enunciate a proposition, we are proposing to inform our listener or listeners about something.

Modern positivism has insisted, to the point of exaggeration, that an authentic use of language should be capable of *verification*. In other words: That which is the object of my affirmation should be able to be put to the test. If for example I say, "There is a cat on the rug," my listener can, in principle, check to see whether this is true. This possibility proves that my statement has sense and meaning: it really does provide information. I am using language correctly, in other words, even if I am using it to tell a lie.

Now if I say, "Napoleon was defeated at Waterloo," my listener certainly will not be able to verify my statement directly. He or she will have to have recourse to more or less trustworthy indices. But there is at least the theoretical possibility of verifying my statement; and once again my listener knows, in a general way, what road to take in doing this. This implies that he or she was able to perceive and determine the content of my statement.

What is worth noting is the fact that as the propositions of language move away from the realm of direct verification by the senses, they move into a realm in which verification is bound up with logic: i.e., with a reasoning process. I cannot verify what exactly happened at Waterloo. But I can figure out that if Napoleon had not been defeated there, he would not have abdicated and withdrawn from the historical scene. In other words: the content of the statement has sense and meaning insofar as I comprehend what would logically follow from its being true, and what would change if it were not true.

Thus when language is not dealing with sense objects, the verification requirement shifts from the control of the senses to the network of real modifications to which the statement alludes.

In the name of this principle, the parable of the invisible gardener (cited in the Introduction of this volume) seeks to point up an inappropriate use of language. If one argues that the sensible arrangement of the flowers requires the intervention of a gardener, the fact is that nothing would change with the existence of an invisible, intangible gardener, and so forth. Hence it makes no difference whether we say "a gardener exists" or "no gardener exists." Such language is devoid of meaning and sense, on the basis of the verification principle.

Now as we have already seen, Christian revelation about Jesus contains a series of statements relating to *factual events*. If we say, "Jesus died on the cross," it may be difficult to verify that statement today. But it falls completely within the aforementioned rules of language. And we do not see why that would change radically if we say, "Jesus rose from the dead," i.e., came out of the tomb alive after being put there dead. The Gospel accounts show that the disciples applied methods of verification to the transmission of these facts. We rely on witnesses for verification of these facts, even as we do for countless past events. Whether they be true or false, adequate or not, the language is converted into testimony and, as such, preserves its rights.[39]

As we have already pointed out, however, mere facts are only the starting point in the language of faith. The most important thing is the interpretation of the facts. To stick with our example of the resurrection, we can cite Paul's words: "If Christ was not raised . . . we of men are most to be pitied" (1 Cor. 15:17, 19).

Here is where the most serious problem of language starts. For, as John Macquarrie points out,[40] believers have long recognized that their language is not direct, literal, and representational. It is a language of symbols and analogies.

The "chance" resurrection of Jesus would not change the piteous situation of which Paul speaks. For his resurrection is a creative and joyous thing only if it is the symbol and analogy of something that God destines for all of us (1 Cor. 15:18).

And it is precisely here that the disturbing element enters the picture. However much importance is given to the Jesus "happenings," if the significance attributed to them comes from my own personal consideration, then that does not seem to resemble Christian faith at all; hence the paschal happening cannot be radically more contagious[41] than any other historical happening.

If, on the other hand, it is something more than that, whence comes this "more" if not from something that is neither my own existence nor the mechanisms of the world?

2. Here is where the problem of language in dealing with the topic of God begins to show up in its authentic terms. In the last section we spoke about a language that provides information about objective things: the cat on the rug, Napoleon's defeat at Waterloo, Jesus' resurrection. But when Poe wrote about a raven "knocking" at his door, he certainly was not trying to provide information about some event. Using analogies and symbolisms, the poet seeks to create in us the same subjective state he feels. Here again the language informs, but by re-creating sensations, emotions, and valuations of feelings and values that are recognized and felt to be such. It is subjective information with its own logic, but it is not arbitrary.

We must admit that the mere discovery of some thing with all its qualities does not, in itself, provide information about the valuation I give it. To provide information on the latter, I can utter a mere exclamation ("Wow!) or compose some complex, symbolic creation (a poem, a parable, a story, etc.).

Nor is it obvious that the language dealing with God combines objective information with subjective information. We need only read a couple of pages of the Bible to see that. The same thing holds true for our own "religious" language. But here we can see that the language used in the latter instance is often devoid of "linguistic" truth, even though it may not be totally devoid of meaning.

We say for example: "God was good to me. He let me win first prize in the lottery." Are we claiming to provide objective information about some divine action with that statement? What possible verification of it could there be? The very indirect one—i.e., the supposition that all pleasant and unpleasant events are doled out by God intentionally—does not seem to be the rule of our language. For the logic of that principle would lead us to say that our neighbor was cursed by God, since he or she did not win. And we do not dare to say that.

Now if we claim to transmit a subjective estimation with that statement, then the logical way of verifying it would be to see what would change if we responded to it with a "no" instead of a "yes." In that case we would imply that if it were not a blessing from God, we would prefer not to have won the prize. But this is obviously not the meaning that we give the statement. In reality we are using the name of God to make our right to the prize absolute and incontestable. The attribution to God plays with language, and plays badly with it. God is used merely to blur the real import of the statement. I would be using language properly if I said something like this: I want this prize at all costs, no matter who gets hurt in the bargain.

Any sociologist can verify the fact that we do this with a considerable number of statements in which we use the term *God*. Indeed this process could be one of the most wholesome and revolutionary things for today's Christian.[42] It might alter his or her life considerably.

The use of the word *God* in such cases as the one mentioned here is inappropriate: not because it is devoid of meaning but because it camouflages the real meaning. A real saint might say: "God blessed me with this event." But he or she would probably be willing to admit that they would reject or devalue the event if they discovered that it was not a blessing from God.

To put it another way: our inappropriate use of the term "God" is related to the superficiality and relativity of the values it symbolizes in our lives. If some value dominates our whole life, our use of language in which the term "God" appears seems to take on a curiously "realistic" and verifiable sense.

Here is where Robinson's attempt at "honesty" comes into the picture. The God "out there" was the God of an objective language. Robinson feels that there is no authentic religious language so long as God does not show up in the center or midpoint from which spring the values that structure our existence.

We could say that here the *Transcendent* is replaced with the *Absolute*. And in this sense every human being, insofar as he evinces any depth and coherent values, structures his or her existence around some Absolute. Robinson points out how important the following remarks of Tillich were for his own thinking:

> The name of this infinite and inexhaustible depth and ground of all being is *God*. That depth is what the word *God* means. And if that word has not much meaning for you, translate it, and speak of the depths of your life, of the source of your being, or your ultimate concern, of what you take seriously without any reservation. Perhaps, in order to do so, you must forget everything traditional that you have learned about God, perhaps even the word itself. For if you know that God means depth, you know much about him. You cannot then call yourself an atheist or unbeliever. For you cannot think or say: Life has no depth! Life is shallow. Being itself is surface only. If you could say this in complete seriousness, you would be an atheist; but otherwise you are not. He who knows about depth knows about God.[43]

And Robinson adds this personal commentary on Tillich's words: "They seemed to speak of God with a new and indestructible relevance, and made the traditional language of a God that came in from outside both remote and artificial."[44]

Here again we meet the question that came up at the beginning of this CLARIFICATION: "Suppose that all such atheism does is to destroy an idol, and that we can and must get on without a God 'out there' at all?" Do not the "atheist" and the "believer" come together in agreement at this point? For, as Robinson puts it: "To assert that 'God is love' is to believe that in love one comes into touch with the most fundamental reality in the universe."[45] Perhaps the ambiguity of the verb *believe* is intentional here. For in fact it does not mean an act of faith but rather some such thing as, "think that" or "be convinced that."

3. The unfortunate thing about this promising agreement and convergence between atheist and believer is that the God who is the "Other" disappears along with the God "out there."[46] What possibility remains for talking about God as *Someone* who summons us, loves us, and judges us? One cannot help but ask this question after reading Robinson's book, even though it represents a fine effort at clarification and honesty.

Robinson writes: "The word 'God' denotes the ultimate depth of all our being, the creative ground and meaning of all our existence."[47] Note that he does not say: "God works *in* the ultimate depth." He says: "God *is* the ultimate depth." And this rejection of the word *in*, and its replacement by the word *is*, is expressly suggested by Robinson on the previous page:

> Yet we are not here dealing simply with a change of symbolism, important as that may be. This is not just the old system in reverse, with a God 'down under' for a God 'up there'. When Tillich speaks of God in 'depth', he is not speaking of another Being *at all*. He is speaking of 'the infinite and inexhaustible depth and ground of all being', of our ultimate concern, of what we take seriously without reservation.[48]

And a few pages later he adds: "A statement is 'theological' not because it relates to a *particular Being* called 'God', but because it asks *ultimate* questions about the meaning of existence"[49] (the first italics are ours).

We must admit that we find it difficult to make this linguistic reduction in the Christian message, to take what it says about three persons so intimately united that they form one being and willing and reduce this to the depth of our own being. By the same token, we find it just as difficult to talk about God without leaving room in the term for that which makes up our deepest and most unreserved interest. We feel much closer to this notion than to some notion of Pure Act infinitely separated from man the creature.[50] But we feel that the linguistic analysis must take one further step.

4. Let us recall once again the words of Saint Augustine: "God is love, *the very same love with which we love*."[51] And in another passage he says that God is "more interior to us than we ourselves are." Now does this God, as described by Saint Augustine, correspond to the form of expression used by Robinson in the passages we have just quoted?

We think not. The grace with which we love is the life of God in us. It is God *in* us. It forms part of our being insofar as our liberty opens up to it. But it is not the ground of our being. It is innerness, to be sure, and an innerness that is greater than ours. But it remains alien so long as we do not dialogue with this "Thou" who stands at the door and knocks. We must open the door to this Thou.

So once again we must inquire into the use of language. And once again we find that the possibility of verifying the content of linguistic statements varies not only between object and subject, reality and value, but also in terms of what we could call "personal attribution."[52]

To say "he loves" has meaning because I can verify whether his behavior patterns are those to be expected when one uses the word *love*. On the other hand, the possibility of verifying the statement, "I love," is very different. Because the content of the latter statement does not signify that I have such and such a behavior pattern, but rather that the meaning and course of my life is different. Someone could have these very some behavior patterns without loving in the personal sense that I give to the word.

What is more, what is involved here is something more than affected subjectivity, something more than a phrase equivalent to a gasp or a "Wow!" If I use the word with complete truth, then I would consider it treason to love anyone else besides the "you" alluded to in it. And, in addition, I can never verify the truth of this "I love" by a process of self-introspection. Because it is the "you" who are the real verifier of love and its unpredictable demands. The laws of language are altered here to the point of the incredible.

Now the tieup between all this and the language we use to name God is obvious. The person, every person, communicates with another person through events that are fashioned into symbols by words. I can regard the universe as a complex of mute happenings. If I speak of God to explain what is happening, then I am using language improperly. But I can also trust that these happenings are the words of a personal being, who need not be "out there" but who is not I.

I can contemplate the deeds of Jesus as does someone who later relates what so-and-so did. But it is also possible that this Jesus may be a Thou for me, indeed such an absolute Thou that my existence depends on interpreting his message and following it.

The point is that the image of "outside" and "other," the image of one and two, is necessary for personal language. That is our objection and our reply to the language of a Robinson or a Tillich. It does not mean that we take this exteriority to be some extramundane transcendence or physical outsideness. But the language of faith falls apart if the identity is turned into something impersonal.

No positivist has ever been able to convince someone in love that his language is inadequate. Something very similar occurs with faith. The Father, Son, and Holy Spirit are not "out there" or "up there." But neither are they my own depth.

NOTES

1. In his now classic book, *The Secular City*, (New York: Macmillan, 1966), Harvey Cox does not adequately distinguish between the two tendencies, although it is obvious that one cannot strictly classify his book as one of the "death of God" works. But a careful reading of his book does enable the reader to distinguish between those aspects of secularization that are presented as obligations proceeding from the Judeo-Christian message, and those which appear to arise from the process which man goes through in the "technopolis."

2. Cox seems to ignore the explicit secularizing theology of the New Testament. He restricts himself to a suggestive but also controversial exegesis of creation, exodus, and covenant (*The Secular City*, Part I, Chapter I).

3. It was the practice of the time to use oppositions to designate totality, and we find this in the present text. But "the present and the future" also contrasts the old order with the new Christian order. We find a clear example of this in another Epistle: "By this the Holy Spirit signifies that so long as the earlier tent still stands, the way into the sanctuary remains unrevealed. All this is symbolic, pointing to the present time. The offerings and sacrifices there prescribed cannot give the worshipper inward perfection . . . But now Christ has come . . ." (Heb. 9:8–11).

4. See Volume I, Chapter V and Volume II, Chapter III.

5. Conrado Eggers Lan, *Cristianismo y nueva ideología* (Buenos Aires: Jorge Alvarez, 1968), pp. 47–48.

6. See Volume II, Chapter III, CLARIFICATION V.

7. The different nature of the two documents could invalidate the comparison. But we feel that the difference is more apparent than real. For the catechism is an exposition of Christianity for adults, while the Medellín documents present a reformulation of the Christian message in terms of the realities of the Latin

American continent. By the same token, anyone familiar with present-day ecclesiastical problems and their formulation will recognize that the two examples mentioned are no more than that: i.e., two examples of a reality that is much broader in scope and that could be confirmed by many other facts.

8. Herbert Marcuse, *One-Dimensional Man* (Boston: Beacon, 1964), Chapter I, pp. 10–11.

9. *Ibid.*, p. 14.

10. César Aguiar Beltrán, "La temática del Sínodo," (II), in *BP Color* (Montevideo), September 24, 1969, p. 12.

11. Alberto Methol Ferré, "Iglesia y sociedad opulenta: Una crítica a Suenens desde América latina," insert in *Víspera*, no. 12, p. 3.

12. Aldo J. Büntig, *El Catolicismo Popular en la Argentina*, Book I (sociology) Buenos Aires: Bonum, 1969), p. 15.

13. Two things are strange about this assessment from the viewpoint of a scientific sociology. 1. It seems to be ignorant of the fact that the evaluation of facts and events do not come from the events themselves (hence not from the sociologist), but in this case from theology. 2. It seems to be unaware of the fact that both a positive evaluation and a negative evaluation of religious phenomena, and even more the absence of any valuation, is weighted with a good dose of "ideology."

14. *A New Catechism*, Eng. trans. (New York: Herder & Herder, 1967). The inclusion of "humanism" and "Marxism" among the "religious" thoughts that pave the way for the Christian message does not diminish the emphasis put on this "religious" preparation (see *ibid.*, Part II, A, pp. 25 ff.). On this whole problem see Volume I of this series and, in particular, Chapter III, CLARIFICATION I.

15. On these points see *Perspectivas de Diálogo*, n. 32. In particular see J. L. Segundo, "¿Hacia una Iglesia de izquierda?" (pp. 35–39), and Ricardo Cetrulo, "Utilización politica de la Iglesia," (pp. 40–44).

16. Here again the reader will recognize ideas that were developed in the previous volumes of this series, particularly in Volume I. Theology is one and does not permit tight compartmentalization.

17. Here we disagree with the analysis of Methol cited in Note 11. We agree that "every theology implies a politics *in some way*." Reasons of a merely political sort can incline us to give a very positive evaluation of Rome's ecclesiastical centralism (for example). But it would be at the cost of sacrificing the specific contribution which the Roman Curia, evaluated in theological terms, can and should make to the fight against man's political enslavements.

18. *Op. cit.*, p. 17. See Note 12.

19. *Ibid.*, p. 19.

20. *Ibid.*, p. 17. Any reader of Paul and his doctrine on liberty (for example) can clearly see that Christianity does not seek to be a universal religion with its "marked tendency to lose doctrinal vigor" (*ibid.*, p. 18). The loss of doctrinal vigor could presumably be compensated for, only by the maintenance of attitudes considered to be "religious." But such attitudes, in Paul's view, do not suffice to enable a person to call himself a Christian. See Volume I of this series, Chapter III, CLARIFICATION I; and Volume II, Chapter III, section III.

21. Priests from Quilmes, Argentina, in J. J. Rossi (ed.), *Iglesia Latinoamericana: ¿Protesta o profecía?* (Buenos Aires: Búsqueda, 1969), pp. 99–100. A similar set of documents has been published in English by Maryknoll Publications under the title, *Between Honesty and Hope.*

22. *Ibid.*, p. 100.

23. *Ibid.*, p. 253.

24. Who often apply the label "rebels" to priests who express themselves in the same terms as these texts.

25. Jean Mansir, O.P., "Révolution dan l'Eglise Catholique," *Lettre*, n. 128, (April 1969), p. 14.

26. Rossi, *op. cit.*, p. 264.

27. *Ibid.*, p. 390.

28. *Cf.* Michael Schmaus, *Teología Dogmática* I, Spanish trans. (Madrid: Rialp, 1960), p. 267. This is the Spanish version of a series of dogma manuals written by Schmaus. As far as I can tell (the translator), it is not a translation of his earlier *Katholische Dogmatic*, but I am not sure. So I have directly translated the Spanish of Segundo's text into English and given the Spanish reference. The reader is advised that a *new* series of volumes by Schmaus is coming out in English under the title, *Dogma* (New York: Sheed and Ward, 1968–). In the Foreword to this English series the author says: "I would like to stress that this work is not at all a summary or revision of my older German text (*Katholische Dogmatik*), but a completely new treatment of theology, based on the developments which have taken place as a result of the Second Vatican Council." So we seem to have three works: his earlier *Katholische Dogmatik*, a more popular series of dogma volumes that circulated in Europe before and around Vatican II, and a new series after Vatican II that is now being translated into English. At any rate the point is that I cannot directly cite an English source for the Schmaus citations used in this series.

29. Pseudo-Dionysius was a Neo-Platonic Christian who was erroneously identified with Dionysius the Areopagite converted by Saint Paul (Acts 17:34).

30. Many expressions of this "negative" theology, often joined with the *via mystica*, can be found in Henri de Lubac, *The Discovery of God*, Chapter 5, "The Ineffable God." See in this volume, Note 4 after the main article of the *Introduction*.

31. *Cf. Cántico Espiritual II*:

RESPUESTA DE LA CRIATURAS	REPLY OF THE CREATURES
Mil gracias derramando,	Diffusing showers of grace
pasó por estos sotos con presure,	In haste among these groves
y yéndolos mirando	his path he took
con sola su figura	and only with his face,
vestidos los jedó de su hermosura.	glancing around the place,
	He clothed them in his beauty
	with a look.

ESPOSA	BRIDE
¡Ay quién podrá sanarme!	Oh who my grief can mend!
Acaba de entregarte ya de vero;	Come, make the last surrender
nos quieras enviarme	that I yearn for,
de hoy ya más mensajero	and let there be an end
que no saben decirme lo que quiero.	of messengers you send
	who bring me other tidings
	than I burn for.

Y todos cuantos vagan,   All those that haunt the spot
de Ti me van mil gracias refiriendo,   Recount your charm, and
y todos más me llagan,   wound me worst of all
y déjame muriéndome   Babbling I know not what
un no se qué que quedan balbuciendo.   Strange rapture, they recall,
                                                Which leaves me stretched and
                                                    dying where I fall.

                                                [*Translation by Roy Campbell*]

     32. *Cf. Coplas hechas sobre un éxtasis de alta contemplación (Verses written after an ecstasy of high exaltation):*

Y si lo queré is oír,   If you would ask, what is its essence—
consiste esta suma sciencia   This summit of all sense and knowing,
en un subido sentir   It comes from the Divinest Presence—
de la divinal Esencia;   The sudden sense of Him outflowing,
es obra de su clemencia   In His great clemency bestowing
hacer quedar no entendiendo   The gift that leaves men knowing
toda sciencia trascendiendo.   naught,
                                                Yet passing knowledge with their
                                                    thought.

                                                [*Translation by Roy Campbell*]

     33. Henri de Lubac, *The Discovery of God*, Eng. trans (New York: P. J. Kenedy, 1960), p. 157.

     34. Both Christian and atheistic existentialism has stressed, perhaps one-sidedly, criticism of reason. In *Ich und Du* (p. 98; Eng. trans., New York: Charles Scribners' Sons, 1937), Buber writes:

> The external "Thou" cannot by its very nature become an "it," for by its nature it cannot be expressed in measure and bounds, not even in the measure of the immeasurable or the bounds of boundless being; by its nature it cannot be grasped as a sum of qualities, not even as an infinite sum of qualities raised to a transcendent level; it can be found neither in nor out of the world; it cannot be experienced; it cannot be thought; we fail to meet him who is when we say "I believe that he is"—"he" is still a metaphor, but "Thou" is not.

We would ask: How does one know this "Thou" is God except by virtue of his *nature*? This passage is cited by W.H. van de Pol, *The End of Conventional Christianity*, Eng. trans. (New York; Newman Press, 1968), p. 176.

     35. *Cf.* J.L. Segundo, *Berdiaeff: Une reflexion chrétienne sur la personne* (Paris: Auber, 1963), p. 165.

     36. The theme of this CLARIFICATION will be treated in greater detail in the next chapter. But the idea of a God who is a *society* required that we make this point about knowledge on the personal level.

     37. On the role of anthropomorphisms, there is this passage in Schmaus, *Teología Dogmática, op. cit.*, p. 266 (see note 28):

This point makes clear the function of anthropomorphisms. They do not at all presume to lower God to the same level occupied by man. Anthropomorphic expressions do not humanize God. They have never been taken in that sense, except in polemics devoid of objectivity. On the contrary, they should be considered as a pathway that leads man toward God. They fashion a possibility for encounter and differences between man and God in the realm of willing. They make manifest the divine personality. They stand in opposition to the error that tends to see God as a still, indifferent, abstract idea, as a principle opposed to man along the lines of a mute, repelling wall . . . W. Eichrodt (*Theologie des AT*, 1933, I, 104–110) . . . states that the revelation of the Old Covenant saw less danger in not spelling out clearly God's spiritual nature than it saw in not manifesting clearly his personal mode of working and operating.

38. John A.T. Robinson, *Honest to God* (Philadelphia: Westminster Press, paperback edition, p. 17, Chapter 1. On the whole matter of "linguistic sincerity," one can also consult Paul Van Buren, *The Secular Meaning of the Gospel* ("based on an analysis of its language"). *op. cit.* We may also profit from reading the article by John Macquarrie, "Religious Language and Recent Analytical Philosophy," *Concilium* 46 (New York: Paulist Press, "The Development of Fundamental Theology," 1969), 159-62.

39. According to Van Buren (*op. cit.*, p. 130), this would be mixing two incompatible languages. "This *is* Jesus" would signify one thing when Jesus is alive, and another thing after his death. We must confess that we do not understand the argument. If the same verb is there when we apply it to a child before the age of reason and to a man who has become an adult, we do not see why the unwonted nature of "resurrection" would prevent us from attributing it to someone who died and now is alive. Nor do we see why that would change the rules of language.

40. Macquarrie, *op. cit.*, see note 38.

41. Hence Van Buren's solution would be logical if the term "faith" were to disappear from language at the same time that the term "God" does. See *The Secular Meaning of the Gospel, op. cit.*, pp. 126 ff.

42. See Chapter IV in this volume.

43. Paul Tillich, *The Shaking of the Foundations* (New York: Pelican, 1962), pp. 63 ff.

44. *Honest to God, op. cit.*, p. 22.

45. *Ibid.*, p. 53.

46. Robinson is aware of the problem: "The abandonment of any idea of a God 'out there' will inevitably appear a denial of his 'otherness' . . ." (*ibid.*, p. 56). But he minimizes the problem when he interprets this "otherness" to be "the infinite qualitative difference between God and man" (*ibid.*). The "otherness" in question serves as the foundation for the *I-Thou.*

47. *Ibid.*, p. 47.

48. *Ibid.*, p. 46.

49. *Ibid.*, p. 49. At another point Robinson rejects the idea of God as a personal being totally distinct from man and living in majesty. It seems to us that his rejection covers all three characteristics, not just the last two.

50. See Chapter III in this volume.

51. *De Trinitate*, PL 42, 957.

52. *Cf.* Maquarrie, *op. cit.*, see note 38.

CHAPTER THREE

God and Liberty

While the theologians and particularly the apologists of the first centuries after Christ were searching for the most correct and intelligible way of explaining the Trinitarian revelation to pagans and neophytes, being embroiled in controversies that were often heated and not always apolitical, the Church as a whole continued to maintain an unshakable fidelity to the Trinity even though it had not yet spelled out the mystery explicitly or applied the term *Trinity* to it.

What was the Church proclaiming and teaching while these errors were circulating? The *symbolon* or creed of that era said simply: "I believe in the Father, the Almighty, and in Jesus Christ, our Redeemer, and in the Holy Spirit, the Consoler; in the Holy Church and in the pardon of sins" (Denz. 1). Nothing more.

Much the same was evident in the liturgy, in the baptismal rite for example. Baptism was conferred in the name of the Father, the Son, and the Holy Spirit. The triple invocation was matched by three ablutions or immersions to give further emphasis to the Trinitarian formula. And three questions were asked of the catechumen to whom the sacrament was being administered: Do you believe in the Father? Do you believe in the Son? Do you believe in the Holy Spirit? Standing on the border of all the polemical talk and outside all the controversy, the baptismal rite continued to affirm the existence of the three divine persons, the revelation of divine love. And all the heretics, both Modalists and Adoptionists, administered baptism in their churches with this same Trinitarian formula and with the threefold immersion, both of which were universal.

We find much the same thing in the most ancient prayers or orations of the Church. There is, for example, the beautiful Vesper hymn ("afternoon prayer") that is believed to date from the second century: "Bright light of the Father's holy and immortal glory, holy and blessed Jesus Christ, as we approach sunset and see the evening star coming out, we sing the praise of the Father, Son, and Holy Spirit of God.

You are deserving, at all times, of hymns of praise from holy voices, Son of God who gives life. Amen." There is not the least shadow of a doubt that this is an affirmation of the divinity of the Son, the Light of Light, even though it does not explain how that fits in with the existence of one unique God.

We also have the testimony of the martyrs, the witnesses *par excellence* to the Christian faith. We have, for example, the official records (called *Acta*) of the martyrdom of Saint Pionius, who says to his judge: "I worship God the Almighty, whom we have come to know through his Word." The judge then asks: "The Word? Who is that? Another god?" And Pionius replies: "No, *the same.*"[1]

Could not the Church stick with this wise, vital, and orthodox understanding of the revelation about God even though it rested on a basic and spontaneous level?

We have already said that it was logical that questions would crop up even within the Church. And it was even more understandable when the apologists tried to explain the Christian faith to people of Greek training and culture. To take some sample questions: How can the deity be one and, at the same time, Father, Son, and Holy Spirit? On the one hand you assert that there is only one God, but on the other hand you also talk about three divine beings, do you not? Aren't they really three distinct gods? Are they not *one* divinity in the same way that the human nature of Peter, Paul, and Andrew is one? May not the fact that only one of the three is called "the God" *(ho theos)* be more important than it appears to be?

To appreciate the difficulty of this whole enterprise, one must remember that these questions were posed by the upper classes of the Greek cultural world. These people would automatically relegate a religion with three gods to the plane of popular superstitions. Hence the deviational tendencies that arose in this area never, for all practical purposes, took the form of conceiving the divine unity as a generic concept in which all three participated just as three human beings participate in one and the same human nature. If the Father is God, the Son is God, and the Holy Spirit is God, what unites them is not the fact of being *three gods* of equal nature.

In the Trinitarian controversies of the first centuries the temptation was to move in the opposite direction: i.e., toward the affirmation of the one and the denial of the three. In other words, people moved toward the facile solution of espousing a monotheism that was not changed one bit by the revelation of the Son and the Spirit.

Thus from the time of the New Testament to the First Ecumenical Council of Nicea (325), the cultural circles of the empire, and the major centers of Rome and Alexandria in particular, were saturated with count-less attempts to divest Christianity of the "three." For these "three" seemed to subvert the interior of the one and only God that would be compatible with this cultural realm.

Two logical pathways were open to this line of thought. They enable the modern theologian and historian to shed some ray of clarifying light on the overall panorama, where groups, personal opinions, and even entire churches confronted each other over terms that were not always used univocally. The two courses open were these: (1) to interpret the three distinct names as different *modes* of operation belonging to one single divine individual; (2) to *subordinate* the relatively divine condition of the Son and the Spirit to the one and only being that was absolutely divine, that is, the Father. Hence we get the twofold classification of Modalists and Subordinationists. While these terms cannot always be used with absolute clarity, they do provide us with a guiding thread that is more comprehensible than the labels based on individual thinkers and their followers: e.g., Sabellianism and Arianism, referring to the doctrines of Sabellius and Arius.

We will begin by considering Modalism in this chapter. In the next chapter we will consider Subordinationism.

Section I

The theoretical name "Modalism" comes from the fact that this tendency tried to reduce the *three* in God to three different *modes* of operating. Salvation history had been carried out in three stages and, as it were, on three planes. This and nothing else was the difference indicated by the three divine names, according to the Modalists.

Let us admit right here that the rise of Modalism is perfectly under-standable, considering the fact that God's work was evidently one single effort even though it was carried out on different planes, and con-sequently in different ways or modes. After all, creation is attributed to Father, Son, and Holy Spirit. It is said of all three that they counsel, sustain, and judge. And their names, rather than distinguishing them or separating them, serve more to show that we are dealing with the same doctrine, the same plan, and the same activity.[2] So why not go a little beyond the purely textual statement and conclude that the three names designate the same being operating differently on the different levels that go to make up our existence: i.e., our relationship with things, our interpersonal relations in history, and our reflection on our own inner life?

With varying degrees of refinement, this was what actually happened in the first few centuries after Chirstianity's propagation. There were three steps or stages in this tendency, as logic impelled it to its ultimate conclusions.

The first step, on a rather course level, was taken very early in the primitive Church. Already around the year 190 the Monarchians appeared in Asia Minor. The name signifies that they espoused "one single prinicple," and in fact they maintained that only one God exists: *the Father.* Hence, according to them, we are forced to believe that it was the Father himself who was born, persecuted, and put to death under the name or figure of Jesus. For this reason the Roman Church applied the ironic name *Patripassians* to them around the year 200. For they "made the Father suffer the passion." Taunting Praxeas, the founder of Monarchianism in Rome, Tertullian said in a humorous vein that he "had put the Paraclete to flight [by eliminating him], and had crucified the Father."[3]

A more refined level of this same tendency, associated with the name of Sabellius, reveals its dominant orientation in a more unequivocal manner. That thrust was to return the Christian revelation of the Trinity to a more refined and cultured conception of God. And we say *return* here quite deliberately because Old Testament revelation, despite it anthropomorphisms, paradoxically enough lent itself to an interpretation that was closer to the monotheism of Greek philosophy. The work of Philo of Alexandria can serve as a witness to this fact.

This regressive tendency was most apparent in the thinking of Sabellius, the most well known of the Monarchians or Modalists, as we indicated above. Hence this outlook was also called Sabellianism. What is worth noting is the fact that as Modalism became more refined and purified, it manifested a clear tendency to avoid the "coarse" error of Patripassianism which, in effect, introduces a "history" into the unique divinity. If one did not admit the possibility of a divine person distinct from the Father through the Incarnation, then why not go all the way and avow the purity of the idea of divinity elaborated by Greek culture?

But there was one more step to take, and we should not be surprised to find that it was taken—by Paul of Samosata. In Antioch, one of the most important cultural centers, he combined the idea of Modalism with the idea that the Incarnation is really God's "redemptive modality" through the divine indwelling or adoption of Jesus of Nazareth, the latter being thereby empowered to accomplish his salvific work.[4] Thus Modalism, which is born of a typically rationalist simplification, tends to end up by denying God-with-us in history. God simply manifested himself and operated through Jesus, but he remained independent of his instrument and infinitely distanced from his sufferings, his commitments, and his and our history.[5]

A decisive step was taken here. All man's rational elaborations of the deity—the "unmoved mover" of the Aristotelian tradition, the absolute One of comtemporary Neoplatonism (Plotinus), and the *logos* of Stoic nature—came rushing through the Modalist breach and converged toward the very center of Christianity.

Perhaps now we may begin to suspect that Modalism had an importance that went far beyond the mere question of whether the "three" in God corresponded to three different "persons" or simply to three different "modes" of operation—a question seemingly without human resonances. We begin to see that even in those days Modalism tended to confirm the hypothesis that some sort of degradation of man lies buried within every deformation in our idea of God—and vice versa. For the fact is that Modalism ends up with what we might call the divine "nature" and calls this the God of Christian revelation.

In this nature it sees only what it can deduce about its infinity, its absolute self-sufficiency, its full measure of possible value; and it identifies all this with serene, unclouded bliss. By taking this nature as such to be God, Modalism separates it in a total and irremediable way from any and every created nature, and hence from all change, all sorrow, and all history.[6] What lies behind this process?

Section II

The reduction of the Christian God to the divine nature (not so much to the "God of the philosophers," as we shall see) is the result of a rational process that "lays hands on" revelation and sets itself up as the latter's judge and jury. Lehmann is quite right in saying: "Any interpretation of the Trinity runs the risk of modalism."[7]

So we are faced with a more general question: By what process does reason lay hands on the theme of God and take control over it?

To begin with, reason starts from the existent and poses the problem whether God, the Infinite Being, exists. The process of proof is really quite simple and, so long as it remains simple, convincing. For no one doubts that a produced mechanism presupposes the existence of a producer, and that this producer should possess greater intrinsic perfection than that manifested by the product. Unless we opt for an inexplicable infinite series, we must conclude that the totality of existents was produced by Someone who possesses the fullness of being: i.e., by the Infinite Being.[8]

Let us assume the validity of this rational argument which starts from the *efficient cause* (i.e., the producer) and concludes that there does exist a being with a divine, unlimited nature. But something else is required at the same time if a cause is to cause, that is, if *someone* is to produce *something*. Not only must the someone have the power to produce; the something must also have value that makes it worthy of being produced. In short, there must be an end in view, a *final cause*.

If either the efficient cause or the final cause is absent, the production will not take place. For it will lack any reason for being. And that brings us to the crux of our question, which can be summed up in a simple statement: creative power in the producer and value in the product are in inverse proportion to each other.

A hypothetical example will clarify this statement. Suppose we have a rancher who produces wool. Now if he does so, he does so because he possesses the know-how and technical skill and means of production (all components of the efficient cause), and also because he lacks wool which he desires and needs (the final cause). If wool ceased to have value for him, he would simply stop producing it. In our world this loss of product value usually results from external causes. But we can imagine an even more radical loss of value. Let us suppose for a moment that the inner perfection of the rancher soars. He can at will convert the air he breathes into food, clothing, shelter, money, prestige, etc. Now he is a far more perfect efficient cause, because his inner production facilities have multiplied greatly. But now he will no longer produce wool! Why? Because now it will have lost the value that it once had for him. Now he *already* possesses what the wool once provided for him. Thus an increase in the perfection of the efficient cause goes hand in hand with a corresponding decrease in the value of the final cause.

And so we see where this reasoning process ends up. The perfect being, the infinite producer, has no reason to produce anything at all. For any value that might presumably be attached to the production of something is a value that he already possesses in an unlimited way. No one and nothing can add one iota to what he already possesses. The perfect efficient cause has no final cause that could prompt him to produce. His will for infinite efficacy is therefore in perfect repose already.[9]

Now the reader may feel inclined to minimize the importance and possible influence of this objection—not so much because it is intellectual but mainly because the problem seems to be resolved even without taking revelation into account. One might say: some finality would remain for creation still because the universe does exist after all![10]

But the danger we are underlining is not that anyone might claim that the created world does not exist for want of sufficient reason. The danger is that in this framework of thought the created universe, and hence human beings with their liberty and history, are left without any positive ties to the infinite divine nature. Or, to express the same idea in the way that a more precise philosophy might: they are left intimately and decisively tied to a nature that is entirely unattached to them.[11]

Granting the fact that man exists, makes decisions, and thereby creates history, it still would seem that reason is forced to acknowledge and define another being at the apex of the pyramid. And this being must remain infinite, inaccessible, immutable, and content, no matter what may be the result of man's history, the destiny of the individual or of mankind, and the use to which human liberty is put.

Perhaps now the reader will sense that the problem here is far from being a merely intellectual one. Man's whole religious attitude and outlook will depend on its solution. What is more, one of the greatest sources of human enslavement and alienation will be overcome or not, depending on whether we overcome to the god of Modalism, the god of reason, the God who is simply a divine nature.

Note that we say "overcome" rather than "suppress."[12] But this overcoming must certainly go further than the mere juxtaposition of incompatible languages such as we often find in our lives as Christians. For example, when revelation teaches us that God became man, rational reductionism prompts us to say that this does not signify any change because God is immutable. When revelation tells us that God gave his life for human beings even unto death, rational reductionism prompts us to say that God, being absolutely simple and inaccessible, cannot have any real relationship to his creatures. When revelation tells us that God truly suffered and died, rational reductionism reminds us that the Infinite Being is the seat of all values and that nothing can make him suffer.

Let us try to bring these two languages into even closer contact, if it is possible. One says: "No one and no thing can add anything to the Infinite Being." The other says: "Here I stand knocking at the door; if anyone hears my voice and opens the door, I will come in and sit down to supper with him and he with me" (Rev. 3:20). One language says: "The supreme will reposes in its infinity." The other says: "My Father has never yet ceased his work, and I am working too" (John 5:17). One language says: "Every created value remains extrinsic to God." The other says: "Father, I desire that these men, who are thy gift to me, may be with me where I am" (John 17:24).[13]

What are we to make of these two opposed languages? And no one can doubt that they are opposed. Operating on some lofty level of abstract speculation, one might be able to show that they are compatible. But we feel that the demonstration would succeed at the expense of the data of revelation, reducing and deforming it in the process.[14]

And there is a more serious question to be faced. What are we to make of these two languages, not in the rarefied atmosphere of speculative theology, but rather in the real-life existence of Christians? Here no one can deny that the two languages are *existentially* incompatible. And by this we mean that the image of God and man that is evoked by one is opposed to the image evoked by the other. To offer one example: the image of a God who is infinitely happy both in the face of man's right use of his liberty as well as in the face of his wrong use of that liberty is, *qua* image, contradictory to rather than compatible with the image of God who stands and knocks at the door of man's heart. In practice one image eliminates the other.

And there is more to be said in the realm of practical living. Even if we presume the coherence of the two languages on the speculative level, the fact is that the images which arise from them are rated differently. The images that arise from one language are judged to be primitive and naive, while the images that arise from the other language are judged to be purified and cultured. Later on in this same chapter[15] we shall have occasion to see how the forms of societal life enter into connivance with these rationally purified types of images. And the fact is that the opposition between these two languages does not end up along class lines, for even the lower classes tend to nurture the latter type of images.[16]

So we are faced with three possible alternatives. We can opt for a rational reduction of the God of revelation that is obviously incompatible with Christian theology (e.g., ancient Modalism, modern rationalism, deism). Or we can solve the problem by taking the easy way out, juxtaposing the two languages in measured doses and alternating between them without offering any internal coherence; this leads to the same reductionism as the first alternative. Or, finally, we can opt for a third alternative.[17] We noted earlier that those things which reason might discover about God-qua-divine nature must be overcome rather than denied (Denz. 523). That means we reject the rationalist portrait of a God-qua-divine nature only, but accept the data of reason on the nature of God. The fact is that revelation does not show us a God with a limited, changing, fickle nature. But it does show us a God who freely *loved and gave himself up* (cf. Gal. 2:20) despite the fact that he did not have to by virtue of his nature. And he carried the logic of this love through to the end.

What in fact is the mystery of the individual person for us? It is that we do not really know his history even though we may have come to "know" his nature more or less. For if he truly is a person and acts as such, his nature is not a mere mechanism that allows us to predict its functioning. A person does not "function," a person decides. Hence only a "revelation" of what he has decided gives us access to what he is at bottom. If we do not know his history well, that does not make what we do know about it false. But we would indeed be wrong to regard what we know as the totality of his being and worth. And it would be criminal of us to follow this logic through to the end, continually reducing what is unique in him to the simplistic unity of a genus or species, and subordinating the person to the undifferentiated value of said genus or species.

The same thing, or something quite similar at least, holds true for our way of looking at God.

Section III

Everything we have said in the preceding section may seem to be speculative and abstract. But before it becomes material for human intellectual effort, it is doubt, anxiety, and drama in man's existence. And it is precisely on this latter level that we should like to take up these ideas once again, comprehend them better, verify them more carefully, and compare them anew with our revelation.

We said above that reason, starting off from created things, speaks to us of an infinite being wherein there exists the absolute plenitude of being and value right from the start. Faced with this already realized plenitude, man is led to ask himself: To what purpose is my liberty, then? It is a question that is asked by saints and sinners, by those who choose to believe in God still and by those who do not want to believe in him, by highly intellectual human beings and by practical people. Indeed it is asked by all human beings who have the time, daring, and depth to approach this abyss, and who are not content with readymade answers. Let us consider three examples here.

In his play *The Flies,* Jean Paul Sartre has Jupiter speak as the Christian God might speak if he really were the infinite nature that we have just been discussing.[18] Jupiter says: "The world is good. I have created it in accordance with my will, and I am the Good . . . The Good is in you, outside of you . . . it is what permits success to your bad undertaking, for it was the brightness of your torches, the harshness of your sword, the strength of your arm. And this Evil of which you are so proud, what is it but . . . a stray road . . . whose very existence is sustained by the Good?" And man responds: "Outside of nature, against nature . . . I shall not return to submission to your law . . . Because I am a human being, Jupiter, and every human being must invent his own path."

We are compelled to reflect briefly on this dialogue. If goodness is in the author of things and then, in a proportional and conditional way, in the order arranged by him for the universe, then the root problem for man is not to produce a good that is lacking but to *attain* one that already exists and is proposed to him.

But why is it necessary to attain it? Or to put the question better: Why is that a *problem?* Because the law that leads him toward the good is not his own internal mechanism, as it is in all the other beings of the universe. Following this order through law and thus attaining the good is left to man's liberty, to man's own decision-making, which is thus put to the test of saying yes or no to the order established by God.

The significance of man's liberty flows from this, according to the reply of the man in Sartre's play. For only two possibilities seem open. Either human liberty can produce something unexpected, something original which is lacking, in which case it is *creative*. Or else it is merely something which sadly and inexplicably separates man from his natural finality, in which case it is a *test* with no value for the world and a worthless piece of cruelty toward man. If the character in Sartre's play chooses the first alternative, he certainly believes he is choosing it against God, in order to confer on his liberty the only positive value that justifies the risk entailed.

A second example is the maxim that Blanche of Castile is supposed to have addressed to her son Louis, the future king of France and saint. For centuries it has been a part of popular spiritual formation. She is supposed to have said: "I would rather see you dead than have you commit one mortal sin."

Here again a brief reflection is in order. It would appear that the protagonist of *The Flies* and Blanche of Castile are saying things that are diametrically opposed. Yet, paradoxically enough, what is becoming more and more decisive is what they agree on rather than what they disagree on. For in reality Blanche of Castile tacitly acknowledges the very same dilemma that is posed by Sartre's play. Liberty is either *creation* or a *test*. The first alternative presupposes a God who in some way needs man's decision-making. On the other hand, if God is perfect and inaccessible, if the good is already fully realized, then liberty can only be a test. If the latter case is true, and if by some escape-clause one can attain the good without having to go through the test (by holding on to one's baptismal innocence in this case), then that is all to the good. And that is true even if it means welcoming death, the definitive nonliberty.[19]

Blanche of Castile would prefer that her son, and *a fortiori* other human beings, opt for nonliberty rather than a specific use of liberty: i.e., choosing evil and that which is opposed to the law. And since one cannot attack a specific use of liberty without attacking it at its roots, i.e., without attacking liberty itself, she would simply prefer nonliberty.

Here we see the anxiety evinced by the religious outlook, even on the most popular level, when confronted with the uncompensated risk that man's decision-making faces vis-à-vis the infinity of the divine. This anxiety becomes more explicit and eloquent in our third example. It is the anxiety of a man who lived this drama on an imaginative scale that took in the whole cosmos, and who was in close and continual contact with the scientific attitudes of nonbelievers. Teilhard de Chardin writes: "What is the point of attaining 'beatitude' if, in the final reckoning, we have made no absolute contribution, through our lives, to the totality of being?. . . You may, by a dialectic of pure act, silence our reason as much as you please, but you will never now convince our hearts that the vast business of the cosmos, *as we now see it,* is simply some gift or plaything of God's."[20]

Another passage, which is even more explicit and precise, establishes the connection between this attitude toward the world and its history and the reductionism that comes from a rationalist conception of God:

> Christian faith, through its mysteries of the Incarnation and even of the Redemption, adorns this world with many charms, but does it not, on the other hand, rob it of all interest—even, maybe, make it contemptible to us—by insisting on God's self-sufficiency and, in consequence, on the complete contingence of creation?. . . "God creates by love" is a fine scholastic phrase: but what is this love, then, inexplicable in its subject and degrading for its object, that is *based on no need* (unless it be the pleasure of giving for the sake of giving)?[21]

Curiously enough Teilhard de Chardin, after falling into the same dilemma that was faced by Sartre and Blanche of Castile, tips the scales in favor of Sartre in the name of revelation itself. He does so, not because he chooses Evil, but because he affirms that the only Christian significance of liberty has to be that of *creation*. He was convinced that "every human being must invent his own path."[22]

If this is to be so, however, we now realize that one must make a choice between the two languages mentioned above. We must select one as the key to knowledge of God. So we shall conclude this section by showing briefly how basic and biblical this exigency is.

We often forget that what the apostles saw during their years with Jesus of Nazareth was a man, a human being. They called him their "master" or "teacher" or "rabbi." Only later, after they had reflected on the whole affair, did they realize that they had "seen" more than that. This reflection of theirs is precious to us. In it, as well as in the words and deeds of Jesus that serve as its basis, we have God's revelation, his self-disclosure to human beings. He did not say to them: "I am God." Instead he enabled them to make God's acquaintance; and when they pondered the acquaintance, *they recognized him.* To put it another way: the apostles' first direct "seeing" of Jesus was transformed into another kind of "seeing," thanks to their reflection on the "signs." They came to realize that what they "saw" did not stop there.

A sign is something that we perceive and think we understand. But then it slips away from us toward something else further away. The apostles "saw" their master, but they soon realized that certain actions of his suggested "something more" and were fraught with signification. For example, they saw him cure illnesses and they soon realized that there was something more than curing involved here. Something was being proclaimed in these cures: "Go and tell John what you hear and see: the blind recover their sight, the lame walk . . ." (Matt. 11:4–5). What conclusion were the apostles supposed to draw? Undoubtedly the same conclusion that was to be drawn by the disciples of John the Baptist, to whom Jesus addressed that reply: namely, that they were *seeing* the "one who is to come" that they were expecting (*cf.* Matt. 11:3), the Messiah that God was to send to his people.

This more profound sort of *seeing* is epitomized in John's Gospel, precisely because in it the seeing had gone much, much further. In the first chapter of that Gospel we read that Philip goes to find Nathanael and tell him the good news. His words here undoubtedly anticipate what will be a long process of discovery: "We have met the man spoken of by Moses in the Law, and by the prophets: it is Jesus son of Joseph, from Nazareth" (John 6:45). The astonished Nathanael replies: "Nazareth! . . . can anything good come from Nazareth?" (John 1:46). And Philip replies with the verb that entails much more than simply verifying events; that entails comprehending their import and significance: "Come and *see*" (John 1:46).

As we noted above, there is much more to "see" here. John begins his first Epistle with these words: "It was there from the beginning; we have heard it; we have seen it with our own eyes . . . the word of life . . . made visible (1 John 1:1). It is the same Word that was in the beginning with God the Father, and was God too (*cf.* John 1:1–2).

But how is it possible to *see* God, whom no one has ever seen (*cf.*

John 1:18)? John explains it to us in a passage that is central to our quest here: "The Word became flesh; he came to dwell among us; and *we saw his glory*" (John 1:14; our italics).

Now for anyone familiar with the Old Testament, the word *glory* suggests simply the sign of the presence of God, of the deity. How did the Jews in the desert recognize that God was accompanying them? In the fact that the glory of Yahweh showed itself unmistakably. They had an unequivocal sign: the cloud and the fire went before pilgrim Israel and protected it. How did they recognize the fact that God was dwelling in the temple they had constructed at Jerusalem? In the fact that the glory of Yahweh filled it on its inaugural day, taking the form of a cloud.

Now then, John the Evangelist must have seen some *sign* of the deity that enabled him to go beyond the verification of Jesus as Messiah, which itself entailed reflection too. For John *saw* the divine attribute of "glory" in Jesus. There is no doubt that the whole teaching of Jesus during his years of living with the apostles slowly opened their eyes so that they might *see* this sign, so that they might comprehend the import and *signification* of the events that were taking place under their eyes in the human happening.

For us, however, the logical road to take must be more rapid. We must try to find out *when* John saw this divine glory, what in the concrete was the sign that enabled him to recognize the fact that he was seeing God. For the reader of the fourth Gospel, there can be no doubt about the answer to this question. Strange as it may seem, John does not locate this privileged moment in the resurrection or even in the passion, much less in any of the miracles or "signs"—even though the latter, framed in their proper context, do lead to Jesus' hour, to the moment of glory.

To see this moment more clearly we should recall what various exegetes have said about the Prologue of the fourth Gospel (John 1:1–18). They have pointed out that it is carefully constructed to bring out two phases: (1) the descent of the Word from the bosom of the Father into human existence; (2) paralleling this, the gradual, step by step ascent of the Word with human beings toward the bosom of the Father.[23] So the question is: What is the moment of return? Which is the moment in which he who loved his own and participated seriously in the world lets them see whence he has come and whither he is going? When does he make known his glory to them?

The answer is plain to see in John's Gospel: "It was before the Passover festival. Jesus knew that his hour had come and he must leave this world and go to the Father. He had always loved his own who were

in the world, and now he was to show the full extent of his love. The
devil had already put it into the mind of Judas son of Simon Iscariot
to betray him. During supper, Jesus, well aware that the Father had
entrusted everything to him, and that he had come from God and was
going back to God, rose from table. . ." (John 13:1–3).

We are at the highpoint and climax of the Prologue. The Word
has come and is now returning. But before he returns he will give fulfillment to John's statement: "We saw his glory." When exactly? Jesus himself
says that it takes place in the scene which follows the passage quoted
above: "Now the Son of Man is glorified, and in him God is glorified"
(John 13:31). The passion and resurrection which will follow are nothing
but a large-scale mute reproduction of what was said and done in this
key scene (*cf.* John 13:32–33).

And what exactly does take place in that scene which manifests the
glory, the divinity, of Jesus? The very first section of chapter 13 tells us,
moving from the words cited above to the heart of the matter: "Jesus
. . . rose from table, laid aside his garments, and taking a towel, tied
it round him. Then he poured water into a basin, and began to wash
his disciples' feet and to wipe them with the towel" (John 13:4–5).

Here we have the extreme measure of love in which the presence
of divinity is recognized. At the moment when he who said he was
one with the Father is returning to him, his greatest preoccupation and
concern is to wipe the grime and weariness of the road from the feet
of his poor friends.[24] John the Evangelist did something that may seem
paradoxical to us, but his logic is clarified and corroborated by everything
that has gone before. He sensed the divinity, not in the indifference
of one who possesses everything, but in the love that turned itself wholly
to him, John, to his liberty as something creative, to his history as the
bearer of something unique in the eyes of one who by his nature could
have prescinded from it.

Section IV

What was at stake in the struggle to overcome Modalism, then, was
the one and only notion of God compatible with the worth of the human
person, liberty, and history. As Berdyaev says so well: "One can say
that the recognition of God as person preceded the recognition of man
as person . . . The doctrine of *hypostasis* [i.e., of persons] in the Trinity . . .
in terms of the problem of the person, occupies a privileged place in
the history of world thought."

In the last paragraph we said "was at stake." But it should be clear to the reader that the significance of man still continues to be at stake[25] in our notion of God. At this point in our reflection we should not be surprised to find this out. To be sure, divine revelation does seem to offer data that is relatively independent, and that is capable of shedding light not only on theological distortions but also on the existential and human distortions that are the foundation for the former. But as Christ himself tells us, it is man's behavior that determines whether he draws nearer to this light and grasps the message: "Here lies the test: the light has come into the world, but men preferred darkenss to light because their deeds were evil. Bad men all hate the light and avoid it, for fear their practices should be shown up. The honest man comes to the light so that it may be clearly seen that God is in all he does" (John 3:19–21).

This suggests quite plainly that the idolatry into which we fall (cf. GS 19) does not result primarily from a defective catechesis. It comes from something much deeper within us. It is not without reason that we have accepted such catechesis—and it is important to see this. For other people, more faithful to the task of acting out the truth, have rejected this catechesis and refused to accept a God of that sort.[26] Over against the rejection we might have uttered, our acceptance of such a catechesis proves that the distortion is in line with something we carry deep within us, with something in our conduct that is not in accord with the truth.

When we retrace this route from the opposite direction, we see that all the deviations and distortions which have touched the notion of God, both now and in the past, proceed from the same source. The fact is that while God did make us in his image and likeness, we fashion for ourselves a rationalist image of him in the image and likeness of one who guides our life and our society.

Let us recall here what we said in Volume II about the starting point for the dynamic work of grace in us. What exactly is the force that puts up opposition to love? How do we protect ourselves from love and its demands? Certainly not by consciously espousing the cause of egotism.

The process is much more subtle. And the Gospel itself alludes to this fact when it suggests that even such holy and honorable occupations as those of priest and Levite can impede us from drawing closer to the lives, the problems and the needs of those who live near us physically.

Who is my neighbor? Who is the one near me? That is what they ask Jesus. And Jesus offers a profound but unexpected response: he is the one whom I draw near to, whom I make my neighbor (cf. Luke 10:29–37).

Our fidelity to Christ's great commandment is not going to show up so much with respect to persons who are bound to me by some imposed proximity. It is going to show up in our acceptance or refusal of the innumerable possibilities of establishing these relationships in the society where we live.

So then the question is: What technique or mechanism do we use to put others at a distance, to avoid drawing near to those who are around us in our everyday world? Sociologically speaking, the answer is not difficult. In the concrete we put others at a distance by putting labels on them, by cataloguing them in neat little pigeonholes.

Once we have branded a certain person as "the bakery man," for example, we can pass by his shop every day for years without feeling close to his personal history, to his irreducibly personal core.

In reality this procedure is familiar to us already from what we have said in the earlier sections. It consists in reducing knowledge of a "person" to the realm of "nature" and what is natural. And the inevitable result is that we reduce the liberty of another person to a *function* of our system, refusing to perceive what can only come from a *history* born of his liberty. In other words: the egotistical procedure *par excellence* consists in substituting "positive" rational knowledge for "negative" (because it is individual) historical knowledge.

We refer to *positive* rational knowledge here because, as we have already seen, it consists in allowing reason, which can only distinguish natures, to present these natures to us as if they were the whole story. And hence we refer to *negative* knowledge because it sets a limit, a "no," on this attempt at rational totalitarianism, leaving room for that which is free and cannot be generalized, for personal history.

And it is symptomatic that the more we distance ourselves from the personal and the historical, the more possible it is for us to relativize, manipulate, and use the being in question.

The label "natural" or "functional" may vary. A person can be removed to a distance by being turned into his or her social function: cop, laborer, president, etc. A given person can be catalogued in terms of some psychic trait: megalomaniac, snob, grouch, etc. Or a person may be labelled in terms of some prevalent ideology: Communist, conservative, preconciliar Catholic, etc.

Each time we use one of these key words, either externally or internally, we remove the *person* to a distance. His personal history is replaced by his usefulness, and the open wound continues to fester at the edge of the road.

Yet how easy it is to have the very opposite experience! With the very first sign of being in love, the label disappears and we see a real person before us—a person with a family, a history, and personal successes or failures.

So it is easy enough to see what we were talking about above. It is easy to see that every approach to a person in terms of nature relativizes him or her, reducing and integrating the person into a system of functions geared to my own advantage. The historical approach, by contrast, says no to this tempting tendency. It takes us out of the center and directs our attention to that other center which each and every person is. In short, it leads us to the absolutely personal.

Thus it does not take too much imagination to realize that the infinite, inaccessible God-as-nature, the creator of an order prior or indifferent to the existence of each individual, is at the same time the projection and justification of our desire and our effort to rigidly structure other people within our societal life. The God of Modalism, the rationalist reduction of God, serves as the backdrop for every unnecessary subjugation of human liberty—what Marcuse happily calls "surplus repression," to distinguish it from the impersonal foundation of order that is a precondition for all liberty and that must be ensured by every human group.

Love has an obligation to be effective. But every attempt to oversimplify things is accompanied by a tendency to inertia, by a tendency to spare a group, a social class, or even society as a whole from the work of according proper value to the minority and the irreducibly personal element. So we must say no to this deviation and set limits on reason. It is an essential part of "doing the truth" vis-à-vis both God and human beings. Only a "negative" theology and a "negative" ethics, which say no to this process of rationalization, will allow us to make room for relationships based on liberty. Only they will enable us to dráw nearer to the absolute that summons us in every encounter.

Nicholas Berdyaev perceived this intimate relationship and described it as follows:

> Cataphatic theology [i.e., positive, rational theology] knows only a God who has been transformed into an object. Apophatic or mystical theology [i.e., negative, historical theology] on the other hand, gets above and beyond this objectification of God. It strips from the notion of God any and all anthropomorphic deformations. It conceives the relations between man and God without tying them to such categories as state, power, judgment, and punishment.[27]

The most suggestive element in this passage is its transformation of the notion of "anthropomorphism." The fear of attributing "too human" elements to God has unfortunately led theology (even the modern theology of the death of God) to "purify" the notion of God by stripping all historical realism from it. Far from avoiding anthropomorphism, this procedure fell right into it—as Berdyaev brings out. Because this "rational" version simply transposed to the divine realm the alienated relationships we have with persons through our use of impersonal, utilitarian categories for societal, political, economic, and juridical life.

Berdyaev is right: "Idolatry is possible, even with respect to God. The social relationships based on domination, which do exist between human beings, have served as the model for [theologically] establishing the relationship between man and God."[28] And in turn, God "conceived as an object . . . has been turned into a fountainhead of enslavement."[29]

Hence the work of modifying our notion of God is parallel and complementary to that which we should undertake in understanding persons: "It is not enough to affirm the truth of apophatic theology. We must likewise affirm the truth of apophatic sociology."[30]

To put it in other words: the notion of God will be purified of its most throughgoing anthropomorphisms and blatant idolatries only in a society where human beings encounter other human beings endowed with history, personality and, if we might use this term, a tinge of the absolute.

NOTES TO CHAPTER THREE

1. Knopf-Krüger, *Ausgewählte Märtyrerakten* (Tübingen), 1929, pp. 49-50.

2. It would have been a different story if the "eternal" relations existing between Father, Son, and Spirit had sprung directly from Scripture itself, thus allowing us to distinguish them from each other independently of their relationship to our history and our salvation. But such is not the case, however obvious classical theology may take these eternal relations to be.

A typical example of the latter approach is the heading of a section on Paul's Trinitarian formulas in a theology manual. Following the usual procedure, it says that these formulas designate the divine persons "according to the order of their eternal relations or the order of their missions." ("Mission" here refers to the tasks carried out by each divine person in the history of salvation.) Now the fact is that in the whole section there is not one Pauline formula that does not refer to the Trinitarian *missions:* i.e., to the divine persons in relationship to our history rather than in terms of their eternal life. The first part of the alternative ("the order of their eternal relations") is a reflex action. The only sound statement comes at the end of the section. There it notes that in the cited passages the divine names "are connected with the *oikonomia* [historical plan] of our salvation."

Displaying much greater precision and theological sense, Paul Lehmann writes: "If the successors of Athanasius had been as clear about the range and intricacy of this panorama of human history as the work of the Spirit as Athanasius was about its focus and foundation, the trinitarian substance of Christian faith could have been spared much metaphysical and liturgical sterility. It is under-

standable that in the environment of classicism, theology should have been dis-
proportionately engaged by an ontological rather than an economic interpretation of the Trinity . . . What God is in himself can only be hinted at from
his self-disclosure in his activity" (*Ethics in a Christian Context*, New York: Harper
& Row, 1963, pp. 107–08).

3. *Adversus Praxeam*, 1.

4. It is worth pointing out that when he wanted to describe the divine
unity through the three names, he said that Father, Son, and Holy spirit constitute
one and the same substance (*homo-ousios*). But he meant it in the twofold sense
mentioned in the previous chapter: one single substance or thing, *and* one single
substance or individual or person. So when the local Council of Antioch condemned Paul of Samosata, it also condemned the term *homo-ousios*, which would
later be solemnly approved at the Council of Nicea. But as we indicate, Modalism
had been overcome by then; so there was no longer any possibility of confusing
the divine persons, even though no such term as "person" or *hypostasis* existed
as yet.

5. Paul Van Buren (*The Secular Meaning of the Gospel*, New York: Macmillan,
1963) offers these remarks:

> The patristic conception of man was modeled on the patristic picture of
> the process of nature. Suffering involved change, and to change was to
> decay (p. 40).

> The patristic idea of God colored the whole development of classical
> Christology and has posed a problem for theology ever since. The Fathers
> insisted at all costs on the impassibility of God and his Word, for change
> was the mark of the imperfect, the sign of corruption and decay (p. 42).

> The Johannine assertion (John 14:9) that he who had seen Jesus had seen
> the Father, formulates a major New Testament theme which was also crucial
> for the Fathers: Jesus as the full and adequate revelation of God . . . Although
> the Fathers missed something of the dynamic historical note of this theme
> and worked with categories which seem too static or metaphysical, they took
> seriously this central affirmation of the New Testament (p. 43).

This would be an overstatement if it were not for the reserved tone of the
last statement. The Fathers did manage to juxtapose the only existing philosophical language of their day with fidelity to the truths and even the mode of expression of the Old and New Testaments.

6. If we simply take into account the nature of the creator and the nature
of the creature, the nature of the Infinite Being and that of a limited being,
then we must draw the same conclusion that Lateran IV did: "We cannot affirm
any degree of similarity between Creator and creature without having to affirm
an even greater degree of dissimilarity" (Denz. 432). But this poses a serious
problem of language. When we attribute to God any quality we derive from
our own experience, the dissimilarity-greater-than-the-similarity would logically
lead us to use a "no" or a "not" to describe it. We would not even be able
to speak of God if it were not for the fact that God is more than a "creative
nature" and an "infinite being." Hence one would be just as mistaken to draw
the following conclusion on the basis of Lateran IV's statement: "God is not
good, not better, not best. It is as wrong for men to call God 'good' as to call

white 'black.' " This error, attributed to Meister Eckhart, was condemned by John XXII (Denz. 528; see also Denz. 555).

7. Paul L. Lehmann, *Ethics in a Christian Context*, (New York: Harper & Row, 1963), p. 108.

8. De Lubac, *Por los caminos de Dios*, p. 284 (see note 4 of the Introduction to this volume) cites this observation of Descoqs in his *Praelectiones theologiae naturalis:* "It seems to me that all the proofs are to be reduced to one, and involve the process of efficient causality as the only apodictic one on the level of scientific discourse."

Two observations should perhaps be made about this "apodictic" proof. 1. There is no certainty that it will not be open to countless objections and counter-arguments when it leaves the empirical plane. Resisting it or not is much more a matter of "proportion" or balance. 2. A related matter is the fact that there is a prior problem in connection with this proportion, as Nicolas Berdyaev points out. It is the problem of justifying God. The proofs will appear more valid than the objections only if the notion of God is the notion of Something or Someone who is desired greatly.

9. Thomas Aquinas is well aware of this problem when he joins Aristotle in affirming that God is the unmoved mover, and asks whether God has volition—in particular, the possibility of willing something that is not himself or something he does not already possess (see, for example, S.T., I. q. XIX, art. 1 and 2; and q. V, art. 4). His solution typically bears witness to the (not always logical) "infiltration" of elements from Christian revelation—or, from the Christian mentality, if you prefer—into Greek philosophy. The Christian mentality takes the latter as its handmaid, but does not always maintain control over it.

From Pseudo-Dionysius Thomas takes the idea that while it is certain that a will either seeks the good it does not possess or rests in the good it does possess, one can just as well say that it does not rest in the good it possesses because "the good is diffusive of itself." In other words, the will that possesses this good feels a need or a desire to spread it around. That is how we are to explain creation, according to Saint Thomas (q. XIX, art. 2, resp.).

Strict logic might go much further in its subsequent deductions. It might say the good which is not communicated *still lacks something of value:* viz., that which can give finality to creation (which would seem to be incompatible with what was said above). In any case we must admit that even if "the good is diffusive of itself," it is so only to a certain point! The world created by God is not the totality of possible perfection (S.T., I, q. IV, art. 1 and 2). As Schmaus says: "Absolute optimism is a limitation on the divine creative free will, which is difficult to mesh with the teachings of Catholic dogma . . . When Leibniz affirms that divine goodness and wisdom require the creation of the best possible world by the creator, he is guided by the false idea that God must fulfill all the possibilities available to him in creating the world and give the best he can give" (*Teología Dogmática*, p. 95; on this book see note 28 at the end of the CLARIFICATIONS for Chapter 2 of this volume).

10. The age-old problem of why the "many" exist alongside the "one"—that is, the problem of the origin of what exists—has not found a rational solution. Outside of pantheism, of course, which suppresses the many. But pantheism is not very rational either, even though it makes the subsequent task of reason easier. The finality of creation for the Creator has spawned many theological efforts, which end up by concealing the difficulty under seemingly correct

phrases that really offer the same contradiction to the analytic mind. (Consider, for example, the whole theme of "external glory.")

As we shall see from all that follows, the honest position of people like Schmaus is far better:

> Because of his absolute independence, perfection, and felicity, God could not have created the world in order to augment and enrich his ontological, noetic, and moral perfection through his creative activity. As we have just seen, he is not incited or impelled to create—neither by an external good distinct from himself nor by some internal deficiency. The motivation for God's will to create lies in God himself, and it has *neither presuppositions nor causes.* God creates because he chooses to create. We could say: *He chooses to because he chooses to.* Freely and voluntarily he is of the mind to flesh out his goodness and perfection in the external sector [sic], in a finite way, permitting beings distinct from himself to participate in them (*op. cit.* . p. 100).

11. *Cf.* S.T., I, q. XIII, art. 7 c; q. XXVIII, art. 1 and 2; etc.

12. In line with what we have been saying, we could take the following statement by John Damascene about God's nature and apply it to the authentic life of God that is defined by his freely proffered love: "Everything we say about God in positive terms spells out, not his nature, but what *surrounds* his nature" (PG 94, 800).

13. These two languages are juxtaposed to such an extent that the theology commonly taught in seminaries and faculties of theology studies *separately* the tract *De Deo Uno* and the tract *De Deo Trino*! The same criticism can also be levelled against such innovative works as the *Initiation Théologique,* which was put together by a group of eminent theologians and published in 1952. It not only divided the two tracts but also entrusted them to different collaborators. This dissociation allowed each mode of language to be carried to its ultimate possibilities without a hitch. It was left to the reader or seminarian to synthesize them. But what usually happened was that they were put into different mental pigeonholes, to be used on equally different occasions. One could not preach a sermon on the "Seven Last Words" with the vocabulary of *De Deo Uno* no more than one could take part in a philosophical discussion with the language of *De Deo Trino.*

14. So, for example, it may be possible to say that God remained immutable in his Incarnation, because his human nature remains distinct from his divine nature, and it was the former that suffered, died, and went through a history. But if we choose to go further and ask whether this history, suffering, and death of a human nature affected God, the reply is difficult. If we answer "yes," that response does not seem to be compatible with God's immutability. If we answer "no," not only do we make little of the statement "God became man and dwelt amongst us," we are also condemned by the Third Ecumenical Council (Ephesus, 432) which was explicitly concerned with this radical question of language: "If anyone distributes . . . the words contained in the apostolic or evangelical writings . . . accommodating some to the human being apart from the Word of God, and others—as worthy of God—only to the Word of God the Father, let him be anathema" (Denz. 116). So this "communication of languages" (as the theologians call it) is a Catholic dogma.

15. See Section IV further on in this chapter.

16. One must not forget that the primitive religions are nature religions. Something of that persists in the religion of Israel. And we have had occasion to point out that many attitudes of those who bear the name of Christian in our countries do really belong to pre-Christian stages of religion. See J. L. Segundo and J. P. Sanchis, *As Etapas Pré-cristãs da descoberta de Deus: Una chave para a análise do cristianismo* (latinoamericana). (Petrópolis: Vozes, 1968).

17. Here we must take note of the major work of Karl Barth and its decisive impact in our day. If what we say in this volume is true, a "natural theology" that judges and even goes so far as to "abridge" the theology of faith is not Christian. This is all the more true because, as we have already seen and will see again, "natural theology" and man's sinfulness cannot be separated as if one belongs to the speculative order while the other belongs to the moral order. But Barth, especially in his criticism of Bultmann, does not seem to recognize the fact that God speaks and sends out a summons to us from within our structures of language, thought, and existence.

18. Those who have read Volume II in this series (*Grace and the Human Condition*) will be familiar with this passage from Sartre's play. They will also be familiar with the more general theme of liberty as an unjustified risk if it is a test and not a creation. See Volume II, Chapter I, CLARIFICATIONS IV and V.

19. It is said that the Curé d'Ars found it impossible to commiserate with mothers whose children died at an early age, feeling that the child's time of struggle had been reduced and it was able to enjoy eternal bliss that much earlier (François Trochu, *Vida del Cura de Ars,* Spanish trans. (Padre Las Casas: San Francisco), II, 158; citation not found by this translator in the English translation, *Life of the Curé d'Ars* (Westminster, Md.: Newman, 1950).

One viewpoint calls up the image of another, its opposite in this case. We get a different picture from an unbeliever:

> The existence of a creation without God, without final aim, seems to me to be less absurd than the presence of a God who, existing with all his perfection, creates an imperfect human being to make him run the risk of punishment in hell . . . Because if I understand what my parish priest and you say, the situation is this: This God, whom Paul preached twenty centuries ago . . . seems to have created human beings to drop them into the most hazardous world a human brain could contrive. His world is a dark labyrinth studded with forbidden temptations at every turn. And unless one manages to slip through a trapdoor into eternal bliss, one falls through another trapdoor into an eternity of sufferings . . . (Armand Salacrou, *Théâtre,* 4th ed., Paris: Gallimard, 1954, VI, 209–211)

Assuming the veracity of the testimony, however, we will find that the Curé of Ars spoke a very different laguage on another occasion (see CLARIFICATION IV in this chapter).

20. *Christianisme et évolution,* unpublished, 1945; cited by Emile Rideau, *The Thought of Teilhard de Chardin,* Eng. trans. (New York: Harper & Row, 1967; p. 508.

21. *Contingence de l'univers et goût humain de survivre,* unpublished, 1953; cited by Rideau, *ibid.,* pp. 508–509.

22. We feel that the examples provided will bring many others to the mind of the reader, relating to different levels of religious expression and indicating

that this notion of God and its corresponding image of man has invaded many different areas of life: education, politics, spirituality, etc.

23. Marie-Emile Boismard offers one example of this exegesis in his article, "Dans le sein de Pére," *Revue Biblique* (1952), pp. 23–39. There he presents this basic schema for reading and interpreting John's prologue. 1. In his descent *the Word is with the Father (John* 1:1–2); in his ascent the Word introduces us to the Father (v. 18). 2. In his descent the Word presides over creation (v. 3); in his ascent the "grace and truth" he gives us in place of the law constitute the new creation (v. 17). 3. In his descent the Word gives life and light to everything existing in the world (vv. 4–5); in his ascent it is said that we all have received from his divine treasury (v. 16). 4. John the Baptist bears witness to him, both to his descent (vv. 6–8) and to his ascent (v. 15). 5. In his descent the Word slowly draws nearer to the world (vv. 9–11); in his ascent he reveals to his intimates his personal glory as the only Son of the Father (v. 14 b). 6. Finally it is the Incarnation that makes God a son of man and men sons of God (vv. 13–14).

24. In *Honest to God* (Philadelphia: Westminster 1963), pp. 76–77, Robinson writes:

> Jesus is 'the man for others', the one in whom Love has completely taken over, the one who is utterly open to, and united with, the Ground of his being. And this 'life for others, through participation in the Being of God', *is* Transcendence. For, at this point, of 'love to the uttermost,' we encounter *God*, the ultimate 'depth' of our being, the unconditional in the unconditioned. This is what the New Testament means by saying that 'God was in Christ' and 'what God was the Word was.' Because Christ was utterly and completely 'the man for others,' because he *was* love, he was 'one with the Father,' because 'God is love.' But for this very reason he was most entirely man, the son of man, the servant of the Lord. He was indeed 'one of us.'

25. We hope it is clear to the reader that here as elsewhere the activity of the Spirit does not consist in articulating the whole content of revelation "all at once," but rather in fashioning a continuing dialogue between it and the new problems posed by history. In that process question and response, search and revelation, render "mutual service" to each other.

Hence we feel that the following assertion by Schillebeeckx, dealing with the statements of the magisterium on social questions, oversimplifies far too much: "We are concerned here with the theological value of the 'historical decisions' contained in such documents, in other words, of the value of non-doctrinal, somewhat 'hypothetical' pronouncements by the Church's highest authority, Pope, or Council. The words 'somewhat hypothetical' refer to the fact that such texts also depend on nontheological information and speak of a contingent secular reality" ("The Magisterium and the World of Politics," *Concilium*, New York: Paulist Press, 1968, 36:36–37).

We would rather say that the activity of the Spirit, even though it may not disclose aspects of revelation except when they serve for "counsel" and "judgment"—two essential functions of the Paraclete according to John 16:7–8 —does keep alive in the Church the conditions which permit this suggestiveness to find an echo. This matter is discussed in CLARIFICATION III of this chapter.

26. "Our pastoral solicitude nevertheless prompts us to probe into the mind of the modern atheist, in an effort to understand the reasons for his mental turmoil and his denial of God . . . They sometimes spring from the demand for a more profound and purer presentation of religious truth . . . We see these men serving a demanding and often a noble cause . . . impatient with the *mediocrity and self-seeking that infect so much of modern society*" (Paul VI, encyclical *Ecclesiam suam*, n. 10; our italics).

27. *Dialectique existentielle du divin et de l'human* (Paris: Janin, 1947), p. 63.

28. *De l'esclavage et de la liberté de l'homme* (Paris: Aubier, 1946), p. 91

29. *Ibid.*

30. *Ibid.*, p. 18

CLARIFICATIONS

I. GOD DOES NOT SPEAK? OR MAN DOES NOT THINK?

If God is not the one we are to question about the "how" of natural processes, then his reality must be framed in terms of the "wherefore" or "what for?" of things. As we have just seen, this is the fountainhead of meaningfulness, critical evaluation, and value. But we have also seen that if there is a question before which the God of reason stands mute and "dead," it is the whole question of the "wherefore" of the creature and its liberty.

So let us indulge in a little suspicion. If we maintain such a God, is it not an indirect way for existing society to avoid certain critical questions about its meaningfulness and value? And if obvious questions are avoided, what is the reason for this?

In the main sections of the preceding chapters we have already dealt indirectly with the so-called "death-of-God theology"; and we have dealt with it more directly in some of the CLARIFICATIONS. The name itself is rather misleading and sensationalist, for in reality none of those who propound it envision the death or disappearance of God from the human dilemma and its problems. They are theologians, after all. And depending on their bent, they talk about the death of a specific kind of God who is associated with some qualifying word: e.g., the mythical God, the supernatural God, the conventional God, the God described in terms that are out of date linguistically.

In all of these cases, they are trying to replace that God with a God who is undoubtedly more authentic. But the result of the replacement, admitted and proclaimed quite openly, is that it is impossible for *modern man* to continue to accept and relate to the God that is so understood.

1. This character, the "modern man," appears countless times in the writings of those who pursue this general line of thought. To begin with, we can cite Bultmann: "An action of God is not visible to the objective viewpoint, and it cannot be established as intramundane happenings are."[1] To put the conclusion in more popular terms: "We cannot use electric lights and the radio, call upon medicines and hospitals in

time of illness, and at the same time believe in the spiritual and miraculous world of the New Testament."[2] Bonhöffer has this to say:

> Man has learned to cope with all questions of importance without recourse to God as a working hypothesis . . .Efforts are made to prove to a world thus come of age that it cannot live without the tutelage of "God." Even though there has been surrender on all secular problems, there still remain the so-called ultimate questions—death, guilt—on which only "God" can furnish an answer, and which are the reason why God and the church and the pastor are needed. Thus we live, to some extent, by these ultimate questions of humanity. But what if one day they no longer exist as such, if they too can be answered without "God"?[3]

Bonhöffer attributes this "coming of age" in particular to Darwinism[4] and the overall technological organization of nature.[5]

Ogden carries the logic of Bultmann even further than the latter himself did. He proposes the basic principle that demythologization, imposed of necessity by the situation of modern man, must be accepted as an unconditional exigency.[6] And Robinson has this to day:

> The signs are that we are reaching the point at which the whole conception of a God 'out there', which has served us so well since the collapse of the three-decker universe, is itself becoming more of a hindrance than a help . . . The final psychological, if not logical, blow delivered by modern science and technology to the idea that there might *literally* be a God 'out there' has *coincided* with an awareness that the *mental* picture of such a God may be more of a stumbling-block than an aid to belief in the Gospel.[7]

Cox and Van Buren draw an even better portrait of this "modern man" who stands up against the gospel message about God, proud of his own way of thinking and living. Says Cox:

> We should not be dismayed by the fact that fewer and fewer people are pressing what we have normally called "religious" questions. The fact tht urban-secular man is incurably and irreversibly pragmatic, that he is less and less concerned with religious questions, is in no sense a disaster. It means that he is shedding the lifeless cuticles of the mythical and ontological periods and stepping into the functional age. He is leaving behind the styles of the tribe and the town and is becoming a technopolitan man.[8]

> Tillich speaks to those who still feel the need to ask "religious" questions even when we ask them in nontraditional ways. These are questions he believes to be inherent in the very structure of human existence. The difficulty, however, is that they are obviously *not* questions which occur to everyone, or indeed to the vast majority of people. They especially do not occur to the newly emergent urban-secular man . . . We begin by accepting pragmatic man as he is, and this means we must part company with Tillich.[9]

Finally, we can cite these remarks of Van Buren:

> The first of these assertions is another way of making Bultmann's point that myth is no longer tenable; the idea of the empirical intervention of a supernatural "God" in the world of man has been ruled out by the influence

of modern science on our thinking. In making such statements, we reveal our own commitment to modern science, and we would only add that modern thought tends to grant the validity of the findings of the natural sciences. For those holding these commitments . . . Linguistic analysis challenges the qualified theism of Bultmann and Ogden as much as that of more conservative theologians . . .

This clarification [i.e., by linguistic analyses] has been accomplished by a frankly empirical method which reflects the thinking of an industrialized, scientific age.[10]

Van Buren adds another characteristic to the one cited already, and it too still maintains its importance: "We do not reject the insights which existentialism has contributed, but we cannot forget that our English-speaking culture has an empirical tradition and that the world today is increasingly being formed by technology and the whole industrial process."[11]

And so we can sum up all this briefly. This "modern man," who asserts his very refusal to take a stand on the problem of God, is a very determined man. He is the man of the great urban centers in the Anglo-Saxon industrial empire; an urbane, pragmatic man molded by scientific and technological thought and bound up with the notions of progress and affluence. And as we have seen,[12] what he cannot accept is a transcendence pictured as intervening within the boundaries of this world that he knows, uses, manipulates, and dominates.

In other words, he is not man as such, the univocal and necessary representative of the human species, but the product of a specific and particular history. And his history is as least as ambiguous as the history of belief in God.[13]

2. In his instructive book, *Religion and the Modern Mind*, W. T. Stace suggests that this history *begins* in the seventeenth century with the scientific discoveries of Copernicus, Kepler, Newton, and others.

Various authors have noted the fact that the shift from the cosmic system of Ptolemy to that of Copernicus was not brought about by a demonstration of the former's *erroneousness*. The simple fact is that the calculations required to explain the same mechanisms were much shorter in the second system. In the scientific realm, efficiency and truth begin to be interchangeable, with surprising results.

Newton was not yet able to explain the planetary system as a perfect mechanism. Being a believer, he had recourse to divine interventions to explain and correct the irregularities left by his calculations. According to Stace, it is the last time that a great scientist tried to offer a supernatural intervention as the cause of some observed phenomenon.[14]

When Laplace was able to explain these supposed irregularities and thus the whole planetary mechanism, he could say that he no longer needed the hypothesis of God. An era had come to an end. But in fact this statement leaves much to be desired from a strictly logical point of view. Considering it just from the viewpoint of efficient causality alone, it still leaves unanswered the question of the origin of this "machine." In any case it is clear that from the time of Newton on the natural world comes to look more and more like a giant machine to the awe-struck eyes of Western man. Its interior mechanism becomes more and more comprehensible, and its resources become more and more manageable. Within this general context the problem of more remote origins, which do not alter current explanation or exploitability, can be regarded as nonexistent for all practical purposes.[15]

Another point remains obscure in the statement of Laplace. According to him, the hypothesis of God is no longer necessary once the machine is functioning. The very fact that he draws this conclusion is significant. For if we assume that the world and everything in it is a machine, then everything that occurs in it can be explained in mechanistic terms and a *teleological* explanation is ruled out or rendered superfluous.

Here we have a process that pervades the further development of occidental civilization. With the growing efficacy of a more or less mechanistic explanation and its accompanying manipulation, the question of finality and the wherefore of things is banished from the scene. Insofar as God does not interfere with the mechanism, there is no need to know why he made things (if he did make them, which is now a question of little interest). Teleology is excluded from science in the seventeenth century, and mechanical causality alone is scientific causality. Hence, as Stace points out, teleological explanations cease to have any value for the modern mentality and are regarded as absurd.[17]

The fact is that this proclivity is even more logical than Stace seems to think. The industrial, technological, and capitalist world of the West made this "leap" from efficacy to truth, not so much because it "seemed" logical, but largely because it served its interests wittingly or unwittingly.

It is not coincidental that science has dropped concern for the wherefore of things, that Western man in the developed countries has become pragmatic, and that he cannot conceive any breakthrough of the transcendent into the mechanisms that he controls. We have already seen how readily and inadvertently he has moved from denying divine interventions in the order of natural phenomena to denying any and all divine intervention in the world—even if such intervention might be intended to help man ponder the why and the wherefore of what he is doing, even if it be intended as a *judgment* rather than a miracle.

3. We have summarily examined how the history of this "modern man" began. We have seen how he began to deny any and every intraworldly representation of transcendence that might pass judgment on his world. Now let us examine this history from the other end, looking at where it has arrived now. Herbert Marcuse certainly offers an accurate description of this world that is no longer concerned about the why and wherefore of things: "Today we can turn the world into a hell, and we are well on the way to doing just that as you all know."[18]

There is no doubt that at a certain point in history nature began to yield to man's technological know-how in an increasingly mechanical and docile way. But as Teilhard de Chardin points out, the world of technology is a new synthesis of the same energy available in humanity. Every synthesis has its cost; and the cost of the man-machine synthesis is paid by another human being who is used, dominated, and alienated. The history of man's *dominion* over nature is also the history of the *domination* of some human beings over other human beings. And the aim of this process was to have the latter group assume the cost of the "modern world" while the former group would enjoy the results.

For some time, as Marcuse points out, scarcity was able to serve to some extent as the pretext for this domination. In the end someone had to guide the whole process and consume its best results. Why should it not be those who were most adept!

As pragmatism and scientific efficiency become more and more successful, however, it is at least possible for scarcity to be overcome completely. In this context domination over human beings appears to be unnecessary,[19] and repression must then explicitly assume its planetary role: that of permitting *modernization* at the expense of *humanization*.

In terms of its etymology, the word "modernization" suggests an accelerated thrust toward new possibilities of humanization and the future. But in the present-day world such acceleration is possible only if the majority of people on this planet give up their sluggish pace in searching for solutions to age-old problems of man's basic needs: food, housing, basic education, marginal living, etc.

On the other hand modernization entails *factors, mechanisms, and costs* that run counter to the solution of the aforementioned problems. The factors that go to make up a modern civilization are essentially technological factors bound up with heavy industrialization. Thus modernization comes down to the centralization of industrial capabilities, so that the world is divided up generally into "modern" countries and countries that produce raw materials, into countries endowed with creative technology and countries with merely applied technology.

With respect to mechanisms, the basic mechanism of modernization is to concentrate economic and technological processes within an overall complex that is governed by the same rules. Through their interaction they continually produce new processes and new solutions, and this in turn opens up ever new possibilities.

Finally, the cost of modernization necessarily concentrates it. People celebrated man's first walk on the moon with legitimate pride. They found it odd and offensive that many other people seemed to be less enthusiastic about this event, contemplating instead how many human lives could have been spared and enriched with the costs of that single trip to the moon. Are the former group of admirers insensitive louts? No, certainly not, at least in the main. For it is the accepted logic of modernization that these costs must be paid, and that they prove to be useful in the realm of modernization itself.

Imbedded in the term "modernization," therefore, is the tendency for it to be the modernization of a restricted group of people within the human race. This group will say that the results are outstanding and should be imitated. But it will not stop to think that the very elements of modernization have been drawn off from the possibilities of humanization. If we are to make every human being a subject of his own destiny rather than its object, this presupposes that we are going to reduce the speed with which some few nations are experiencing the ultimate possibilities of the universe. To speed up the pace is to lose sight of the human race.

Now is it not just a bit naive to expect that the message of God might be spoken to "pragmatic man as he is," when his very pragmatism protects him from the questions that would shatter his tranquillity and ask him about the wherefore of it all?

Experience also proves that a mere shift from individual ownership of the means of production to state ownership of them (i.e., a shift from capitalism to socialism) does not invalidate this dilemma. What does one do after the revolution in a world where power continues to be associated with industrial modernization and its underlying mentality?[20] An overly simplistic Marxism, which is often strikingly akin to the "new man" described by Cox and others, is again faced with problems that Marxist "science" thought it had resolved. As Marcuse poses it: "If I might offer a provocative formulation of this speculative idea, I would say that we have to at least consider the notion of a pathway to socialism that runs *from science to utopia* and not, as Engels believed, from utopia to science."[21]

But what is "utopia" except the breakthrough of some transcendence, depicted in terms of this world, into the midst of our societal pragmatism? The theology of the death of God has been too uncritical in immersing itself in the overall societal context of the planet. It has not grasped the fact that "the function of science and of religion has changed—as has their interrelation . . . Where religion still preserves the uncompromised aspirations for peace and happiness, its 'illusions' still have a higher truth than science which works for their elimination."[22]

So it is clear that religion must fight against its own tendency toward idolatry. Like the Old Testament prophets, we feel that this fight is far more critical and decisive in the process of liberating people from being considered as objects than the whole problem of knowing which language about the divine can be accepted by human beings to whom domination and repression do not provide an inescapable "wherefore."

II. A GOD OPPOSED TO SOCIETAL COHESIVENESS?

1. The mental set of those who view persons under some category or label is in large measure the product of society. This has been verified by many experiments in the field of social psychology on the whole

matter of racism, for example. It has dealt extensively with such phenomena as Nazism in Germany and segregation in the United States.

Earlier hypotheses assumed that "race" resided in the biosomatic constitution of man and investigated the coincidence of genotypes. Nazism said that the "Aryan" race was more perfect and superior. It measured such features as height, form, cranial cavity, facial type, and blood type—any feature by which one might distinguish races in somatic terms. Then all these variables were correlated to intellignece quotients. No scientific result could verify these hypotheses. Hence the concept of "race" does not derive from any somatic or psychosomatic reality; it derives from a psychosocial reality.

Typical of this whole process is the study made of the first stirrings of a segregationist attitude in young children living in the United States. In its early years the child does not notice the skin color or complexion of its playmates. When questioned about the color of its playmates, the child is unable to give any precise answer. It is only when its parents begin to forbid it to play with Negro children, or issue some similar prohibition, that the child begins to notice the difference. Gradually it becomes used to making this differentiation, considers it normal, and develops a stereotype. This develops to the point where school children, looking at photographs of huge mansions and gardens, will say that they see a Negro gardener at work in them. Thus differentiation in terms of skin color comes to constitute a social differentiation as well.

Gradually the child enters a world where human beings are considered in terms of the group to which they belong. They are classified in terms of "status" (employer, employee, manual laborer), "function" (doctor, butcher), nationality or "race" (foreigner, half-breed). With this summary classification of individuals, which reflects the attitudes of adults, the child goes about the work of constructing his own evaluations and thereby integrating his personal experiences into a formal framework.

Stereotype, then, is equivalent to *prejudice:* that is, to a value judgment made before knowing a concrete person and his or her relationship to this value. Some of these prejudices are called "natural" because they well up more spontaneously. Such would be one's feeling about a dirty, ill-kempt man in a society that sets value on cleanliness and comeliness. Other prejudices are learned, determining people's attitudes toward some group that is considered perverse: e.g., Jews, dwarfs, the Mafia, etc.

These prejudices, which are oversimplifications of personality types, are means used to achieve practical ends: e.g., defense, aggressivity, etc. To cite a typical case: Negroes were once lynched in some parts of the United States because the crop had turned out poor. The black man was made culpable for everything that went wrong. He became the scapegoat around which was polarized all the diffuse aggression resulting from the economic misfortunes of the region. The Jews suffered a similar fate in Nazi Germany.

The social function of this collective attitude is wide-ranging. It gives

consistency to the particular group, makes it easy to take a stand vis-à-vis
other groups, justifies the remoteness of relations between individuals
in different categories, and facilitates oversimplified evaluations of persons and the adoption of practical lines of conduct toward them. The
person remains hidden behind the label; so does his complexity, which
would render domination more difficult.[23]

This self-justification of aggressiveness, value-judgments, and dubi-
ous lines of conduct also leads people to set a high value on memberhsip
in the group to which they belong. So we get nationalistic campaigns
that exalt patriotism over some real or imaginary enemy. We get waves
of anti-intellectualism where the intellectual is criticized for his real or
potential betrayal of the nation.[24] These and similar processes of self-
justification seek to bring about greater internal cohesion in the group
and, at the same time, to channel its aggressiveness toward some outer
target. Through the press and the other communications media an
attempt is made to impose attitudes and behavior models. These attitudes
and behavior models are meant to be the group's reaction to certain
concrete facts that have been interpreted in a specific way. Thus attitudes
are canalized in a certain direction, their intensity is heightened, and
they are given a distinctive and easily recognizable coloration.

Now society does need stereotypes. They play an indispensable role
in cementing the fabric of a society. It would be childish to expect the
same result from a considered, personal adhesion that is freely chosen.
The *power* of social stereotypes is so strong that we can count on it
alone for the salvation of human community in certain specific cases
and alternatives.

The propaganda of the Nazis intensified the national stereotypes.
It justified aggression as the way to defend them, and German society
integrated this outlook into its own attitudes. It accepted and went along
with bellicose actions and unjust repressive measures. During the war,
the "Allies" made stereotypes out of "the defense of liberty,"
"democracy," and "civilization," and symbolized their opposition to the
"Nazi monstrosity." If between 34 and 38 million people in Europe
and 20 million in Asia gave their lives for these "stereotypes," we can
begin to realize the tremendous power they wield as forces for cohesion
and adhesion. And we can see how impossible it is to do without them
when we are trying to get people to pay the human cost of any great
historical synthesis.

It is important for us to realize that these costs do not apply solely
to the work of maintaining an existing order or synthesis. They also
apply to the creation of a new and superior order or synthesis. In other
words, the force required to produce a revolution cannnot be whipped
together in society as a whole without new stereotypes.

Now in both cases,[25] one of the most effective ways to fabricate
the stereotypes that are considered essential for maintaining or changing
the social order is to attribute the stereotype to a valuation given by

God himself, to a valuation given by the one who makes the ultimate and absolute decision about all values. Here we have a conception of God in conformity with the aspirations of the national group, and we find this conception in certain stages of biblical history too. He is seen as a God who fiercely defends the group, who is cruel to the "enemies" that must be destroyed. This conception of God fortifies the group's aggressive tendencies, channels it outward, and inhibits internal aggressiveness by dividing it up between different groups and interests. He can even be seen as a God who is "cruel" for the sake of goodness and justice![26] God thus fulfills a social function on the basis of a psychological projection of the group's aspirations and needs.

2. In the realm of social psychology there is no doubt that it is hard to find a foothold for a universal God who is conceived differently. What if we conceive God as being universal, not because he is the keystone of a mechanism in which one or more groups dominate other groups, but because he turns each individual human being and each human community into an absolute and thus poses a radical obstacle to any and all use of people as mere tools? What if God calls, loves, and values all human beings as equals? What if he demands that we know them as they really are, rather than through the glasses of our own prejudices? Such a God cannot fill the social role of justifying the stereotypes that are the basis for social cohesion on the mass level. Such a God will not give cohesion to the group, channeling its aggression outward toward real or imagined enemies. Such a God will not offer an easy solution to the problem of collective security.

A God who is love will instead call for the overcoming of our insecurity. He will launch the group into the risky venture of opening up calmly to "others" without losing its own cohesion. If God is indeed love, then none of the social functions analyzed above can correspond to him; none of the social functions based on stereotypes, prejudices, and group security can be related to him. And this even applies to the function of negative cohesion (i.e., group fear and collective defense) and to the justification of spontaneous aggressive reactions to an opposing group.

This leads us to a pastoral conclusion of the utmost importance: it is "popular religion" that fulfills the social functions we have just discussed. And these functions take on visceral force when truly profound and rapid cultural changes (e.g., urbanization) leave people without the security of an ancestral tradition.

The function of Christianity is essentially and dialectically opposed to that one. It presupposes that this psychosocial insecurity has been overcome in large measure. Some people cherish the illusion that popular religion can be progressively transformed and improved until it is turned into an adult Christianity.[27] But it is an illusion, incomprehensible to the sociologist. Only liberation from oppression, insecurity, and passivity toward the phenomena of societal life can pave the way for a mature Christianity. This conclusion of the Medellín Conference is not merely a theological and pastoral *desideratum;* it is a condition *sine qua non* for Christianity to exist.

3. Let us say, then, that the Christian ecclesial community cannot lend itself to stereotyped representations of God or of itself. If this is the case, what will its social function be in times of peace? What will its social function be in times of conflict?

The need to ask this question is obvious. If what we have said so far is true, then there is no Christian and "religious" line running from the rites and formulas that produce and fix stereotypes to the Christian community that is guided by a revelation which liberates man from these very same stereotypes. And since the latter constitute a necessary function of any and all social cohesion to a greater or lesser degree, the Christian community cannot represent an absolute but simply a function that is only comprehensible within the framework of, and in relation to, that totality. And it could well turn out that the social price that must be paid for a God who destroys stereotypes is not recompensed with a new society. The old may simply fall apart, or the transforming, revolutionary forces may disintegrate.[28]

Now in the "normal" situation, in the case of a society enjoying internal equilibrium and moderate prosperity, the social function of the believing community will be rooted in the breaking up of the stereotypes that still play their role of exerting domination over the defenceless, the alienated, and the exploited. This critical function should give rise to plans and efforts for a society in which integration is not achieved by impersonal equality but rather by the singular complexity and complementarity of the creativity inherent in each person and group.

In moments of conflict, the situation is quite different. When the cohesion of the overall society is threatened, two groups appeal to the Church for support. If it is a society which as yet is not reacting against the common values, it can only remain united without changing radically if it re-evaluates the prevailing stereotypes. In such a case we often find some people, who evince indifference or even hostility to the Church, calling for her intervention to "resacralize" the threatened values and to "anathematize" the criticism or violence exercised against them in the name of other values.

A second group, on the other hand, makes another demand. Since the Church has *in fact* carried out the role of reinforcing and sacralizing values in the past, this group asks the Church to exert its "sacral" power in favor of opposition to the existing order, to act in the name of the transforming values that should take first place *today*. In other words, this group asks the Church to create the stereotypes of the revolution or, at the very least, to lend them her sacral overtones and power.

Our feeling is that the first demand is totally unacceptable on principle, and that the second demand is based on a weighty sociological error.

The portion of society that seeks security in religious practices cannot be thrown into insecurity by changes dictated by religious authority. For the latter is authority insofar as it is grounded on the established order and converges with it. To repeat once more: if a person is disposed to follow the Church in criticizing the basic stereotypes of the existing order, he does so because he has overcome the insecurity which that process evokes.

The Church really has only two choices. Either it has to be a mass entity supporting the existing order. Or else it must attack this order through its own process of consciousness-raising that is based on the revelation of a God who destroys stereotypes.

Now, as we have suggested, this latter course or process, carried out with human beings who are not only Christians but also, and first of all, *human beings,* will necessarily produce two types of fidelity that must be recognized, accepted, and valued.

One type of fidelity will support the denunciation of the stereotypes of the existing order in the name of the Christian God. In new, opposing stereotypes it will find the power to carry through a revolution, which must of necessity be on a mass scale if it is to be effective. In such a case it will find it impossible to go further with a Church which insists on criticizing *all* stereotypes, including the new ones. In the name of an effective revolution, it will have to part ways with the Church in the long run.

A second type of fidelity will pursue the denunciation of stereotypes to its ultimate consequences. That will not prevent it from participating in the work of fashioning a new social plan. But in the very act of taking sides it will already glimpse the work of criticizing the new stereotypes, however preferable they may be to the old ones and however necessary they may be judged to be for man's liberation. This course will coincide with that of revolution so long as it is a matter of expanding people's awareness about the false values of present-day society. But the moment will come when this course comes into conflict with the direct effectiveness of the revolutionary movement. If the Christian is consistent enough to continue maintaining his revolutionary position, no matter what it costs, and if the revolution and its leaders manage to maintain sufficient breadth of outlook to appreciate and preserve attitudes that will be required and truly valued later, then Church and social change will have taken a considerable step forward.

As far as the Church, particularly the Latin American Church, is concerned, it will take a great effort at sincerity and profundity to recognize and acknowledge its most authentic function in a process that will seem to be desertion in part and that will involve martyrdom in part. But it will manage to do this in spite of everything, if it recognizes its function in society as a whole and the fact that it does not possess the solutions (GS 16); and if, furthermore, in such moments of tension and crisis, it allows itself to be judged by its God, the God who liberates man from *all* stereotypes *to the extent* that this liberation is made possible.[29]

III. LIBERTY, YES, BUT IN THE CHURCH TOO?

We have repeatedly said in this volume that our idea of God is conditioned by our experience of interpersonal relationships with others in this world. In this chapter we have seen that God, far from being a being who fashions automatons and draws up a plan for each man from all eternity, is one who nurtures liberties that are meant to run the risk of adventure and creation. We have also seen that our conception of God, which views him solely as some immutable, self-sufficient nature without any real interest in what he himself brought about is nothing but the rationalization of our own alienated societal relationships.

So we may well ask: How does the Church act to transmit the revelation of the Christian God? Is the Church a medium of liberation that calls our false rationalizations into question? Or does it act to the contrary, confirming and sacralizing our alienations through its own structures of domination?

Here we shall again consider some of the Latin American documents that are collected in the anthology compiled by Father Rossi.[30] We shall focus on those which deal with pastoral structures, that is, with the way in which the Church organizes her specific activity of proclaiming the word of God entrusted to her. These documents will indicate how difficult it is for the Church to effect her own transformation, despite the import and thrust of such official documents as those of Vatican II and the Medellín Conference that would seem to assume definite and wholehearted commitments: "This assembly has been invited 'to take decisions and establish programs only under the condition that we are disposed to carry them out as a personal commitment even at the cost of sacrifice' " (Medellín Conference, Introduction to Volume II, *Conclusions*, n. 3).

Let us begin with that sector of pastoral effort in Latin America where the postconciliar effort at renewal is more in evidence through plans worked out on the diocesan or national level. Such plans are criticized in a document which three hundred Brazilian priests sent to their bishops' conference:

> We notice that the principal lines of the pastoral renewal run from above to below. It is a vertical movement. There is no elaboration or review of plans, no real emancipation, no real participation by the priests who are in contact with the people and do pastoral work at the grass-roots level. What bishop really talks to his priests about the topics that should be discussed and the decisions that should be made at diocesan and regional meetings? Who lends an ear to their needs, suggestions, and aspirations? Many priests

want to speak out, but they are not allowed opportunity or full freedom
to do so. Why is it so difficult to listen to them? The Good Shepherd knows
his sheep. No stimulus is given to new initiatives or experiments, much
less original ideas. No encouragement is given to the spirit of inquiry. Everything is determined in advance. There are more executors than creators.
We are objects of pastoral activity rather than subjects of it. More confidence
is placed in the strength of well-organized structures than in the creative
activity and charisms of the spirit.[31]

Is it not evident from this testimony that even though official pastoral
structures may speak the language of renewal, they continue to manifest
a lack of appreciation for the liberty of those to whom God addresses
a liberative message?

When we leave the realm of general plans and consider pastoral practice, we find that the failure to pose crucial questions about God gives
rise to a series of aberrations. These aberrations are mentioned and
denounced in several documents.

Still speaking in general terms, a group of Bolivian priests had this
to say to this bishops' conference: "The pastoral ministry, as it is conceived
and practiced in present-day structures over a large part of the Catholic
world, and even more in regions of questionable faith such as certain
parts of Bolivia, is false and illusory. At times it can even be an injustice
that leads to a real alienation of humanity."[32]

Some documents spell out this latter aspect in greater detail, denouncing the utilization of stereotypes proper to an alienated mass. Religion
confirms these stereotypes, sacralizes them, and may even use them
for commercial purposes. This is what the Brazilian priests call "religious
exploitation":

> It is impossible to overlook the exploitation of certain popular devo-
> tions . . . This is religious exploitation insofar as it is readily accepted by the
> people, who are attracted by graces and promises, by the naive consolation
> of filled churches and crowd gatherings, and by the equally naive illusion of a
> living faith. It is commercial exploitation because these popular devotions
> provide good cash receipts, which facilitate the building of sanctuaries and
> parochial churches and the maintenance of other works. We wonder if this
> does not justify the accusation that religion is the opiate of the people.[33]

Pursuing the same line of thought, a document composed in Santo Domingo has this to say: "Certain popular devotions to national patron saints
are exploited. They are based on the ignorance of the people and on
material promises. They nurture the bureaucratic apparatus of the parish
and the 'pastoral machinery,' involving the priest still more in the
administration of the sacraments and in external cultic practices."[34]

Now all these efforts at taking a clear-eyed look at the existing situation
do have shock value, although the sad fact is that people are more
shocked at the accusing statements than they are at the facts themselves.
But it would be merely shock value if they were not accompanied by

some clues for further analysis. The fact is that almost nobody around fails to recognize and deplore these facts. Yet there is a weighty obstacle that crops up when an attempt is made to put an end to the present deplorable situation.

The documents quoted would indicate that the Church does not seem to value the liberty and creativity of its own members, that it permits practices which rebuff this liberty. So let us proceed to a realm where this problem crops up quite plainly: the realm of morality.

There is no little significance in the fact that the aforementioned documents are relatively silent about this topic. Despite the fact that their denunciations cover a wide gamut of features in the life of the Church, they say little or nothing about the fear of creative liberty that is embodied in the morality which is generally offered to Christians in current pastoral practice. Yet it is obvious that the Christian will not measure up to his mission in Latin America, if he does not manage to formulate a morality that is based on the creative demands of love. And this love will have to confront unexpected situations that cannot be foreseen by any law.

A document composed by Latin American priests who held a meeting in Peru breaks this silence and focuses directly on the obstacles that confront the Christian who is trying to be an authentic revolutionary:

> [The Church] would need to formulate a coherent line of thought that could give a direct and effective response to the urgent needs of revolution, instead of assuming a sharply critical and belated attitude toward them. The latter course was evident in Cuba when Castro needed collaborators who had precise solutions based upon real facts and events. These collaborators were not Christians. But to achieve this coherent line of thought will require a radical revision of the prevailing concepts of morality, the point of contact between doctrine and action. We have not reflected sufficiently on Christian morality in terms of today's world. Consider these topics, by way of example: the notion of property in an industrial, technological society which is no longer the traditional agrarian society of yesteryear; the notion of suicide, which was so hotly debated at the time of the last war. But this revision cannot be complete without the collaboration of the laity, when we are dealing with a very complex temporal world in which they are actors and protagonists.[35]

This allusion to morality, which our readers will readily relate to the main section of this chapter, brings us back to the practices of a ritualistic religion. For the morality criticized in this document is a species of ritualism, and we can now try to see what lies hidden behind this enslavement of liberty. Here is what a group of Argentinian Christians have to say:

> Instead of Masses, processions, and costly pilgrimages, the vast majority of the faithful have hoped to receive from God things which fit in with their own power to demand and correct. Sacred Scripture vigorously emphasizes that material liberation is a prior condition for spiritual liberation

from sin and its consequences. Yet not a few priests and Catholics are deeply involved with the representatives of liberal capitalism and government officials, and preaching deals with resignation, patience, and a misunderstood notion of the cross. This has debilitated the liberative power of the gospel, impeding the establishment of a regime of justice.[36]

Following the same line of thought but perhaps going even further, this observation by Brazilian priests has been quoted often: "The spirit that underlies many fundamental aspects of the people's lives is markedly conformist and fatalistic. 'It is the will of God.' That is the habitual way in which most priests interpret the happenings of life for their people. Does that not nurture this mentality instead of combatting it?"[37]

Finally, these same Brazilian priests arrive at a point in their analysis that is directly related to our theme and that is central to our discussion:

> All this commercialization is possible because the "devout" are unaware of *God's way of operating with man*. They do not realize that God acts through indirect causes. They do not realize that man is the subject of history, that his vocation is to master the material world and place it in the service of human beings. The only idea of God they have is that of a paternalistic God who leaves everything readymade. And when he does not do this, he is an arbitrary, vengeful God. We must tell the people of Brazil what the exact and correct notion of God's way of operating is. We must tell them of a God who respects man's dignity and liberty. The people of Brazil must take cognizance of their dignity, and of the possibility of directing and guiding events. Only then will we have liberated our brothers from witchcraft and superstition. Hence the enormous importance of the gospel in the work of liberating people from all their enslavements: the enslavement of fear, insecurity, and feelings of inferiority.[38]

What holds true for everything else also holds true for the structures and practices of the Church. If God had set them up in advance, prior to man's vocation, as means and conditions for man's right use of his liberty and successful passing of the test for salvation, then no renewal of pastoral practice could make the Church a medium of liberation. It could never be a human atmosphere where human liberty is not only respected but also valued above everything else.[39] Only the Christian God can obtain this evaluation from us. But first he must be preached.

IV. GOD NEEDS HUMAN BEINGS

In the preceding CLARIFICATION we cited documents that discuss concrete examples of the devaluation of liberty in the life of the Church. We saw that this devaluation implies an idea of God elaborated by reason alone.

It is our feeling that in the main section of this chapter we showed that in this idea reason does not express the full potentialities and limits of human knowledge. Indeed we said that this idea expressed a type of relationship existing between human beings wherein the freedom, creativity, and unforeseen possibilities of the other person constituted a latent threat and danger to me.

Christian theology certainly gave in to this tendency. It did so partly because it depended on Greek thought, which was suffused with rationalism. But it also did so because it fitted in with a dominant human tendency in the Church, which appeared to be coextensive with society and identified in practice with it.

But the Church was never *that kind of Church alone*. Her saints always were the sign of a contrary tendency, a clear and decisive sign however incomplete and incoherent.

But the problem is, as Urs von Balthasar points out in a valuable article,[40] that theology went its merry way and left aside one part of tradition (in the deepest and most theological sense of that word): i.e., the experiences of the saints. And it is obvious that the saints in turn were tributaries of the prevailing theology, particularly when they tried to express the connection between their own experiences and Christian *doctrine*. Saint John of the Cross bears witness to this fact, for example.

However, theology could have enriched and corrected its treasury with something else that is the very life of the Spirit, who leads the Church to the full truth as Christ promised. It could have been wise enough to take in these experiences, expressed in their more immediate and direct languages, and to incorporate them into its own methodology—as biblical theology does with the literary genres of Scripture, for example.

Now the thing worth noting is that this direct language is evident, despite theology's insistence on God's immobility and his lack of any real relationship with his creatures. In simple, direct verses that well up from his own experience, Angelus Silesius writes: "It is said that God lacks nothing and has no need of our gifts. To be sure, but then why does he want to have my poor heart?"[41] In another place he writes: "I know that without me God cannot exist for a single instant. If I should disappear, he would give up the ghost out of sadness."[42]

Within their own literary genre, these statements express a truth which we would say is not equal but superior to many of the disquisitions on God in the *Summa Theologica*. And this is hardly an isolated case.

To consider one example, let us take an essential topic in this whole area: namely, the reciprocity that God himself has established in his relations with human beings. While rationalist theology and mass-oriented practice were denying this reciprocity, the experience of the saints was affirming it. Consider this dialogue between Saint Ignatius Loyola and Diego Laínez:

> [Ignatius] said to Laínez: "Tell me . . . What do you think you would do if our God made this proposition to you: If you want to die now, I . . . will give you eternal glory. But if you want to live longer, I will give you no

guarantee of how you will end up. You will be on your own . . . It being
understood that if you remained some time in this life, you could do some
great and notable service for his divine majesty, what would your reply
be?"

Laínez replied: "I must confess . . . that I would choose to insure my
salvation and rid myself of the dangers attached to such an important affair."

Then our father [Ignatius] said: "I certainly would not do that. If I
felt that by staying alive I could render some singular service to our Lord,
I would plead with him to leave me in this life . . . And I would focus my
eyes on him, not on myself, without considering my own danger or security."
And he added: "Because . . . what king would not feel deeply obligated to
such a servant? And if that is the case with human beings . . . what could
we be afraid of? . . . I cannot imagine any such thing about such a good
and grateful God."[43]

The reader can readily see the following points in the above passage:
(a) Laínez's view of liberty as a danger to salvation; (b) Loyola's overcoming of this view with a creative notion of liberty which is tied up with
the possibility of doing something important *for God;* (c) this presupposes
faith in the Pauline sense, that is, reaching God through a life on the
personal rather than merely natural level; (d) it is this personal type
of life which permits us, by analogy, to comprehend the Christian God,
and to apply to him such categories as "gratitude" toward his creature
without any false fear.

Earlier we cited the feelings of the Curé of Ars about a child dying
before it had reached the age of reason. Here he presents us with a
much more profound aspect of his outlook on the whole matter of
God and liberty. It is almost an exact reproduction of the comments
of Ignatius above:

"Father," the missionary asked one day, "if the good God gave you the
choice, either to go up to heaven at once or to go on working as you are
at present doing for the conversion of sinners, what would be your decision?"

"I should stay on. In heaven the saints are happy indeed, but they are
like men who live on their income. But they have laboured well, for God
punishes laziness and only rewards work; however, unlike ourselves, they
cannot by their labours and sufferings, win souls for God."[44]

Such statements help us to understand the reverse side of the coin:
i.e., the complaint of another Christian whose experience was deeply
spiritual. Here we shall quote in full a passage of Teilhard de Chradin
that we presented earlier in an abridged form:

What is the point of attaining "beatitude" if, in the final reckoning, we
have made no absolute contribution, through our lives, to the totality of
being? At the same time, from the Christian point of view, we can no longer
understand why a God could have committed himself, out of mere
"benevolence" to such a flood of sufferings and vicissitudes. You may, by
a dialectic of pure act, silence our reason as much as you please, but you
will never now convince our hearts that the vast business of the cosmos,
as we now see it, is simply some gift or plaything of God's.[45]

We do not claim that this resolves the problem of evil. But we do indeed feel that the Christian God offers elements that are critical to understanding its import and meaning: (a) evil is the price to be paid for a human liberty that is placed before the universe in all seriousness; (b) something absolute depends on the responsibility therein confided—even for God; (c) in the meantime, God shares with man all the sorrow of this gestation—the supreme guarantee.

V. GOD AND THE LIMITS OF REASON

After what we have said above, we have every right to ask one final question: Can reason alone arrive at knowledge of God, that is, of the true God? To put it another way, reason comes to call something "god" by starting from the nature of creatures and operating in its own way. Is its "God" the God that Christians adore and love?

An ounce of prevention is worth a pound of cure, so note how we have phrased the question. We did not say "human knowledge" but "reason," and we did not say "starting from creatures" but "starting from the nature of creatures.

Having stipulated these reservations, we would not hestitate to answer no to the question we have just asked. And we would readily give the same answer if we were asked about reason's possibility of knowing any living human person in a concrete, personal way.

To get to the real problem, however, we should perhaps be more precise and say that a radical depreciation of liberty and history comes about only when reason ignores its proper ambit and tries to travel the road of efficient causality to God. In other words, when reason takes as its basis the natural perfection that corresponds to God as cause. Reason is capable of more than this ratiocination about efficient factors that are apprehended in the comportment of *things*. As we have already pointed out, reason itself can point out the faulty logic of a finality which explains the existence of the creature simply in terms of the nature of God and the creature. The conclusion which reason should arrive at through this appraoch is that it is confronted with a fact which cannot be explained solely in terms of the divine nature.

This should lead reason to comprehend its limits—and not just when it is a question of the divine. Its limits are not just "the mysterious" or "the infinite." It is not simply a matter of coming to a standstill before the power, majesty, and infinity of the divine. It is a matter of the same limits we run into with respect to each and every human being. There is a dividing line between that which we know about the person by virtue of his *nature* and that which we learn about him from his *history*. Reason certainly cannot recount this history to us, precisely because it does not stem from nature but from the liberty that goes to make up each and every person. In general, nature can be the object of positive, rational knowledge. But that which relates to liberty, history, and personal reality calls for a rational knowledge that is real but negative. It must recognize a limit beyond which reason cannot go without contradicting itself. In this new domain reason can operate only by using analogies relating to personal and affective life.

It is only in terms of this complete sense of the word "reason," which includes both its positivity and its negativity, that we are obliged to echo the statement of Vatican I: "If anyone says that the living and true God, who is our lord and creator, cannot be known with certainty by the natural light of human reason, through the things he has made, let him be anathema" (Denz. 1806). If things and persons do exist, then it is certainly because God is something more than an inaccessible, self-sufficient, unmoved mover. The good must really be diffusive of itself, although not in the manner of a machine. God must not be content to hold it in himself and for himself. Like us, he must not be able to be happy without giving of himself (cf. GS 24) Any human being can intuit or glimpse this, even if he is not a philosopher. And the philosopher must give up opposing the Christian God to the God of the philosophers. We must be bold enough to describe the latter as the God of bad philosophers.

Now that we have reached this point in our reflection, however, the explanation that a "bad philosophy" is responsible for the obstacle which stands in the way of knowing God lacks any solid support from a sociological viewpoint. As Michael Schmaus points out: "One cannot object to the decision of Vatican I on the grounds that outside of the biblical sphere natural reason has not managed to find any sure pathway to the living God."[46] Once again we recommend his series on dogmatic theology to readers of this volume. In connection with the theme being discussed here, readers of his work will see how far rational and natural knowledge of God can go.[47] They will see that this positive content allows man to recognize something of God's essence, or to put it better, God's nature. Then they will see the difference—a very important difference here—between the domain of nature and the domain of the person insofar as human knowledge is concerned.[48] Finally the reader will see that the *personal* and historical life of God is revealed to us uniquely in the Trinity.[49]

For all that, Schmaus's initial response seems to be a more facile than realistic way of ducking the statement of Vatican I—the latter appearing to be overly optimistic at first glance. To say that human knowledge has the power to arrive at certainty about God but in fact has never found a way to do this is to reduce the problem to a search by professional philosophers for authentic proofs of God's existence.

We feel that the search must be conducted in a different direction. In affirming this possibility, Vatican I meant to set aside the tendency to turn knowledge of God into a difficult task for intellectuals alone. We should not look for the difficulty in the plane of knowledge as such.

The same tendency that inclines us to deform God also leads us to avoid encountering him. And this obstacle does not go by the name of "transcendental illusion" or anything of that sort; it goes by the name of *sin*. In this context it is Karl Barth who has made a major and decisive contribution to the whole question of God. Knowledge does not function in some isolated, aseptic region of our being.

Let us test this hypothesis by asking some questions. To what extent are we sensitive to the personal element that palpitates all around us? To what extent and frequency do we glimpse in the products we buy the human countenance of the worker who produced them? Is it odd to us that the whole world is losing any trace of personal resonance and becoming a mere mechanism with no suggestion of persons? If it is not, then we should not be surprised to find that our ratiocination about the author of the universe, however simple and correct it may be, leads us nowhere.

We should not be afraid to attribute to sin—and to societal sin—our failure to arrive at a God who does not lie buried in our knowledge. We should not be afraid to do so because sin is not the private preserve of the person who denies God's existence. To repeat the wise remark of Henri de Lubac: "Whether incredulous, indifferent, or believers, we compete with one another in ingeniously guarding ourselves against God."[50]

And it works the opposite way too. Just as reason distorts the picture when it conceives God in terms of purely "natural" categories, so these same categories are transformed when we are willing to subordinate reason to the revelation of the personal.

To conclude this section, we should like to offer two concrete examples that support what we have said. One comes from the Bible, the other from a theological work.

We find the first in Paul's Epistle to the Philippians. The absolute and inaccessible perfection of the divine nature is maintained. But in the context of revealed personal history it leads to knowledge of God, precisely because God freely renounced it to live our life: "For the divine nature was his from the first; yet he did not think to snatch at equality with God, but made himself nothing, assuming the nature of a slave, bearing the human likeness, revealed in human shape" (Phil. 2:6–7).

The second example comes from the work of Schmaus. The immutability of God, taken as the terminus of knowledge about the Christian God, leads us to denigrate and even demolish the import and reality of the Incarnation. On the other hand, the immutability that follows rather than precedes the gift of self, which God *is* rather than gives, leads us to an essential feature of all his work: i.e., his fidelity:

> The immutability of God does not imply an attitude of indifference or immobility toward the fate of man. Nor is it rigidity or inertia . . . Sacred Scripture bears witness to the immutability of God's being and volition . . . In his Epistle to the Romans, Paul describes in detail the immutable fidelity of God.[51]

This is how rational knowledge is integrated with that other, superior knowledge which revelation directs to man's full power of comprehension. The latter does not prescind from reason, but neither is it reduced to reason alone.

NOTES

1. Rudolf Bultmann, *Kerygma und Mythos*, ed. H. Bartsch (Hamburg:Herber Reich-Evangelischer Verlag), II, 91.

2. *Ibid.*, I, 18.

3. Dietrich Bonhoeffer, Eng. trans. *Prisoner for God* (New York: Macmillan, 1967), pp. 145–46.

4. *Ibid.*, p. 156.

5. *Ibid.*, p. 178.

6. Schubert M. Ogden, *Christ without Myth* (New York: Harper & Row, 1961), p. 127.

7. John A. T. Robinson, *Honest to God* (Philadelphia: Westminster, 1963), pp. 15–16.

8. Harvey Cox, *The Secular City* (New York: Macmillan, 1966), pp. 69–70.

9. *Ibid.*, pp. 79 and 81.

10. Paul Van Buren, *The Secular Meaning of the Gospel* (New York: Macmillan, 1963), pp. 100 and 102.

11. *Ibid.*, p. 17.

12. *Cf.* Chapter I, CLARIFICATION IV.

13. "Whether incredulous, indifferent, or believers, we compete with one another in ingeniously guarding ourselves against God" (Henri de Lubac, *The Discovery of God*, Eng. trans., *op. cit.*, p. 151.

14. W. T. Stace, *Religion and the Modern Mind* (Philadelphia: Lippincott, 1952), p. 76.

15. Stace states that Newtonian science produced a growing feeling of the *remoteness* of God. It now seemed that after his initial work of creation, God did nothing more. Gravitation and the laws of motion do everything. See *ibid.*, pp. 94–95.

16. *Ibid.*, p. 108.

17. *Ibid.*, p. 109.

18. Herbert Marcuse, *El fin de la Utopia,* Spanish trans. (Mexico: Siglo XXI, 1968), p. 1. The translator of this volume has not consulted the English version of this essay, "The End of Utopia," which is now available in Marcuse, *Five Lectures* (Boston: Beacon), 1970.

19. "Industrial civilization has reached the point where, with respect to the aspirations of man for a human existence, the scientific abstraction from final causes becomes obsolete in science's own terms. Science itself has rendered it possible to make final causes the proper domain of science . . . Instead of being separated from science and scientific method, and left to subjective preference and irrational, transcendental sanction, formerly metaphysical ideas of liberation may become the proper object of science" (H. Marcuse, *One-Dimensional Man,* Boston: Beacon Press, 1964, pp. 232–233).

20. *Cf.* the interesting statement of Milán Machovec, a Marxist and former

professor at Charles University in Prague: "Once the more complex social problems have been resolved, there will remain this enormous movement molded
by an atheistic tradition. For this very reason it will find itself obligated to undertake another quest, no matter how difficult it may turn out to be. In different
ways it will have to make a thoroughgoing survey of all the human dimensions
that now exist or that can be envisioned as possible. Having given up on God,
Marxism will sooner or later have to pick up once again the heritage of the
'human mystery' " (in *Lettre,* May 1969, p. 3).

21. Herbert Marcuse, *El fin de la Utopía, op. cit.*, p. 2.

22. Herbert Marcuse, *Eros and Civilization, op. cit.,* pp. 65–66. But we would
be unfair if we did not recognize the fact that the European church is quite
aware of the problem being discussed here. Consider this statement by Claude
Geffré, O.P. ("Recent Developments in Fundamental Theology: An Interpretation," *Concilium* 46, New York: Paulist Press, 1969, p. 21): "It seems clear from
the more recent and significant studies in the field that authors have clearly begun
to see the limitations and dangers of this inflation of anthropology. There is a
fear that we may make man the measure of the Word of God. It is also said against
the use of the transcendental dimension that it puts transcendental subjectivity
before man as an historical and political being, and that it therefore overcomes
idealism only in appearance" (our italics).

23. *Cf.* the brilliant observations of Richard Stith in his letter to a professor
concerning calculator-type knowledge as opposed to human knowledge of
people: "Respect signifies diversity (rather than a single scale) and unity based
on diversity (insofar as we concern ourselves with the *singularity* of each person).
Contrary to a unity based on alikeness (e.g., the same race, the same profession),
the community is *one* because it is diverse. And because we trust others even
without understanding them, we can never eliminate them or judge *a priori*
that their expression has no value . . . And "anti-community" would have the
contrary features. . . Just as the community is grounded on an attitude of service,
so the anti-community is grounded on an attitude of dominion and *control.*
One who controls has no ear for any need, and feels tht everything can be
manipulated . . . So he does not hesitate to label people in his desire to control
and dominate them. The kind of knowledge of the world required for an attitude
of service is radically different from that required for an attitude of control.
And the latter tends to eliminate the former. I think that perhaps the principal
reason behind our loss of a community sense is the fact that we have allowed
knowledge for the sake of domination to spread to the point where it has practically eliminated knowledge for the sake of service" (in *Perspectivas de Diálogo,*
May 1969, n. 33).

24. *Cf.* Richard Hofstadter, *Anti-Intellectualism in American Life* (New York:
Knopf, 1963), Part I, Introduction.

25. But much more in the first case, because the stereotypes on which any
radical transformation is based presuppose some start at criticism, however simplistic it may be.

26. *Cf.* Volume I, Appendix II, A: The Israel of the Covenant. There is
a more developed treatment in Segundo and Sanchis, *As Etapas Pré-cristâs da
descoberta de Deus: Una chave para a análise do cristianismo (latinoamericano)* (Petrópolis: Vozes, 1968), Chapter 2.

27. "This is the price to be paid by any Church, which as such is called
to universality, the consequent institutionalization in society as a whole, and

acculturation in the surrounding sociocultural world. Hence in every Church we will find a diminution of the tension, without that necessarily implying an adulteration of the values it transmits" (Aldo Büntig, *El Catolicismo Popular en La Argentina*, Buenes Aires: Bonum, 1969, p. 104).

The general statements we make here are in no way intended to disregard the complexity of the human attitudes that converge in the religious sphere. We know of many people who are incapable of moving out of the traditional mold, but who do find in the Christian message, understood in what is undeniably a human sense, a springboard for goodness, sacrifice, and solidarity. Even though these persons belong to the people, we should not talk in their case about "popular religiosity" (*cf.* Chapter II, CLARIFICATION I. We would reserve this term for the deformation of Christianity that is due to basic exigencies of societal life: security, aggressiveness, etc. Even in the latter case, however, we must carefully separate the social function of such a Christianity from what it should be in the authentic sense of Christ's message. The superstitious practice of a tribe may fulfill a human function that is socially useful while certain societal conditions last, but that does not mean that it should call itself "Christian" merely because it invokes the name of Christ or makes external use of the Christian sacraments.

28. See further on, Chapter IV, CLARIFICATION II.

29. We fully realize how deeply critical is the question of the unity of all Latin American societies, and how difficult is the socio-pastoral problem of a more authentic Christian syntehsis. The reader can explore this question further in Volume I, Chapter V, CLARIFICATION III. He may also consult the book by J. L. Segundo, *De la Sociedad a la Teolog*ía, (Buenos Aires: Carlos Lohlé), Part IV.

30. Collected in J. J. Rossi, *Iglesia Latinoamericana. ¿Protesta or profecía?* (Buenes Aires: Búsqueda, 1969).

31. *Ibid.*, p. 188.

32. *Ibid.*, p. 162.

33. *Ibid.*, p. 184.

34. *Ibid.*, p. 355.

35. *Ibid.*, p. 33.

36. *Ibid.*, p. 115.

37. *Ibid.*, p. 184

38. *Ibid.*, pp. 184–85.

39. *Cf.* Gustavo Gutiérrez, "Libertad religiosa y diálogo salvador," in *Salvación y Construcción del Mundo* (in collaboration with J. L. Segundo, J. Croatto, B. Catao, and J. Comblin) (Barcelona; Dilapsa-Nova Terra, 1968), pp. 11–43.

40. Hans Urs von Balthasar, "Théologie et sainteté," *Dieu Vivant*, n. 12, p. 15 ff.

41. Cited by Riwkah Schärf, "La Figura de Satanás en el Antiguo Testamento," from C. G. Jung, *Símbología del Espíritu*, p. 111. On this article, see note 51 below.

42. Cited by Berdyaev. See J. L. Segundo, *Berdiaeff, op. cit.*, pp. 152–53.

43. P. de Rivadeneira, *Vida de San Ignacio de Loyola* (Madrid: Ap. de la Prensa, 1920), pp. 492–93. This reciprocity is also a key element in the motivations of Loyola's *Spiritual Exercises*.

44. François Trochu, *Life of the Curé d'Ars*, Eng. trans. (Westminster: Newman, 1950), p. 550.

45. See note 20 on p. 119.

46. Schmaus, *Teologia Dogmática, op. cit.,* p. 217.

47. *Ibid.,* pp. 281 ff.

48. *Ibid.,* pp. 292 ff.

49. *Ibid.,* pp. 299 ff.

50. See note 13.

51. Schmaus, *Teología Dogmática, op. cit.,* pp. 501 and 504. On the other side of the coin one should consider the interesting exegetical hypothesis suggested by A. Lods and elaborated by Riwkah Schärf in an excellent analysis of various texts of the Old Testament. According to this hypothesis, man's growing maturation in his idea of God, a maturation guided by God himself, leads him to separate and eventually contrast certain attributes over against God himself. In the beginning man had confused and identified these attributes with God. So man is gradually led to attribute to Yahweh's angel certain actions that become more and more clearly incompatible with Yahweh himself, but for which he cannot find anyone else to take the responsibility. In line with this thought, Satan represents strict justice and right as opposed to the grace and mercy of Yahweh: that is, impersonal and demonically mechanical response as opposed to an inexplicably gratuitous personal relationship.

Schärf develops this hypothesis by studying in particular: 2 Sam. 16:10; 19:23; Zech. 3:1; Num. 22:22; 2 Sam. 24:16; Job 1:6 ff; 2:1 ff; 1 Chron. 21:1; 2 Sam. 24:1; 1 Kings 22:19.

Schärf's article (see note 41 above) discusses the figure of Satan in the Old Testament. Similar comments on the figure of Satan can be found *passim* in the collected work of C. G. Jung. See, for example, C. G. Jung, *Psychology and Religion: East And West* (New York: Bollingen, 1958).

CHAPTER FOUR

God and the World

Another converging line of thought, which sought an easy way out in giving expression to the Christian God, was Subordinationism. According to it, the Word made man, who was immersed in time and matter, could only be a subordinate, secondary, delegated God. Here again the divinity, in its fullest sense, was restored to absolute oneness. Only the Father was strictly God.

At first sight this deviation may hardly seem to differ from the one analyzed in the prvious chapter. And in fact they were not always distinguished from one another. The Council of Rome (382) calls them "the same impiety" (Denz. 61).

First of all, they do seem to be identical in principle. They are a response to the same difficulty: How does one avoid a coarse and absurd "tritheism" in confronting the refined circles of Greek culture? The early apologists, that is, those who were charged with the task of presenting the new faith before the tribunal of contemporary educated pagans, keenly felt the difficulty in explaining the basis for the adoration they paid to Christ.

If Christ is a *divine being,* then only one of three explanations seemed fitting. Either he was the Father manifesting himself and operating in another way (Modalism). Or else he was a divine being by adoption (Adoptionism). Or else, even more radically, he was a divine being by creation, a second-string God destined to penetrate the world of human beings.

Here again the underlying intention was pastoral. In their effort to explain the Christian faith to pagans, the apologists were especially concerned to present its monotheism in vigorous terms. They wanted to preclude the danger that these people, with their propensities toward polytheism, would turn the Father, Son, and Holy Spirit into three gods. So for men like Origen, the Trinity was pretty much a bothersome obstacle. Origen himself often talks about the Son as a second-ciass God. The Son is God, but not God like the Father is; he is *inferior to the*

Father. The "God-God" is the Father. Christ is God too, but less so. He is God, but not as much as the Father.

In contrast to the Adoptionists, the Subordinationists proclaim that Christ is the Word. But the Word is a secondary God created by the Father. And there is the catch. For if the Son, the Word, is created by the Father, then he is a creature, a halfway God, a satellite God, a star without its own light that merely reflects divinity. Once again the divine signification of Christ is obscured in order to salvage monotheism. Once again there is not real Trinity in God.

Origen insists a great deal on the fact that the Son is the instrument of the Father's will, who came to execute the latter's orders. In one sense Origen is right in saying this. Christ says repeatedly that he has not come to do his own will but to carry out the will of the Father who sent him. But Origen takes what is a free and voluntary surrender in Christ and turns it into a relationship of substantial dependence. He talks about Christ as if he were a secondary God. Christ had no recourse but to submit to the Father, because he was by nature inferior and subordinate to the Father.

Origen confuses the Son's relationship of filial dependence vis-à-vis the Father with the subordinate relationship of a being inferior by nature vis-à-vis another being of a superior nature. In generating the Son, God curtailed the divinity. He did not transmit or communicate all of his divinity to the Son. Only the Father is fully God.[1]

We encounter the same difficulty and confusion in almost all of the apologists. It will leave the door open for later deviations. One apologist says: "We adore and love the Word *after God*." Another apologist, Justin, says: "The Word is set up *below* God the creator."

We must appreciate his difficulty. The doctrine of the Church's magisterium had not yet been formulated or elaborated—much less with respect to this exceedingly difficult point.[2]

What is more, even though the problem of the Spirit and his divinity had not yet been posed, it was logical to think that what was said of the Word was essential for understanding the situation of the Holy Spirit in the Christian revelation of God. Later the Macedonians would extend the Arian deviation to the theme of the Holy Spirit, and they too would be condemned as the Arians had been (Denz. 62).

However, the imprecision and ambiguity of many apologists continued to be no more than that until it converged with one of the great religious currents of that period and became a massive force. It was only then that the imprecision turned into an open deviation and, as one author puts it, the Church woke up to find that it was Arian. Arianism is the most well known and popular form of Subordinationism.

Once again we must ask ourselves: What exactly were Christians debating so heatedly at the start of the fourth century? Why were they so passionately taken up with what seems to be a very abstract problem—whether the Son had been generated or created, whether he was equal to the Father or subordinate to him?

Section I

Arius affirms that there is only one God; the Father alone. He is absolute and eternal. He cannot communicate his being, his substance—not even by generation. God is not a body; hence he cannot be made up of parts or be divisible. God cannot beget a son. Arius even rejects the traditional expressions of Christianity that could be taken as allusions to generation: e.g., "light of light," "life of life," etc.

Everything that exists besides the one and only God has been created by him out of nothing. God willed to produce the world; in order to do this he first created an intermediary to be the instrument of creation. We call this intermediary the Word. He is before all creatures that are properly so called; he is before time. But he is not eternal because he did not always exist. There was a moment in duration in which he did not exist, in which he passed from nonexistence to existence. The Word is created; he is not engendered from the Father's substance. Hence the Word is a creature; he is not the natural son of God but rather his adoptive son. He is not truly God. He is alien to, and distinct from, the substance of the Father.

Thus the Word is subject to God. By nature he is mutable, that is, subject to change and fallible. To be sure, he is not a creature like human beings; he is a perfect creature. But he is a creature. When he became incarnate he took a body without a soul, he himself occupying the place of the latter.

As the reader can see, in the teaching of Arius a definitively heretical form was given to the Subordinationism that had been more covertly suggested in the work of the earlier apologists. The Son is inferior to the Father. He is not God as the Father is; he is a creature. There is not and cannot be persons, and hence a trinity, in God.

Arius had not invented anything new. But he took what had been scattered currents before him and converted them into a "popular movement."

To understand this fact, we must keep in mind certain traits of Arius' personality. He was a "saint," an enlightened man, a man capable of long fasts and great mortifications. His doctrine was attractive because of his person, and because it showed up as the doctrine of purity and holiness, of contempt for the temporal and the fleshly. It said that the Son, who had been incarnated and made man, who had been *tainted* by taking on the body of a human being, could not be God like the Father who is incorporeal, nontemporal, and pure.

Thus Arianism was doctrinally and psychologically inserted into one of the strongest religious currents sweeping through the western borders of the Mediterranean world. This current propounded the dualism between matter and spirit.

It is quite possible that very few readers of the New Testament notice that its authors, particularly the later ones, were already obliged to warn Christians against organized heresies that passed themselves off as the purest version of divine revelation. For example, the second Epistle of John echoes the thought of his first Epistle when it declares: "Many deceivers have gone out into the world, who do not acknowledge Jesus Christ *as coming in the flesh* (our italics; the phrase could be translated "as true man"). These are the persons described as the Antichrist, the "arch-deceiver" (2 John 7; *cf.* 1 John 4:2–3).

In this case we are dealing with an error called Docetism, which regarded the human figure and history of Jesus as one of mere appearance. But it was only one form of a general tendency that divided the world into two opposed realms: good and evil, spirit and matter, God and the world. This current is known to us as Gnosticism, but it is even more familiar to us in its extreme form: Manichaeism.

Manichaeism teaches that there is a radical opposition right from the start between two realms that are conceived vertically: the lofty and the base, eternity and time. Totally in contradiction to this view was the view of a God who was fully God, but who had to be discovered by interpreting the impure and ambiguous history with which he had become consubstantiated and from which he spoke to us. This "contradiction" was the strong point of Arius.

In the year 325 we see these two conceptions clashing head on at the First Ecumenical Council in Nicea. At that point in time, perhaps two-thirds of the Christian people were Arians. There was passionate, heated debate. Neither side made any concessions, as the Emperor Constantine had hoped they would when he convened the Council. The bishops listened to the solid line of arguments presented by the patriarch Alexander, and especially by his young secretary, the deacon Athanasius, who was the major theologian of that Council. The majority of the bishops thoroughly condemned the doctrine of Arius and proclaimed the formula of faith known to us as the Nicene Creed.

The words of this creed are known to us from the Mass, but we may well be unaware of the history and significance that lie buried within them. The Nicene Council begins with an affirmation of monotheism. Indeed the Trinity is affirmed as the most absolute unity. If we leave out the passages relating to each one of the divine persons in particular, the formula would be this: *"We believe in one God, the Father . . . and in the Son . . . and in the Holy Spirit*: (Denz. 54). Here the Council sticks to the vocabulary of the Bible in which God with the article "the" is always the Father. To believe in the Father is to profess monotheism.

What are we to think of the Son, then? Here again the Council employs the most biblical name. To be sure, the term *Word* is used in the writings of John, although not very often. But the name Son points more forcefully to his personal character than does the term *Word*, for the latter could be taken to mean a function of the Father's person. Alluding directly to the language of Arius, the Nicene Council says this about the Son. He is the "only begotten of the Father, that is, of the Father's substance, God of God, light of light, true God of true God, begotten not made, consubstantial with the Father" (which means, of the *same* substance rather than of a *similar* substance). Despite this fact, or perhaps we might better say because of this fact, "for us men and for our salvation he came down from heaven and was made flesh, became man, suffered death, and rose on the third day."

So it is not a creature or a halfway God who, without ceasing to be God (Denz. 54), became a human being like we are and took deep root in our own history. This is the import of another phrase that dates from the same epoch and is directed against the same tendency. It was added to the so-called Creed of Saint Cyril, and then incorporated into the Nicene Creed at the Second Ecumenical Council (Constantinople): "And his kingdom will have no end" (Denz. 86). Being man is not a temporary mission for the Son of God, who is truly God. It is not a tangential contact with man's history, earth, and matter.

Vatican II will later express this fact in a much more categorical way: "By His incarnation the Son of God . . . worked with human hands . . . thought with a human mind, acted by human choice, and loved with a human heart" (GS 22), because no human being is a solitary entity but is bound by ties of solidarity to the human race. His human hands and mind and choice and heart will ultimately come to rest only in the new earth of mankind: "He will dwell among them" (Rev. 21:3).[3]

Section II

However, this definitive and wondrous elevation of our history is not without its inconveniences.

We have already alluded to the easy way out that meant dividing reality into two realms that are opposed in their functioning and value. The false and deceptive clarity of Manichaeism, devoid of shadings and shadows, is the psychological basis of Arianism. It did permit people to confront the options of personal and societal life with a certain ease. Man is presumably a mixed being who cannot prescind completely from matter, time, and history. But God, standing outside of these things, lets man see his interests and his eternal, spiritual values. In the mishmash of a confused and ambiguous history there appears from above, in vertical fashion, the judgments of God, the interests of God, the messengers of God.

Jesus had to confront this eternal religious tendency of man toward oversimplification. He had to make himself known to man through the process of interpreting his work, that is, through what happened in the concrete, mixed, ambiguous, and politicized history of Israel—a Roman colony under the sway of Tiberius. What do his interlocutors demand: "The Pharisees and Sadducees came, and to test him they asked him to show them a *sign* from heaven" (Matt. 16:1; our italics). And Jesus, speaking from within the borders of history, gives this response: "In the evening you say, 'It will be fine weather, for the sky is red'; and in the morning you say, 'It will be stormy today; the sky is red and lowering.' You know how to interpret the appearance of the sky; can you not interpret the signs of the times?" (Matt. 16:2–3).

The image speaks volumes. The same color, shaded differently or framed in different settings, can have completely different meanings. Man can be led to the incarnate God only if he uses his capacity for interpreting things.[4]

Perhaps now we can understand the odd characteristic that the evangelists, particularly Mark, point to. The public life of Jesus is marked by a shifting rhythm of revealing himself and hiding himself in turn. This rhythm has been called "the messianic secret," perhaps improperly.[5] It is as if Jesus wanted to intrigue those who saw him perform his liberative wonders: "The blind recover their sight, the lame walk, the lepers are made clean, the deaf hear, the dead are raised to life, the poor are hearing the good news" (Matt. 11:5). He wants to arouse their curiosity, not so that they will take refuge in some sacred name—Messiah, prophet (Mark 8:28–29), delegate of God (Mark 1:24), son of God (Mark 3:11–12), but so that they will ask questions about the signs of a history where liberation already appears as a victorious reality.

There is no doubt that the incarnate God seriously complicated the lives of his closest contemporaries and their choices with respect to him. We often entertain a false and idyllic image of those few years in human history when one could run into God-made-man on the street corner. And the falseness of the image derives from a false starting point and presupposition: i.e., that we would have already identified him and known who he was at the start. His contemporaries and even his closest friends—perhaps the latter more than any others—were confronted with the terrible difficulty of recognizing him in, and in spite of, limited human realities that were impure and ambiguous in themselves (however pure and holy the interior intention of Jesus might have been).

We need only recall a few passages in the Gospel, starting with one that only Mark dares to put down: "When his family heard of this, they set out to take charge of him; for people were saying that he was out of his mind" (Mark 3:21).

But there is another passage that strikes us even more forcefully: "When he heard that John had been arrested, Jesus withdrew to Galilee" (Matt. 4:12). John the Baptist is his precursor, his friend. He proclaims and defends the same principles that Jesus will later defend. And he defends them against the established authority that wants to silence his voice. He is put in prison for these principles by an unworthy governor whom Jesus himself will call "that fox." Yet Jesus gives no hint of solidarity with John. He departs from there and goes to preach elsewhere.

Many of us would probably be more inclined to recognize truth in an act of solidarity, whatever the cost might be. We might well recall the words that a poet directs to Eve, the mother of all humanity:

> You have interred so many in their graves,
> Dead out of some great loyalty.
> You have buried them in layered waves,
> When they were one short step from felicity.[6]

Perhaps we would have preferred the image of a Jesus who died younger than he did, making a commitment of solidarity with someone who opposed an unjust authority. Why not! But the fact is that Jesus, from within his limited and ambiguous situation, chose *one* of the possibilities open to him. And the one he chose was limited and ambiguous too. He chose to carry out another mission. It too would lead to death, but it would allow his own message to reach maturity. He knew that any number of interpretations were possible at that moment. But he was truly man, and he had to decide as such.[7]

A third passage in the Gospel might be noted here. When the Pharisees are confronted with what we might call "the Jesus phenomenon," they choose to attribute his work to the power of Satan and his realm rather than recognizing God in him. We could say that they identified Jesus with the Anti-God, that is, with the power that he came to combat. In response to this charge, Jesus points out that the decisive and absolute judgment of human beings will center around him: "He who is not with me is against me, and he who does not gather with me scatters" (Luke 11:23).

While it may sound anachronistic, there is no doubt that we can say that the tendency of the disciples toward oversimplification and Manichaeism led them to identify absolute negation of Jesus with the blasphemy of the Pharisees. For the language of the Gospels does tend to hypostatize vertically, to associate with certain individuals or groups tendencies that really are at work in every individual and every group. Hence Jesus had to tell them the parable of the wheat and the chaff, to destroy the illusion that *in history* one could make a distinction between the good and the bad, between God's friends and his enemies.

So when the Pharisees do blaspheme, Jesus takes advantage of the occasion to teach his apostles that the decisive option for "human beings" does not reside in recognizing or not recognizing the "son of man" for what he was. Precisely because it is incarnated in human realities, what is said against him in the ambiguity of history will be pardoned at the judgment.

On the other hand, there is an absolute option vis-à-vis him. It is the choice that goes against the dynamism which he represents, embodies, and reveals. Whether one recognizes and acknowledges the Son of Man or not, one can sin against the Spirit:[8] i.e., against the force that incarnates the divine in history. It is not without good reason that the Synoptics connect the passage cited above with another that depicts the power of God overcoming that other power which holds man in bondage. Luke, in particular, brings out the logic that unites them (Luke 11:15–23). The crowning point of this victory is the disarming of the enemy and, according to Luke, the apportionment of the things he had usurped among those who are supposed to receive them. In other words: the divine power vis-à-vis which every man is judged absolutely is the liberation of man, the process of humanization.

In reality our God is known only with the movement and process of de-alienation, creation, and love that he himself enkindles in man.[9] He is never known prior to, or outside of, that process. No heavenly sign points him out to those who do not scrutinize the ambiguity of history in search of their common liberation.

To "gather with God-made-man" is to contribute in some way or other to the work of providing a whole world of possibilities to man's creative love. To "scatter" is to hold man back from this task, however "religious" one may be.

So Jesus chooses the moment of clearcut, *verbal* denial to correct the incipient Manichaeism of his disciples and the later Manichaeism of his followers: i.e., their tendency to identify the decisive option for God with the religious realm. The Absolute has become incarnate and belongs to history in a definitive way.

Several other Gospel passages tell us the same thing in a clear and explicit way. For example, there is this passage in Matthew's Gospel: "A man had two sons. He went to the first, and said, 'My boy, go and work today in the vineyard.' 'I will, sir,' the boy replied; but he never went. The father came to the second and said the same. 'I will not,' he replied, but afterwards he changed his mind and went" (Matt. 21:28–30). Then Jesus asks a question, the question posed by God-made-man. It would seem to be absurdly obvious, if it were not for the fact that we obstinately continue to simplify life for ourselves by making declarations that are not framed in real life and time: "Which of these two did as his father wished?" (Matt. 21:31).

Jesus makes the same point when he tells us: "If, when you are bringing your gift to the altar, you suddenly remember that your brother has a grievance against you, leave your gift where it is before the altar. First go and make your peace with your brother, and only then come back and offer your gift" (Matt. 5:23–24). It is obvious that Jesus wants us to recognize many people as his who are far from his altar. It may well be that they will spend their lives far from his altar because one can spend his life making peace with his fellow men who have different ideas or are of a different race or social class!

Section III

What then was it, in the last analysis, that Christians were debating so heatedly at the start of the fourth century? Why were they so worked up about the question whether the Son had been begotten or created? Why did Saint Athanasius allow himself to be persecuted and exiled rather than give up one iota in those formulas that seem so speculative and abstract to us?

To begin with, we can say that they realized, however obscurely, that they were defending something more than a precise formula. They sensed that Arianism was attacking and undermining the vital center of human existence conceived as a totality.

The fact is that the cornerstone of the Trinity revealed in the Christian message is the full divinity of the Son, of God with us, of the Word made man. There is a Trinity only if Christ is God, as much God as the Father is. Only then are we set free. We are not set free *from* our human nature, our human matter, or human history. We are not summoned to the rarified zone of pure ethereal and spiritual realities. What is set free is our nature, our matter, our history.

Thus Athanasius, the great opponent of Arianism, was aware that the total destiny of man depended on the question of Christian revelation and the degree of its influence. If the incarnate Word, the Word made truly man, was truly God, then we would not have to look for the Absolute outside of our human condition. As he put it, our flesh is "Verbified."

Carrying on the work of Nicea, Epiphanius offered this explanation: "The Lord Jesus Christ, Son of God, uncreated, consubstantial with the Father . . . for love of mankind and for our salvation came down and was made flesh. That is to say . . . he was made man . . . That is to say, he took on man totally: soul, body, intelligence, and everything that pertains to a human being." And Athanasius goes on to stress the breath and scope of the human totality which this implies: ". . . not in the way in which he inspired, spoke, and worked through the prophets, but by making himself completely and perfectly man . . . because the Lord Jesus Christ is one and not two . . . who suffered in his flesh and rose to heaven in his very body . . . who will come in his body in glory to judge the living and the dead, and his kingdom will have no end (Denz. 13). There is only one explanation for the insistence that pervades this statement. Its author is aware that he is formulating something of decisive importance for human existence in its totality—right down to its biological basis.

So when the creed reminds us that the Word was "begotten" and not created, the Church is condemning every trace of escapist dualism in us. It is condemning all our efforts to oversimplify things by making sharp separations. It is condemning ascetic separations between body and spirit, functional separations between temporal concerns and eternal concerns, between sacred concerns and profane concerns. It is condemning juridical separations between the realm of temporal jurisdiction and the realm of spiritual jurisdiction—with its casuistry of "mixed questions," prudent juxtapositions, and pastoral weights and measures.

The formula "begotten, not made" signifies that Christian revelation ushers man into the one and only task that goes to make up his entire vocation (GS 22), into the one and only task wherein he will encounter God's revelation as a guide for his creative and liberative activity.

Admittedly no one today explicitly relates his attitudes to the dogmatic expression of the Trinity that was propounded by Arianism. But we can say that the image we fashion of God today, like that earlier one, is in large measure a reflection of underlying attitudes whereby we seek to dispense ourselves from the task of being human beings.

There is in all of us a trace of the crowd mentality that fashions for itself an image of God which will facilitate the inevitable historical options. And this God has all the basic characteristics of the Arian God.

There is something more. It is said that Constantine convened the Council of Nicea in the hope that it would reach a solution which, if not totally Arian, would at least be composed of some Arian elements. It seems he saw a more secure support for his imperial authority in Arianism than in orthodox Christianity. Why?[10]

We have already mentioned the Manichaean basis of the Arian deviation. Well the fact is that it is one of the constants in human societal conduct. Reducing God and value to heaven[11] and the human in history to earth proves to be a facilitating norm for conduct when one can establish the instrument with which God vertically communicates his guidelines on value[12] to the lower realm. In other words: when one can pinpoint the values to be cherished and the actions to be performed without having to go through the work of interpreting the horizontal values that history proposes, then a large part of man's difficulty in orientating himself in societal existence disappears. Man is mutilated by this approach, of course, but he finds his mutilation to be convenient for himself.

To really answer this question, however, we must go even further. Simple and ready integration into a given society requires that the person carry out certain functions regularly and easily. These functions presuppose options and choices. In general, they presuppose that the person is in accord with the fundamental values of this concrete form of living together in society. On the individual level, they presuppose that the person will unhesitatingly orient his activity to fulfill the expectations embodied in the function that each one carries out in the social mechanism.

In all this man desires two things. He does not want to abdicate his human dignity and be turned into a robot. And he does not want to critically oppose the society on which he depends. How can he achieve both goals? He can do so by attributing to himself and to his ego values that in reality come to him from above, from a super-ego. And the most satisfactory way of identifying and justifying this super-ego is to picture it as God. But this God is a God who establishes an order from outside of history; to it must be subordinated all the values that present themselves as human, historical, and relative. Every incarnate value is subordinated to a nonincarnate value.

Now if Arianism was the true Christianity then, by virtue of his function, the emperor represented the order subordinate to God. If Athanasius and his party were right, then God spoke from within history and the emperor became merely one more element of this history. He too was subject to the interpretation of "the signs of the time."[13] So we can say that the best defense of the established social order resides in the Manichaeism that was the basis of the Arian God.

Here is how it operates in the sociopolitical realm. When a new social structure appears as a possible substitute for the prevailing one, one must assume that the first task will be to "desacralize" the existing order.[14] On the mass level the existing order is defended, not by comparing it intellectually and critically with other possible models, but by the irrational mechanism of vertically declaring that the existing structures and values are sacred.

This self-defense put up by the existing political and social structure then leads to a religious devaluation of the intellectual function. By this we do not mean some specific level of culture and education on a rather high level. We are referring to a capacity that exists in every class and culture: the capacity not to take the habitual for granted, the capacity to stay open to critical questioning from the Absolute which summons us from within the mixed, ambiguous realities of history.

Now this critical capacity, directed toward the social structure, is not subjected to criticism in turn. Instead it is considered irreligious *a priori*. And because the new plans for society clash with this type of motivation and justification, they explicitly attack the religious foundation of the conservative mentality. In reality they are thereby attacking a distorted form of Christianity.

Authentic and *orthodox* Christianity goes directly against any such Manichaeism. It values man's intelligence applied to history because it is there, and nowhere else, that the definitive revelation of God took place; and because it is there, and nowhere else, that this revelation will continue to penetrate deeper and grow clearer.

On the other hand, the search for security at any price will lead to the absolutization and, at present, the sacralization of total and simplistic options. As Richard Hofstadter points out: "One reason why the political intelligence of our time is so incredulous and uncomprehending in the presence of the right-wing mind is that it does not reckon fully with the essentially theological concern that underlies right-wing views of the world."[15] This mentality

> is essentially Manichaean; it looks upon the world as an area for conflict between absolute good and absolute evil,[16] and accordingly it scorns compromise (who would compromise with Satan?) and can tolerate no ambiguities. It cannot find serious importance in what it believes to be trifling degrees of difference: liberals support measures that are for all practical purposes socialistic, and socialism is nothing more than a variant of Commun-

ism which as everyone knows, is atheism . . . It cannot think, for example, of the cold war as a question of mundane politics—that is to say, as a conflict between two systems of power that are compelled in some degree to accommodate each other in order to survive—but only as a clash of faiths.[17]

It is highly interesting to set over against this *theological* description of the conservative mentality one of the most radical *political* teachings of John XXIII in *Pacem in terris*: "Again it is perfectly legitimate to make a clear distinction between a false philosophy of the nature, origin, and purpose of men and the world, and economic, social, cultural, and political undertakings, even when such undertakings draw their origin and inspiration from that philosophy" (n. 159).

The encyclical tells us that it is perfectly legitimate to make such distinctions. But the Church will continually fail to do this in confronting events so long as it does not, at the same time, question the idea it holds about God and his incarnation; so long as it does not pay heed to its decision to be faithful to its own message, no matter what this may cost in terms of its political position or its power on the mass level.

NOTES TO CHAPTER FOUR

1. However, this is only one aspect of the thought of Origen, bearing witness to the indecision of an era. To do more justice to Origen, and even more to show the vacillation of the whole Christian community, we quote this conclusion drawn by A. Ehrhard in *Urkirche und Frühkatholizasmus* (cited by Schmaus, *Theologia Dogmática, op. cit.*, p. 376): "Origen's doctrine of the Logos represents a decisive step forward by comparison with that of his predecessors. But his doctrine has two features. One affirms quite clearly the full divinity of the Logos and Son of God. The other tends to consider him as a secondary God, as an intermediary member between the uncreated and the created." Neither should one forget that it was apparently Origen who invented the formula *homo-ousios* ("consubstantial") that was later adopted at Nicea.

2. When the popes must confront heresies directly, we note both the firmness of their faith and the difficulty and confusion they have in expressing themselves. They lack concepts, words, categories. The two popes who followed directly at the start of the third century faced a burgeoning Modalism and an incipient Subordinationism. They condemn both doctrines and speak of a one that is two. But they cannot say two *what;* they speak of two who are one single "thing." They find no other word but *thing* to express the unity, the condition of identicalness, between the Father and the Son. On the Pre-Nicene Fathers see Schmaus, *Theología Dogmática, op. cit.*, p. 373.

3. At the beginning of the nineteenth century a Chilean theologian was in exile in Europe. He was Manuel Lacunza, a member of the then disbanded Society of Jesus. He wrote the following words about the "new heaven," which

together with the "new earth" forms the perduring horizon of Christian hope. The literary and theological style of his book is that of his age, but its content is astoundingly current and topical today (*La Venida del Mesías in gloria y magestad: Observaciones de Juan Josaphat Ben Ezra, hebreo cristiano, dirigidas al sacerdote Cristófilo*, (London: Charles Wood, Fleet Street, 1816).

The master and his pupil are discussing heaven. The pupil asks where heaven will be located physically, besides being extended throughout the universe:

> My friend, I will tell you unreservedly this specific, real, and physical place that you ask for so insistently. The court of the Supreme King and the unifying center of this great kingdom will undoubtedly be forever located in some specific place or in one of the innumerable orbs that go to make up the universe . . . But which will be the most privileged orb of all? None other, Christophilus, in my humble opinion, than this very planet on whose surface we dwell. It will forever be the one most attended, frequented, and honored by God and all his creatures; and hence the most glorious and happy place at least in terms of accidental and secondary glory, which can hardly be small after the universal resurrection. I can almost hear you exclaiming: "This is a hard saying. Who can believe it?" Our miserable planet which the Lord cursed, our vale of tears and sickness and sadness and iniquitous corruption: will it one day be the court and unifying center of the whole kingdom of God and the vast kingdom of heaven?
>
> Yes, my friend, so it will. There is no reason why you should be surprised by this proposal, which far from being opposed to Sacred Scripture or right reason, is safeguarded and stoutly confirmed by both. Here briefly are the reasons that militate in favor of our planet over all others. Firstly, the God-Man Jesus Christ, our Lord, or the Supreme King who is the "universal heir through whom and for whom all things exist," is of this very same earth "which God entrusted to man's hands." Here he became man, though being God. Here he united himself intimately and indissolubly with our poor, infirm, vile nature. Here he "emptied" himself, taking the form of a servant, fashioned in a human form and acting as a human being. Here he was born "of the Virgin Mary . . . of the house of David according to the flesh." Here he preached and taught and died. Here he suffered the greatest affront and the most undeserved disgrace that has ever been witnessed, dying naked on an infamous cross as one of the most wicked of men: "And he was counted as a criminal." So here it is fitting as well that his full honor be completely restored. Here ought his innocence be made manifest eternally, along with his justice, his goodness, his infinite dignity, and everything else that can be included under the term: God-Man.
>
> Is it not fitting for God that his infinite grace and goodness and grandeur and magnificence should abound and superabound on this same globe where "the Word was made flesh," where he "emptied himself," where he "was crucified, died, and was buried"? (IV, 418–29).

4. See the dialogue in Luke 20:1–8: "The priests and lawyers, and the elders with them, came upon him and accosted him. 'Tell us,' they said, 'by what authority you are acting like this; who gave you this authority?' He answered them, 'I have a question to ask you too: tell me, was the baptism of John *from God or from men?*' This set them arguing among themselves: 'If we say, "from

God," he will say, "Why did you not believe him?" If we say, "from men,"
the people will all stone us, for they are convinced that John was a prophet.'
So they replied that they could not tell. And Jesus said to them, 'Then *neither
will I tell you by what authority* I act" (our italics).

In reality the answer that Jesus did not choose to *tell* was being made manifest
in history. Jesus was dispossessing the one who had enslaved humanity in order
to distribute his spoils to humanity itself. See Luke 11:20–22 as well as the
next section of this chapter.

5. The attempt to explain this secret as the progressive discovery of his
own mission clashes with internal criticism of the texts. The latter shows this
"secret" to be a kind of dialectic in which Jesus draws near until his message
and work are made present, and then moves away to prevent his listeners from
assuming too quickly that they know both well and then making religious or
political "use" of Jesus. See CLARIFICATION II in this chapter.

6. Charles Péguy, "Eve," *Cahiers de la Quinzaine,* Dec. 28, 1913.

7. A "draft" document composed by the Latin American Confederation
of Religious points out that the activity of religious communities should be carried
out with the witness of a life that is truly poor: "Poverty, which in its personal
dimension is a real renunciation of all goods to follow Christ, embracing his
own poor and destitute style of life." In consequence, "we must live *evangelical
poverty* . . . ridding ourselves of anything and everything that is not the indispensable minimum for life, living as the most disinherited of the area . . . "

It is not for us to say whether this counsel is timely. What is not valid in
it is the recourse to "evangelical poverty," that is, to the example of Christ.
The poverty of Christ was a relative and ambiguous value, if it is taken independently of his concrete mission. An artisan of Nazareth was practically a man
of the lower middle class in a world where millions and millions of people
were slaves, and where they were sold and used and destroyed as such. In
fact Jesus did not live "as the most disinherited" of his country or epoch. But
that does not mean we ought to choose the social class today that would correspond to his either. To say it once again: What we are supposed to do today
is not decided beforehand in heaven, nor even from the letter of the Gospel.

8. Much ink has been spilled by people trying to pinpoint this fatal sin
among the gamut of sinful acts. The most simplistic identification was made
by Pope Leo the Great in Sermon LXXV, when he attributed the blasphemy
against the Holy Spirit to the Macedonian heretics who denied his divinity.
In reality what the New Testament says about sin is that any and every human
act can be pardoned if the person repents of it. When Jesus makes a distinction
between what is pardonable and what is not in people's attitudes toward him,
he is trying to make clear to people what the real opposition to him is in general
terms. And that, without calling into doubt man's capacity to repent of it and
obtain pardon.

9. The Medellín Conference points this out in positive terms: "For all of
us who possess the first fruits of the Spirit, we too groan inwardly as we wait
for our bodies to be set free. God has raised Christ from the dead, and therefore
also, all those who believe in him. Christ, actively present in our history,
foreshadows his eschatological action not only in the impatient zeal of man
to reach total redemption but also in those conquests which, like prophetic
signs, are accomplished by man through action inspired by love. Just as Israel
of old, the first People (of God), felt that saving presence of God when he delivered

them from the oppression of Egypt . . . so we also, the new People of God, cannot cease to feel his saving passage" (Medellín, Introduction to the final documents, nn. 5–6; the documents of the Medellín Conference are available in English translation, under the title *The Church in the Present-Day Transformation of Latin America in the Light of the Council*, 2 volumes, from the Latin American Bureau of the United States Catholic Conference, Washington, D.C. Where possible, their translation is used now in the volumes of this series. For the text cited here, see II, 48–49.)

We do not distort this text if we carry it through to its most obvious conclusions: Israel did not know God *except from within* a process of liberation which God guided and in which the Israelites *collaborated* by the total commitment of their lives.

10. In a very suggestive article ("La Trinidad: problema político," in *Mensaje* 176, January-February 1969, 27–30), Julio Vidaurrazaga agrees with E. Peterson (*Der Monotheismus als politische Forme*) that "it is not by chance that Arianism found support from the autocratic emperors at the end of the empire" (p. 28, footnote 1).

For all that, we do not feel that its subordination of the Son to the Father was the decisive element in this support. We feel it was the logic of thought and attitude that served as the basis for this subordination: i.e., the attempt to decide the historical reality through some type of "divine right," independently of historical evaluation and criticism.

11. And presumably *liberty* as well. There seems to be an obvious parallel between what we say here and the following comments of Gurvitch on the philosophical plane: "We can thus say that we must consider as over the era when man was content to project liberty into a noumenal world, just as the era of monistic determinism is over . . . Any and every conception that projects liberty onto God, substance, necessity, or transcendental reason was merely an *escapist* view. They exiled real liberty to some place where this terrible nuisance could no longer cause any trouble, sending it off with all the honors due to its rank" (Georges Gurvitch, *Déterminismes sociaux et liberté humaine*, Paris: PUF, 1955, p. 10).

12. In his course on the Trinity, Leopoldo Malevez rightly used to point out the similarity between the danger represented by Arianism and the danger represented by the Judaizers in the early apostolic Church. In the latter case the extraworldly and metahistorical Absolute was codified in the *Law*. In line with Christian revelation, Paul re-introduces law within the creative, transforming possibilities of man in history. See in this series Volume I, Chapter V.

13. Hence the desperation and despair of all imperial representatives when faced with a Church that again discovers its task of finding God's decisive word in history. To cite one example among countless others, note the apocalyptic tone of the director of *Visión* when he sees the new social sensitivity of the postconciliar Church: "Now we see that the most ancient monarchy, founded on the rock of the first bishop of Rome, is faced with a subversion of its sacred values. And it is not the silent, scandalized laity but the clergy that is breaking the rigid bounds of its evangelical service. Quite often it is espousing the cause of opening-up to Marxism, with all the ferocity and incontinence that converts traditionally boasted of . . . And they are anti-imperialists, like their comrades, whose slogans they repeat without batting an eye. They are lured on by the spell of not having to speak to the people with the archaic and ingenuous parables

of the Gospel, nor with references to the Fathers of the Church . . . And in these circles where this process is going on, where the Church is being dedicated to resolve here and now the conflicts and sorrows of the human race, on this earth rather than after death, they talk about everything under the sun—especially about Marx, the United States, the blacks, and Vietnam—but very, very seldom about God") Vol. 36, May 9, 1969, p. 17.)

14. In his novel *Man's Hope* (Eng. trans. by Gilbert & Macdonald, New York: Bantam Books Paperback, 1968, Chapter 20, p. 324), André Malraux writes these significant words: "The great intellectual is a man of subtleties, of fine shades, of evaluations; he's interested in absolute truth and in the complexity of things. He is—how shall I put it?—'antimanichaean' by definition, by nature. But all forms of action are manichaean, because all action pays a tribute to the devil; the manichaean element is most intense when the masses are involved. Every true revolutionary is a born manichaean. The same is true of politics, all politics."

It seems to us that two observations should be made with respect to this passage. Firstly, the manichaeism of the revolutionary masses should not hide the fact that manichaeism serves much more often to maintain the masses within the existing order. And in the event of revolution it should be destroyed quite rapidly lest one fall back into immobile, reactionary oversimplifications. Secondly, the "great intellectual" should not make us think of someone with a superior education or culture. It is the intellectual function as such, at whatever level it may be, which opposes oversimplification and exercises historical criticism in accordance with the range and the instruments appropriate to its particular brand of historical responsibility. This will differ, depending on whether one is a labor leader or an atomic scientist, for example.

15. Richard Hofstadter, *Anti-Intellectualism in American Life* (New York: Knopf, 1936), p. 134.

16. See the pastoral letter of Bishop Pérez Serantes, cited in CLARIFICATION II in this chapter.

17. Hofstadter, *op. cit.*, p. 135.

CLARIFICATIONS

I. WAS GOD "NONVIOLENT"?

One of the most common ways of acting with the Manichaean mentality is to take some value that is yet to be achieved and declare it a legal norm or right. Take the case of someone who used a club to gain possession of some merchandise. He will immediately proceed to invoke the *right* of property ownership in order to prevent someone else with a bigger club from taking the merchandise away from him or getting it back. Everyone knows the technique and only a fool would fall for it.

But something that is obvious in a particular situation or over the short run loses its evident nature when it is utilized on an international scale and over long periods of time.

For example, no one denies that the Declaration of the Rights of Man, together with the rights and obligations it sets forth, constitutes an ideal. But one would have to be very naive not to realize that in seeking to convert it into a norm applicable to all *today*, it is being used to defend those who first—and by other means—were able to arrive at the point of declaring something to be a right which for others is only an ideal.

And that is how Good and Evil, thus absolutized, are recognized in history. The "good" are those who recognize these rights. The "bad" are those who deny them. In reality, however, where appearances may be quite ambiguous, we discover that this same ideal is alive and well in people who, out of their desire to achieve this ideal, do not want to deprive themselves of the means that will effectively lead to it when the status of right is still to be won.

So true is this that we are confronted with this interesting paradox. The country where human rights have been proclaimed and codified, and where this type of judgment is most deeply rooted,[1] is also the country that has exported thousands of films which glorify the same situation: the hero, if he is to be a real man, must give up the instruments of law and right and let his fate and that of his family depend on the speed of his draw. San Francisco 1948, forgetting the Wild West!

163

We come closer to our theme when we consider that something similar on the plane of absolutization—but this time in the name of the Christian message—took place in the first phase of the so-called "social doctrine" of the Church. It is indisputable that this doctrine was considered to be a demand of justice in the context of developed countries and within the framework of the capitalist system. None of its concrete orientations are, strictly speaking, applicable to a context of under-development. And to say it once again. It is not because the principles of subsidiarity, private ownership of consumer goods and production facilities, etc.,[2] are not Christian ideals; it is because the effort to make them count as "rights" on the periphery of an economic empire, instead of making them serve the cause of the poor, leads us down a blind alley.

Now when any other solution is proposed, we find ourselves confronted with a disembodied absolutization: God is love, *therefore* the Christian is nonviolent, *therefore* he must not make use of violence. To be sure, the content of the Church's most recent social doctrine[3] is not this sort of absolutization. But the interests of those in power and the naive oversimplification of the Christian message converge there.

Was Jesus really a nonviolent person? Did he preach nonviolence—or if you will, passive resistence—as an attitude to be adopted in the face of any and all eventualities?

Our reply here is necessarily the same one it was in the main section of this chapter. Jesus was God *incarnate*. And total, exclusive opposition between love and violence is not historical.

1. The fact is that love and violence are the two opposite poles of any interpersonal relationship. To love is to give something to a person. To do violence is to obtain something from a person. To love is to make that person the center of our action. To do violence is to make that person an instrument for obtaining something.

Pure violence, then, would be egotism: i.e., the total relativizing of others so that they are seen only in terms of one's own advantage. But we say "would be" because in reality we must assume that there are no absolute and universal egotisms. And on the other hand we know, and this is the important point here, that there is no concrete love without violence.

Love progresses. For awhile it progresses in establishing bonds with more and more persons. But in this progress, as the Lord himself says, it moves out from our neighbors: that is, from those nearest to us. The most simplistic solution with respect to our neighbors is to declare them "persons" and to declare all other human persons "things" (i.e., to relativize them) in order to be able to obtain from them what will serve those I consider to be my neighbors. This is the most economic "system" of force.

We have already seen in the main section of this chapter what process I can use to achieve this end. Physical violence is not the only one.

Any and every denial of the unique, central, irreducible worth of each person is a certain violence. To win over people to my projects—of love—it is as effective to use a club as to employ impersonal legislation, a prejudice, or the refusal to proceed further with dialogue on pending questions, until finally I have convinced them.

Hence Teilhard de Chardin is quite right in saying that the process of hominization, founded on love and directed by it, consists in fashioning ever more complex "systems" of love in which each individual person is a center. Progressive "synthesis of centres":[4] that is the direction and thrust of *history* both in the hearts of men of good will and in the Christian message.

2. To become incarnate means to penetrate into this historical condition that affects every human being: every effective love utilizes a certain dose of violence, and progresses by trying to replace this dosage with systems that maintain its efficacy while making more and more use of the history, interests, and creativity of more and more people.

Perhaps we have not reflected often enough on the fact that Jesus, the God-Man, the man for others, presents himself to us in this way. He does not present himself in the guise of some extraterrestrial and inhuman love. We are indulging in silly oversimplifications if we depict him as a nonviolent prototype, or if we challenge this depiction by adverting to the one episode where he drives out the merchants from the temple with a whip.

Let us take as our guide the Gospel of Mark. For this evangelist is much more interested than are the two other Synoptics (Matthew and Luke) in getting as close as possible to the spontaneous, emotional reactions of Jesus.

Now the first and primary feature of Mark's Gospel, noted by all exegetes, is the stress that Jesus puts on what has been called "the messianic secret." Jesus, it seems, does not want to be known and individualized as the Messiah, as "he who is to come." And this, despite the fact that he is continually performing the very deeds that will inevitably lead his spectators to make this identification.

Why?[5] What is going on here? The Gospel of Mark bears witness to a kind of dialectic with respect to the way in which Jesus communicated his message. In a systematic way he first dazzles and attracts people to him, and then moves away from them and puts them at arm's length. For example, he has just fed five thousand people with five loaves of bread and two fishes: "As soon as it was over he made his disciples embark and cross to Bethsaida ahead of him, while he himself sent the people away" (Mark 6:45; no doubt the disciples had no such intention themselves!).

This procedure is even more evident when he is dealing with those whom he helps, cures, liberates, and saves. Followed by a great multitude (Mark 5:31), he goes to the house of the president of one of the synagogues and finds his daughter already dead. He is met by another crowd of relatives, friends, and mourners. He raises the child from the dead and then inexplicably: "He gave them strict orders to let no one hear about it" (Mark 5:43).

We do not have sufficient space here to dwell upon the reasons behind what we feel to be the solution to the problem posed by this disconcerting attitude. So we shall restrict ourselves to a brief summary.

According to the two other Synoptic writers, when the disciples of John the Baptist ask Jesus if he is the one who is supposed to come, Jesus replies by alluding to the works of his to which the crowd can attest: "Go and tell John what you hear and see; the blind recover their sight, the lame walk, the lepers are made clean, the deaf hear, the dead are raised to life, the poor are hearing the good news (Matt. 11:4–5).

Mark does not cite this reply. As he sees it, Jesus was somehow more prudent in the whole matter of letting himself be identified by the wondrous works he performed for the sake of those in need. That, in fact, is the crux of the question.

In order to proclaim a salvation that is supposed "to liberate all men from the slavery to which sin has subjected them—hunger, misery, oppression, and ignorance,"[6] Jesus employed the most obvious and eloquent word of all: deeds. He liberates people in fact. The miracles are not strictly miracles, they are signs. "All liberation is an anticipation of the complete redemption of Christ."[7]

But there is such a basic need and visceral urgency in the blind to see and the lame to walk that the good news cannot help but become violence to a certain degree. Who can "choose"—or even more, "not choose"—the kingdom when it is proclaimed by the solution of the concrete person's most substantive need? And, on the other side of the coin, how can the good news of liberation get through to a person driven by the urgency of his immediate material and corporeal needs, if it does not start off by liberating him from that which is oppressing him more than anything else?

However divine his message may be, however centered it may be around interpersonal love, Jesus nevertheless finds himself forced to play a terribly dangerous[8] game; his message strikes out at the basic, impersonal needs of man. In any process of evangelization there is necessarily a good dose of violence.

Now one may say that this kind of violence is good because it cures rather than destroys. But have we not seen already that the fear of losing one's sight is as "violent" as the desire to recover it, insofar as they are motives behind a person's actions? And furthermore: if a person gives sight to a blind person in connection with his message, does he not refuse it to others?

But Jesus knows that taking this path would turn his message into a mechanical thing, a rite. Hence he must set limits on it, even though they cannot be clearcut and definitive. He must break through this violence. He must leave room in it for reflection, for deeper thought and gratuitousness, for a truly interpersonal relationship.

By the same token Jesus must also violently restrain the desire of the masses to get their hands on his beneficent power. He must do this too in order to create the needed room. So he does: "The leprosy left him immediately, and he was clean. Then he dismissed him *with this stern warning*: 'Be sure you say nothing to anybody' (Mark 1:42-44; our italics).

Here, it seems to us, is the explanation of the dialectic that accompanies his whole ministry: sign and secret. Indeed it is offered by Christ himself in the parable of the sower (Mark 4:16 ff).

3. Violence is shouldered by Jesus by virtue of the very condition he is in: a human being immersed in history. And it shows up even more clearly in his attitudes than it does in the way he brings his message.

As a human being, Jesus turned his life into a labor of love, a concrete labor of love. And, like any human being, he could love all men in theory. But he began by *being sensitive* to the proximity of some people: those close to him.

This love based on closeness and proximity is intimately bound up with violence. First of all, it is a closeness based on truly knowing the personal reality of those who can precisely and explicitly express their personhood to us. No human being can love effectively without setting limits to this nucleus of persons who are really *persons* by virtue of being *near* to us. Only gradually do we come to know others as persons.

Jesus grew in wisdom (*cf.* Luke 2:40). And if he had lived three hundred years, his active and indefatigable love would have led him to know more and more new people as persons in other races and cultures. But as a human being, he had only one life and limited possibilities. However unwittingly, he had to put up with these factors that would condition the efficacy and equilibrium of his love. This conditioning situation opens the doors to personal knowledge of some people and closes it on others—at least for the moment until a new encounter takes place. And among the factors that play an important role in this conditioning are *prejudices*. Our patriotism for example, which binds our love to concrete persons brought close together in a common country, is fashioned not so much out of restrictions as out of prejudices.

There is nothing strange or surprising in the fact that Jesus, a real human being who grew in wisdom, spent his whole life overcoming prejudices: that is to say, holding on to them:

> Almost at once a woman whose young daughter was possessed by an unclean spirit heard of him, came in, and fell at his feet. (She was a Gentile, a Phoenician of Syria by nationality.) She begged him to drive the spirit out of her daughter. He said to her, "Let the children be satisfied first; it is not fair to take the children's bread and throw it to the dogs" (Mark 7:25-27).

How easy it is for us to evade the impact of this passage! To our mind, a Phoenician from Syria and a Martian are scarcely different. But would we not be profoundly shocked if the comparison between children and dogs had been made between Israelites and Americans, or Israelites and Englishmen, or Israelites and Canadians?[9]

Is this not violence, this barrier that discriminates before knowing who a person is, what his personal history is, and what attitudes he holds?

When the possessed gentile of the country of the Gerasenes asks Jesus if he can go with him, Jesus would not allow it and sent him back to his own people (cf. Mark 5:19). God incarnate, the man for others, had to do what every human being has to do. He had to establish limits within which other people would have access to his innermost life. In theory any human being—with his or her personal responsibility, inner creativity, and irreplaceable liberty—could have been a companion of Jesus. But Jesus "appointed twelve as his companions" (Mark 3:13). Starting with them Jesus would go out to look for other persons, and to give them what he had to give: his life and his message.

But right here we also begin to see more clearly the most important factor that establishes violence in the very heart of love: time.

The span of time at his disposal for dialoguing with a person or a group is not unlimited. So there develops a sensitivity to the fact that a dialogue which really got down to the most intimate personal level would simply require too much time. And the resistance of the other party rises to confront the project of a man tied down to time and its limitations: "They had nothing to say; and, looking round at them with anger and sorrow at their obstinate stupidity, he said to the man, 'Stretch out your arm' " (Mark 3:5). On another occasion, "he was taken aback by their want of faith" (Mark 6:6).

Jesus is faced with resistance which he cannot overcome through a truly personal relationship, because of the time allotted to him as a human being. So, like every human being, he must inject into his personal plan and project the measure of violence and impersonal action which love requires to be as effective as possible. Not even he can fashion a synthesis in which each and every man is a center.

Hence he must judge people en masse, which is an obvious form of violence: "Isaiah was right when he prophesied about you hypocrites in these words, 'This people pays me lip-service, but their heart is far from me' " (Mark 7:6–7). Hence he must give up a dialogue that would go on indefinitely; he must speak so that "they may look and look, but see nothing . . . hear and hear, but understand nothing" (Mark 4:12). He must break off the dialogue at a given moment lest he renege on his mission and his project of love: "With that he left them, re-embarked, and went off" (Mark 8:13).[10] He must refuse to answer questions (Mark 11:27–33). Finally, he must even go so far as to use physical violence, without any dialogue, on the merchants in the temple (Mark 11:15).

To what end? So that in the bounds of time, and with the powers of his human life, he might be able to get across to us the message that is to serve as our guideline; the message that is meant to orient us in the right direction through the course of history, so that we will look for ways to replace violence with love insofar as new possibilities open up to us.

"Violence is neither Christian nor evangelical."[11] It is the inevitable remnant of the hominization process which makes love possible and which, insofar as it is possible, desires to be replaced slowly and gradually by love. Once again: God does not dictate from outside of history in terms of some love-hate dichotomy. He lived both, indissolubly tied together in his incarnation. And he taught to give us life, so that love might guide and correct and eventually overcome violence. When the God who is Love became man, he revealed himself as love in history. And, like any and all love in history, it sought fulfillment in the best possible proportion between its two inescapable components: violence and personal acknowledgement.[12]

II. TWO LATIN AMERICAN EXAMPLES

Here we should like to bring up two examples of judgments made from within the Church—in actual fact, by the ecclesiastical hierarchy—about new sociopolitical realities in Latin America. We feel that they can help us to appreciate how God plays a role in them, thanks to the disembodied or disincarnate idea of him one has.

The first example is closer to us in time. It was the time when Cuban Christians were faced with the task of knowing and deciding what to think—and then what to do—with respect to Castro's revolution when he had just seized power.

We have no data to suggest that the hierarchy asked the faithful to judge, first and foremost, what type of society he was setting up or desired to set up in the country. On the contrary, even before Fidel Castro had declared himself to be a Marxist-Leninist (which itself would not have exempted people from the critical judgment alluded to above either),[13] we find the following guidelines in a pastoral letter of Bishop Pérez Serantes. They are a typical example of the mechanisms employed:

> The struggle has not exactly started between Washington and Moscow, the two formidable military powers that meet each other face to face with death-dealing arms such as the world has never seen or dreamed of before. If it were this, and Washington were not flanked by Christians, the battle would be considered lost. The battle is really going on between Rome and Moscow, and Rome could lose it only if the Christians were to cease being the vigorous leavening of the dough. Moscow could only win this battle sooner or later if its opponents, *the forces of Rome and its closest allies*, were to lay down their arms, the Decalogue, the sacraments, and prayer . . . [or] to desert the ranks of Christ.[14]

Leslie Dewart makes these remarks by way of conclusion:

> For the Universal Church the problem posed by the history of the Cuban
> revolution is not, I believe, whether the Cuban hierarchy was prudent or
> not in allowing its voice to become discredited. It is more important to consider
> whether the Cuban Church was ready to meet *social and political change of
> any radical sort*. But recent Cuban history raises for Catholics everywhere
> an even more basic problem: How did the Cuban Church come to so conceive
> itself and its relations to the secular world that the question whether the
> revolution was or was not communist became the only matter worth judging?
> (our italics)[15]

We feel that we can answer that last question by referring the reader to
what we have been saying about our idea and vision of God.

However, we do not want to close the door on this issue without
seeing how two other observers, from very different religious viewpoints,
pose what we might call "the Cuban challenge" to the reflection of Christians and to our struggle against our own idols—a struggle that certainly
will not end with us.

We mentioned earlier that a more orthodox idea of God cannot
be dissociated from another search: i.e., how to overcome our
improverished and socially compromised conception of the "private"
realm. Well one Christian, Charles Rivière, had this to say about the
reality of Cuba in *Etudes*:

> To be a *revolutionary* is essentially to open oneself up to the rest of mankind.
> This implies a profound conversion . . . How seriously this profound conver-
> sion is desired can be seen from the insistence with which young people
> are taught the idea that separately they cannot forge the best possible future,
> that they must pave the way for it by a common effort, that they must
> fashion a joint future by each person putting all his capabilities at the disposal
> of his comrades and his country . . . This anxiety to stimulate the participation
> of each individual in all initiatives is simultaneously accompanied by a sum-
> mons to a sense of dignity and responsibility, awakening people to take
> cognizance of the creative power of the masses.[16]

Now there is no doubt that lack of information, or observation of other
facts even with emphasis on those mentioned by Rivière, could lead
the reader to form a different judgment on the overall reality of Cuba.
But it seems to us that one thing is undeniable: the kind of things
that Rivière observed, however much they may be intermingled or coun-
terbalanced by other things, present us with a reality which requires
the Christian—the person deeply committed to the Trinitarian God—to
form a value-judgment that is much more serious and complex than
the atrocious oversimplification embodied in the aforementioned pastoral letter. And such oversimplification is not exhausted by that one
letter.

This is all the more important in the light of another fact. Scarcely
had the new social reality been implemented in Cuba when the tendency
to oversimplify and absolutize its gains showed up, was noticed, and was

criticized—at least to some degree—by the revolution itself. One can point, for example, to Castro's repeated allusions to the oversimplistic dogmatism of many followers—revolutionaries by definition, conservatives in fact.

The simplistic judgment of the Cuban reality by the aforementioned pastoral letter, uttered "in the name of God," contrasts sharply with the observations of a Christian such as Rivière. It also contrasts sharply with views formed about the Cuban reality from a non-Christian angle. Here is what Michel Bosquet writes in *Le Nouvel Observateur*:

> I ask myself: Would one have to have received a certain kind of Catholic education to carry the rejection of capitalism so far, to believe so passionately that *Good* can overcome *Evil*, and will, by the power of example alone? Apparently not. Because Che, who was never a Christian (in contrast to Fidel), said that one of the fundamental aims of Marxism was to bring about the disappearance of individual interest as a psychological motivation . . . *To convince by the Good*. That could well be the slogan of this curiously Christian revolution in a country that was never deeply Christianized.[17]

Is it possible that these questions are of interest to everyone except Christians, precisely because the latter know from the start that there can be no common ground between the God they worship and the formal denial of that God by official Marxism in Cuba?

Now we must return to another question posed by Leslie Dewart because there are those who believe that this problem does not arise, or does not become an issue, except in the confrontation with Marxism. Is the Church ready to meet *social and political change of any radical sort*?

Our second example, which dates back further, is instructive here. Back in 1945 Juan Domingo Perón first presented himself as a candidate for the presidency of Argentina. The hierarchy of the Catholic Church advised the faithful that voting was an obligation. Then it went on to offer the following guidelines:

> Among the various candidates or slates that are acceptable from a Catholic point of view, one must vote for those who, in conscience, seem more apt to procure the greater good of religion and the country . . . When all the candidates or slates are unacceptable from the Catholic point of view, one must vote for the least unacceptable.

Now however much we may be suspicious of the phrase "Catholic point of view," up to this point the statement does summon the Christian to make a critical analysis of historical realities: not only to look for the greater good but also to try and determine the lesser evil. But this whole critical effort is wiped out when it runs into vertical principles that point out limits which derive directly from the religious realm through the intermediary of the Church. Despite what was said above:

> No Catholic can . . . vote for candidates who write the following principles into their platforms: (1) separation of Church and state; (2) suppression

of religious oaths and of words in our Constitution that invoke the protection of God . . . (3) laicization of the schools; (4) legal divorce.[18]

Why—or better, how—do these four points escape the work of relative evaluation and become absolute categories? What idea of God lies hidden underneath a value-system which would logically lead the Christian—in the case where only one candidate maintained the status quo with respect to these four points—to vote for him even if it would mean disaster, exploitation, and injustice for the country?

There is no concrete judgment of Perón in that. What interests us here is to show that there was no judgment or evaluation of his characteristic features. Peron came and went, one more episode in the relations between Church and state—a fairly typical episode of Church-state relations in Argentina. And we can rephrase Dewart's question in terms of Perón: How did the Church come to so conceive itself and its relations to the secular world that the question whether these four points were or were not maintained became the only matter worth judging?

Medellín sees redemption and salvation embodied in Christ, who came "to liberate all men from the slavery to which sin has subjected them—hunger, misery, oppression, and ignorance, in a word, that injustice and hatred which have their origin in human selfishness." In doing this, it is certainly uttering an implicit criticism of the conception of God as savior that gave rise to the document cited above. But we must realize that if this criticism is not explicated in a clearer and more systematic way on the pastoral level, the existing notion of God is going to be stronger and more decisive in a given concrete case than any vague, general recommendation.

III. POLITICAL AWARENESS AND THE GOSPEL

According to what Christ says in the Gospel, the "signs" of the time form something like the human *locus* or locale where the word of God can be *heard* and *spoken*.

That fact is that if Jesus was able to speak a language that made sense to his listeners, it was precisely because they "knew how to interpret the signs of the times"; for what Jesus said was nothing more nor less than *one* interpretation of these same signs, and not a message dropped vertically down from above (i.e., a "sign from heaven").

Thus whether the word of God is spoken among human beings or not depends on a twofold conditioning of the pastoral work of the Church, that is, of the community that has received this word to transmit it to history. Let us look at these two factors that condition the Church's pastoral work.

1. The whole question of the relationship between evangelization and literacy is not new. But today it has taken on greater depth as its whole scope has become clearer.[19]

For a long time, and even today in many areas, teaching people to read and write was made an almost mechanical process of learning signs. In this frame of reference, the illiterate person was and is regarded as an inferior being (an ignoramus) who is to be brought to a different cultural level by training him in a visual and manual technique that would permit him to read and write.

This conception of literacy-training has been severely criticized for its dehumanized and dehumanizing character. First of all, the illiterate person—and we are referring to adult illiterates in this section—is not a complete ignoramus. He has his own culture, training, and experiences. Frequently we find he possesses a profound wisdom that cannot be overlooked or scorned. His illiteracy does not stop him from working, creating, establishing personal relationships, loving, fighting, etc. To define a human being exclusively in terms of his illiteracy is a grave error in perspective that makes the solutions distorted.

In this distorted framework, the teacher (or teachers) comes from "outside," bringing along a cultural world that is alien to the prospective pupil. Besides teaching signs and words, the teacher transmits a world of values, beliefs, principles, and images which are not those of the illiterate group. Its "world" is relegated to the background, where it exists vaguely alongside the juxtaposed universe. The result is personality dissociated in the pupil. He is "alienated" in another world that is not his own by birth, upbringing, or personal creation. So his value-system and cultural forms remain submerged under a sea of silence. And even when the teachers belong to the same milieu, they arrive with a "technique" for teaching pupils to read that does not incorporate the pupil's vital interests. So the same phenomenon is reproduced in broad outlines.

There is another aspect of the problem that is highly important. These illiterate people make up the world of the poor and the oppressed. The cultural world transmitted to them by literacy-training is, in many cases, the world of the society which is oppressing them. And this does not necessarily imply a proselytizing attitude on the part of the teacher. An example may clarify what we have been talking about. In Chile, where they are in the process of putting through an agrarian reform, the peasant who has not gone through a process of consciousness-raising (or "conscientization," to use the word coined in Brazil) tends to reproduce on his plot of land the same situation that he lived through on the large landed estates. He tends to turn himself into a landlord, and his employees into serfs. This is due to the fact that the world in which he has lived his life presents this type of structure as the "normal" thing, as "the way things are supposed to be." A process of literacy-training that is not incorporated into a process of consciousness-raising tends to maintain the prevailing social structures. (We shall see more about this in what follows.)

Thus today literacy-training tends to be viewed in a very different contextual framework. The starting-point is to consider the illiterate pupil as a person with his own cultural baggage which the educator must recognize and respect and comprehend. This starting point determines the basic attitude of the educator: he must allow himself to be educated by the pupil. The teacher is not someone who comes to talk; he is someone who comes primarily to listen. It is the logical attitude for anyone who comes from afar or outside. One must make it possible for the new world—with its values, appreciations, and language—to penetrate one's own frontiers by empathy. And this can only be achieved by an attitude of receptivity, which in turn is composed of a spectrum of related attitudes: Here are a few:

a) Esteem and respect for the cultural world of the pupil. If I regard the other person simply as an ignoramus because he lacks certain elements of expression, I am poles apart from an attitude of receptivity.

b) An anticolonialist attitude. This means that I am firmly resolved not to impose my own culture or my own personal outlook on reality, but to collaborate in the elaboration of a more human vision that will be the work of others.

c) Familiarity with a series of "techniques" (understanding this term in a very generic sense) that will permit me to realize this authentic communication. Today the sciences that deal with man have calibrated an instrumentation, in both the psychological and social fields, that makes this task feasible.

In this way the process of literacy-training is situated within a process of consciousness-raising. It becomes the way for permitting man to speak his creative word, which is action and reflection on that action, critical viewing of his own reality and also critical efforts at transforming it. Within this context, literacy-training is the teaching of a visual and manual technique that enables the pupil to write down his creative word (which only he can express), and to read other visions of the world in a critical way.

To put it in other words: it is not possible to give the gospel as it really is, that is, as a liberative interpretation of history, without making man a *subject* of that history rather than an object of it. Without this process of consciousness-raising, the task of evangelizing and catechizing runs the risk of being a cultural invasion: i.e., the learning of new words that do not correspond to life's realities, and mere conceptual games that leave intact old alienations stemming from fear, enslavement, and ideology. Needless to say, we have not always successfully avoided that risk.

This intimate and necessary connection between evangelization and political conscientization—not in the sense of taking party sides but in the sense of leading man from being an object to being a subject of his own *polis*—destroys any false hope of having an "aseptic" evangelization.

An evangelization committed to man's liberation is deeply tied up with the new form of literacy-training: i.e., one incorporated within a process of consciousness-raising. This new form of literacy-training, as a process of liberation, possesses an educational technique in the service of man that is completely similar to those of the evangelization process. We should not even think of two different processes, but of one single movement for the gradual liberation of man within which evangelization is effected.

Perhaps one of the most difficult but fruitful choices for the Church in Latin America to make would be for it to decide whether it should or should not leave aside conscientization at this critical moment, on account of its political implications, and proceed directly to the kind of evangelization of adults that is open to it in the sporadic and superficial contacts occasioned by "religious" mandates: baptisms, marriages, funerals, etc.

2. Man will encounter the living God only *in* man, *in* his history. He will not encounter him in the skies or in the beyond. On the other hand, however, he will not manage to lay hold of the living God solely by *starting from* the history of man. God reveals himself *in* history but he does not surface *from* history.

This revelation is a light shed on history, a word spoken somewhere about history. Now this light and this word are not intemporal or of the present day. They come to us from a past. They speak a specific mental idiom to us, utilizing categories, images, and stereotypes of another age.

The Church as a whole is a community which, under the guidance of the Holy Spirit, should unceasingly be about the work of creatively translating this message, *spoken* in different circumstances, in terms of the problems that are posed today by human beings who are subjects of history. All the functions and structures of the Church, from the magisterium to the sacraments, from the papacy to the laity, have no other meaning than this work of translation.

For a long, long time this task was not felt to be necessary. The elements of the Church were communicated as things that were intemporal and repeatable; they were not harmonized or related to the process whereby man turns himself into a subject of societal life. As a result we see a counter-position at work today: in many circles people tend to make a flat identification between conscientization and evangelization.

Today we find an emphasis on re-examining and revising one's life-style, as *the* method for Christian community, which seems to ignore the fact that the Christian receives a message which transcends the situation in which he currently finds himself. Consequently people attempt to identify all the other functions of the Church with the lay function, so that the former may speak the language of real living human beings. A certain mystique of the priest, as a man with a job distinct from his priestly functions and enshrined in a family, does indeed evince the correct realization that the functions of the priest have been detached from human problems. But it seems to presume rather naively that this was due to ignorance of the price of things (for example), and not to the fact of entertaining an idea of God which makes him the representative of an alien world. By the same token, this same notion of God—as experience proves—produces the same incapacity for Christian dialogue with reality in those who have families and lay jobs.

A Christian community centered around the creative work of the laity might well experience the inadequacy of an acquaintance with the Christian message that is reduced to the demands now being presented. It might once again attribute real value to the ecclesial functions that have a more direct relationship with the transcendental aspect of the message, because the latter would no longer presume to be valid by itself in isolation. Once clericalism was overcome the clergyman, far from disappearing from the scene, would regain his true significance and importance.

NOTES

1. *Cf.* Leslie Dewart, *Christianity and Revolution: The Lesson of Cuba* (New York: Herder & Herder, 1963), pp. 249–250 and *passim*; also Richard Hofstadter, *Anti-Intellectualism in American Life* (New York: Knopf, 1963), pp. 134 ff.

2. We understand private ownership of the means of production in the sense of an insured responsbility, not a right to use and abuse. The reader will find an explanation of this in my article, "Social Justice and Revolution," in *America* (New York), April 27, 1968, pp. 574 ff.

3. The encyclicals *Mater et Magistra*, *Pacem in terris*, and *Populorum progressio*.

4. See note 15 at the end of the main section of Chapter II in this volume.

5. One fashionable interpretation in the school of liberal Protestantism at the end of the last century was to presume simply that Jesus himself was not aware, at the start, of being the Messiah; that he acquired this awareness as his listeners did—and partly thanks to them—through the deeds he performed. Even prescinding from other theological criteria, the problem with this hypothesis "in spite of" what the evangelist says is that it cannot possibly be verified in any way. Mark, who writes from within the faith of an existing community, presents a Jesus who is *always* conscious of his mission, but who *always* demands an almost improbable secrecy. Not only after the prediction of his passion (Mark 8:37) but even later, in fact after the transfiguration episode, he again asks that it be kept secret (Mark 9:9). What is more, Mark returns repeatedly to the problem of this strange mandate and relates it, not so much to Jesus, as to the disposition of his listeners.

6. Medellín Conference, Document on Justice, n.3; Eng. trans., II, 58; see note 9 in the main article of this chapter. See also GS 22.

7. Medellín Conference, Document on Education, n.9; *op. cit.*, II, 100.

8. "Kingdom," a word that seems harmless and antiseptic to us, was as explosive a term in those circumstances as "revolution" is today. For having employed this term, which is ambiguous but also capable of attracting people to his message, Jesus will die (*cf.* Matt. 27:37).

9. Later Paul will rightly say that Christ's message puts an end to all differences between Israelites and non-Israelites, freemen and slaves, men and women, in God's eyes. The barriers that divide human beings do not exist for the new reality borne by Christ. But this is what ought to be, and that is one thing. Something else again is the human condition, which causes us all to move only slowly and gradually toward discovering the personal and unique worth of beings who are distant from us in culture, geography, and ideology.

10. On a similar occasion Matthew employs an even harsher word which does not mean "leave" or "depart" so much as "leave in the lurch."

11. Address of Pope Paul VI in Bogotá; cited by Medellín, Document on Peace, n. 15, *op. cit.*, II, 78.

12. "Every man, be he Christian or not, bears violence within himself. Only the use of it is different . . . No one can know this pathway and journey from the starting line (Roger Schutz, Prior of Taizé, *Violence des pacifiques*, Les Presses de Taizé, 1968, pp. 9–10).

13. But the very fact that, more than a year before Fidel Castro declared himself to be a Marxist-Leninist, he was already tied up with Moscow without any reservations is itself highly significant. It shows that not only the mechanism of judging on the basis of labels is at work, but also the more radical mechanism of attaching labels in order to be able to pass judgment; or, if you prefer, to spare oneself the work of judging by making use of a prejudice.

14. Cited in Leslie Dewart, *Christianity and Revolution: The Lesson of Cuba*, *op. cit.*, p. 312. The date of the letter is November 13, 1960.

15. *Ibid.*, p. 180.

16. Charles Rivière on "The Cuban Challenge." The original French can be found in *Etudes*, June-July 1968, pp. 43 ff; Spanish translation in *Perspectivas de Diálogo*, n. 30, pp. 291–297.

17. Michel Bosquet, "Fidel Castro est-il un fou?" *Le Nouvel Observateur*, February 28, 1968, p. 15.

18. *Cf. Criterio*, n. 923 (November 22, 1945), p. 497.

19. *Cf.* Roberto Viola, "Alfabetización y Catequesis," *Perspectivas de Diálogo*, n. 33 (May 1969), pp. 67–69.

Conclusion

If we try to sum up in one phrase the major themes discussed in this volume, we could say that they represent *a critical approach to the God of occidental society*.

Section I

We have seen that the notion of God stemming from revelation and our interpersonal relations in societal life condition each other mutually. It is certain that divine revelation puts us in contact with truth, and indeed with the Truth—i.e., the absolute truth. But something else is just as certain. In the journey of this truth from its formulation in the Bible and in dogma to our real life and our comprehension of it, the world of human relationships in which we live societally plays a role—not a determining role but a conditioning role.

Since we are not materialists, we have tried to show that an authentic notion of God, or at least a more authentic notion of God, presupposes that we will tackle the possibility of distortion *from both sides*. We will tackle the matter of conscience, allowing it to turn to the revealed word and be judged by the latter. And we will tackle the human or societal "infrastructure," which must be transformed so that man can better glimpse the face of God through it.

This has led us to recall and evaluate the efforts made by the Church in its early centuries to give clear expression to the Christian idea of God and to free its potential richness from obstacles. And we have tried to show that in these efforts in the occident, a decisive role was played by the value accorded to human history, human society, human liberty, and the human world. The fact is that these efforts defended the one and only notion of God that is in accord with man's liberation: that is, the one and only notion of God that is compatible with the possibility of man being really and truly a human being to the full extent of his capacity, and that would entail being a free and creative person in society.

Now it may well be that our criticism of the modern continuations of the old distortions relating to the notion of God has obscured an important and decisive fact: the effort to maintain this dogmatically correct notion of God penetrated the whole history of the occident. And it cannot be accidental that it was in occidental society that a secret force, often logically opposed to a disfigured form of Christianity, posed the most profound problems about history, society, liberty, and the world.

On the other hand we cannot deny that the theoretical deviations analyzed in this volume did not come to an end with the discovery of a correct formulation. Nor can we deny that this was not due solely to poor understanding or defective theory. What happened is that people projected on to God the great limitations of occidental society. And since this is the case, it is obvious that in the occident and its societal life faith cannot be defined by simply opposing it to atheism.

The fact is that when we talk about atheism, we are not talking about *others*. Something much deeper and more disturbing is involved here. If our Christian existence is really authentic, then it must be a continuing journey from atheism to faith.

To put it in a paradoxical and shocking phrase: *atheism is a necessary element of our faith*.

Section II

Sometimes we think that there is nothing between atheism and faith except the affirmation: "I believe in God." The person who makes this statement is a believer; the person who refuses to make it is an atheist.

Family training and the surrounding religious atmosphere have spared many Christians from the decisive moment when a person consciously makes this statement: "I believe in God." Other people, brought up in an atmosphere indifferent or hostile to God, have had to take this step in a free and conscious way. But both we and they often entertain this notion of a believer: he is someone who one day affirmed God's existence with his whole heart, shifted radically from atheism to faith, and henceforth must *defend* the faith he possesses.

Defend it against what? Against an atheism that seeks to destroy it. So every attempt is made, and quite justifiably, to defend the faith against doubts: e.g., against comments and writings that give false reasons for rejecting religious beliefs, and against one's companions whose ridicule and indifference gradually diminishes our enthusiasm as believers and eventually threatens our faith itself.

We certainly must proclaim our faith and defend it in ourselves and the world. But do we ever fully realize that in order to defend it we must *possess it*? Are we sure that the affirmation, "I believe in God," is enough to transport us totally and definitively from atheism to faith?

When we hear people make professions of atheism, there is no doubt that we have often said to ourselves, or heard someone else say: "This atheist is not really denying God but the idea of God that he has. He is refusing to accept a God in league with capitalism, or injustice, or suffering, or needless waste. But that is not what God is really. This man's denial is really more a witness to the existence of a belief in him. Under another name he worships the same God we do, or perhaps even *A God who is more authentic than ours.*"*

But do we ever advert to the opposite side of the same coin? Do we ever realize that we may be operating with a distorted notion of God? Do we ever realize that we may be injecting into our God the base, egotistical values that rule our lives and that are not God at all? Is it not possible that when we say, "I believe," we are making an act of faith in capitalism, injustice, suffering, and egotism?

In the toil of everyday life we often lower God to the base measure of our own life. By a strange quirk of fate he, who made us in his image and likeness, must accept the fate of being turned into our image and likeness through the idea of him that we fashion.

So, harboring this impoverished idea of God, we go out to others and carry our message of faith. We run into atheism and, poor and

---

*Cf. the encyclical *Ecclesiam suam* (Paul VI): The causes of atheism "are obviously many and complex . . . They sometimes spring from the demand for a more profound and purer presentation of religious truth, and an objection to forms of language and worship which somehow fall short of the ideal . . . We see these men serving a demanding and often a noble cause, fired with enthusiasm and idealism, dreaming of justice and progress, and striving for a social order which they conceive of as the ulitmate of perfection" (n. 104).

If this is the case, then atheism as a tendency to deny God is not in *total* contradiction to the faith: i.e., to the acceptance of the authentic countenance of God. To say that atheism, insofar as it denies God, is *ipso facto* a denial of the *true* God is an oversimplification, as Pope Paul VI points out.

For that reason we do not agree with G. Morel when he says that atheism is forced to remain *outside*, for the sake of clarity, when we talk about faith: "For if the word 'atheism' expresses what it signifies in ordinary language, that is, the denial of God's existence, I really do not see how it could purify the meaning of a God whom it considers to be nonexistent" (*Problèmes actuels de religion*, Paris: Aubier, 1968, p. 38).

ignorant creatures that we are, we think that our duty is to defend
the faith we supposedly possess against it. We think that it is our faith
that separates us from others when in fact it is nothing else but our
own incredulity that separates us!

Perhaps now we can begin to appreciate better what atheism is meant
to be for our faith in God's eyes. We now realize that God is a continuing
inner call within our lives toward authentic solutions; toward solutions
that are more difficult, because they do not result from a false, premature
synthesis that sacrifices truth to compromise and leaves us calm and
satisfied in our mediocrity.

God is a continuing summons in our lives to a never-ending search
for authentic solutions, for sincere solutions that are not a mixture of
good and bad but a discovery of the good in all its purity.

But we are not capable of always attaining the good, the whole,
the integral. So God is the unrest in us that does not allow us to be
tranquil and content, that keeps prodding us toward the better course
that remains ahead of us. It is in this unrest, in this anxious desire
to arrive at authentic solutions, pure values, and uncompromised agree-
ments, that we gradually come to know and recognize the God in whom
we believe. As a Spanish poet put it: "I know you, Lord, when I feel
all the desire and yearning that surpasses me. The void of my discontent
contains the broad dimensions of your immensity."

When atheism is sincere and authentic, then, it is precisely the impossibility of seeing God in man's mediocre work and his base compromises.
And when the atheist refuses to adore this God, whom we would like
to involve in our easy solutions and our hypocrisies, we should remember
that nothing evil is compatible with God.

Atheism should continually teach our faith a radical and important
lesson: i.e., *God is above and beyond our mediocrity* in the most pure and
absolute and total value.

When it is a question of God, only sincere discontent and unrest
with the limited effort we put out in his name can assure us that our
faith truly believes in God, rather than in some impoverished idea com-
pounded of our petty deceits and easy bargains.

What separates us from the atheist who is seeking sincerely? *Nothing*.
Speaking to such a man, Augustine put these words in God's mouth:
"*You would not be seeking me if you had not already found me.*" God is already
present in his soul because he is sincerely seeking a God that is not
in league with man's mediocrity and egotism.

If something does separate us from this atheist, it certainly is not
the God in whom we believe, the God who directs his search and ours.
It is the God whom we, who presume to have found him, stop searching

for; the God whose transcendence we cease to feel; the God whom we accommodate to our easy world of convenience and habit. God can then direct almost the same words of Augustine to us, but this time it would be a condemnation: *"If you had found me, you would still be looking for me."* Because a person cannot say he has found God if he stops searching for him. He can only have found a caricature of God.

If the reader now is capable of realizing more clearly that *atheism is a necessary element of our faith*, then this volume will have achieved its aim. For it can be summed up in one brief statement: our notion of God must never cease to retravel the road which runs from atheism to faith.

Appendices

Introduction to the Series

FORMAT AND ORIGIN OF THIS SERIES

We have tried to make it easier for the reader to approach this series by using a coherent format. The essential aspects of our reflection on a given topic are contained in the initial article under each chapter. They are followed by a section entitled CLARIFICATIONS, in which we try to develop and apply more concretely the central lines of thought, to suggest study topics and related issues, and to go over one or more points in detail. Notes are given at the end of each of these two main divisions.

The notes are meant to be useful to the reader rather than to be erudite. Many of them are biblical, indicating other passages in Scripture which complement the thoughts presented or which can be used for related meditation. Instead of citing numerous scholarly works, we have limited ourselves to a few more accessible sources: e.g., the *Concilium* series. Our series was originally intended for a Latin American audience, and their needs were uppermost in our minds.

The type of theological reflection presented here can give rise to different discussion formats: full-length courses, study weeks, and the like. But we actually tested it in a seminar approach, involving intensive sessions of study, discussion, and prayer. It may interest the reader to know how our seminars actually operate.

As far as length of time is concerned, our experiences confirmed the feeling that the busy layman benefits more from short-term seminars in which he is actively involved than from long-term courses in which he is generally passive. So now we try to run seminars of three or four days that coincide with a holiday weekend. The aim is to provide five or six sessions of four hours each in a relatively short space of time. We also stress that enrollment in the seminar implies that the individual is willing to involve himself in it totally, to participate in all the sessions, and to remain until it is over. The seminar is meant to be a total experience, not mere attendance at a series of lectures.

Each four-hour session operates pretty much like this. It begins with a lecture (which is reproduced almost verbatim as the intitial section of each chapter). The lecture lasts about one hour, and at its conclusion one or two questions are proposed to the various study groups (see Appendix III in this volume). But before they move into their discussion groups, the participants are asked to spend a few moments in personal meditation on the questions. In this way they can make an effort to formulate a personal solution, however provisional it might be, to the questions posed.

The various study groups then spend about forty-five minutes or an hour in discussing the questions. There are no more than ten persons in a given group, so that each individual will participate actively in the discussion. Herein lies the essential aim of the seminar itself, for the participants should move on from formulated truths to a truly in-teriorized truth. In other words, the discussion represents a confronta-tion between what they have heard and what they have learned from their real-life experiences; between that which they accepted uncritically as children and adolescents and that which they have put together into a coherent whole as adults.

Thus the questions proposed are not meant to serve as a review of the lecture material. They are meant to foster a great coherence between that which was provided in the lecture and other aspects or facts of Christian experience. To this end, it is highly desirable that the groups be somewhat heterogeneous in makeup, and that their discus-sion be stimulated by a pointed confrontation with things they may have read in the catechism or heard all their life from the pulpit.

It is also highly useful at this point to have the groups make an effort to reach unanimity on their answers and then write them up as a group project. Such a procedure obliges the participants to engage in real dialogue and to respect differences of opinion. When this period is over, the various groups reassemble at a roundtable forum, and each group presents the answers it has formulated. The reply of the group may take one of three forms: a unanimous group response, a set of differing opinions, or a series of questions formulated by the group. It is our feeling that questions worked up by a group are more useful than those which an individual might formulate alone at the end of the lecture.

During the roundtable forum the lecturer comments on the group replies, tries to respond to the questions of the various groups, and then takes up individual questions if he so desires.

The procedure varies for the final hour. Intellectual effort gives way to a period of prayer and recollection that is related to the theme under consideration. It may involve some form of paraliturgical service, or a biblical reading that is not discussed in great detail (see Appendix II in this volume).

This pattern is repeated throughout the course of the seminar. As circumstances permit, the final four-hour session may be dedicated to a review of what has been covered and a discussion of possible concrete applications in the local or parochial sector.

As the reader will see from the text itself, our aim is not to move on to a wholly different topic in each four-hour session. Experience has shown that it is more useful to return to the same few basic ideas over and over again, relating them ever more deeply to real-life problems. It is useful, in this connection, to sum up what has gone before at the start of each session. One practical way of doing this is to refer to conciliar texts that relate to the material in question (see, for example, Appendix I in Volume I and Appendix II in Volume II). While we do not feel that these texts by themselves are enough to encourage this type of reflection, we do find that they are able to shore up and confirm the work already done. For they come from the universal Church gathered together in our day under the special action of the Holy Spirit.

Finally we would point out that this treatment of our notion of God has been preceded by a volume on the Church (Volume I) and a volume on grace (Volume II). It will be followed by a volume on the sacraments (Volume IV) and a volume on sin and redemption (Volume V). Each year a seminar is held on a new topic, and seminars on old topics are held for those who have not yet attended them. In this way we hope to answer the needs of mature persons who are looking for a theology which is equally adult and open to exploring new pathways related to their temporal commitments.

APPENDIX II

A Biblical Tapestry

The biblical texts presented in the first volume of this series served to show how God prepared his people Israel in order to transform it into the New Israel, that is, to Israel as he was educating them. Education and self-manifestation are two sides of one and the same reality. So the reader will not be surprised to find here once again many of the key texts that highlight this biblical education.

I God as Profound Mystery

The biblical image of God does not well up from a process of reasoning about the origin of the universe. Yahweh is a presence that accompanies the people of Israel in the land they inhabit. This limitation is transported back to early humanity in the texts that speak of the period:

> Cain said to the Lord, "My punishment is heavier than I can bear; thou hast driven me today from the ground, and I must hide myself from thy presence. I shall be a vagrant and a wanderer on earth, and anyone who meets me can kill me." The Lord answered him, "No: if anyone kills Cain, Cain shall be avenged sevenfold." So the Lord put a mark on Cain, in order that anyone meeting him should not kill him. Then Cain went out from the Lord's presence and settled in the land of Nod to the east of Eden (Gen. 4:13–16).

God is not deduced by reason; he is encountered. These encounters have characteristics that show up again and again. Yahweh makes himself known from out of the *mysterious,* which becomes *terrible* if profane man transgresses the line of the holy, i.e., the *sacred:*

> Moses was minding the flock of his father-in-law Jethro, priest of Midian. He led the flock along the side of the wilderness and came to Horeb, the mountain of God. There the angel of the Lord appeared to him in the flame of a burning bush. Moses noticed that, although the bush was on fire, it was not being burnt up; so he said to himself, "I must go across to see this wonderful sight. Why does not the bush burn away?" When the Lord saw that Moses had turned aside to look, he called to him out of the bush, "Moses, Moses." And Moses answered, "Yes, I am here." God

said, "Come no nearer; take off your sandals; the place where you are standing is holy ground." Then he said, "I am the God of your forefathers, the
God of Abraham, the God of Isaac, the God of Jacob." Moses covered his
face for he was afraid to gaze on God (Exod. 3:1–6).

In the apparition on Sinai we find a new element. We find that the
line dividing the profane from the sacred is not absolute. *Intermediary*
people (the priests) and *intermediary* things break across it to offer prayer
and worhsip to Yahweh, under certain conditions:

> On the third day, when morning came, there were peals of thunder and
> flashes of lightning, dense cloud on the mountain and a loud trumpet blast;
> the people in the camp were all terrified. Moses brought the people out
> from the camp to meet God, and they took their stand at the foot of the
> mountain. Mount Sinai was all smoking because the Lord had come down
> upon it in fire; the smoke went up like the smoke of a kiln; all the people
> were terrified, and the sound of the trumpet grew ever louder. Whenever
> Moses spoke, God answered him in a peal of thunder. The Lord came
> down upon the top of Mount Sinai and summoned Moses to the mountain-
> top, and Moses went up. The Lord said to Moses, "Go down; warn the
> people solemnly that they must not force their way through to the Lord
> to see him, or many of them will perish. Even the priests, who have access
> to the Lord, must hallow themselves, for fear that the Lord may break
> out against them" (Exod. 19:16–22).

This required "purity" or "holiness," however, is something ritual rather
than something interior. It is attached to things which please or repel
God. Thus animals are divided up into those which are ritually clean
and those which are not:

> The Lord said to Noah, "Go into the ark, you and all your household;
> for I have seen that you alone are righteous before me in this generation.
> Take with you seven pairs, male and female, of all beasts that are ritually
> clean, and one pair, male and female, of all beasts that are not clean" (Gen.
> 7:1–2).

The same thing applies to things and persons that draw near to him,
that are consecrated (i.e., made *sacred*) to him. They are to be anointed
with a special perfume that pleases Yahweh and is reserved for him:

> The Lord spoke to Moses and said: You yourself shall take spices as follows:
> five hundred shekels of sticks of myrrh, half that amount (two hundred
> and fifty shekels) of fragrant cinnamon, two hundred and fifty shekels of
> aromatic cane, five hundred shekels of cassia by the sacred standard, and
> a hin of olive oil. From these prepare sacred anointing oil, a perfume com-
> pounded by the perfumer's art. This shall be the sacred anointing oil. Anoint
> with it the Tent of the Presence and the Ark of the Tokens, the table and
> all its vessels, the lamp-stand and its fittings, the altar of incense, the altar
> of whole-offering and all its vessels, the basin and its stand. You shall consec-
> rate them, and they shall be most holy; whatever touches them shall be
> forfeit as sacred. Anoint Aaron and his sons, and consecrate them to be
> my priests. Speak to the Israelites and say: This shall be the holy anointing

oil for my service in every generation. It shall not be used for anointing
the human body, and you must not prepare any oil like it after the same
prescription. It is holy, and you shall treat it as holy. The man who compounds
perfume like it, or who puts any of it on any unqualified person, shall
be cut off from his father's kin (Exod. 30:22–33).

Even those who draw near to Yahweh experience the terrible side of
his divinity if they introduce something profane into his vicinity. It can
be a simple gesture, as it was in the case of Uzzah:

> They mounted the Ark of God on a new cart and conveyed it from the
> house of Abinadab on the hill, with Uzzah and Ahio, sons of Abinadab,
> guiding the cart. They took it with the Ark of God upon it from Abinadab's
> house on the hill, with Ahio walking in front. David and all Israel danced
> for joy before the Lord without restraint to the sound of singing, of harps
> and lutes, of tambourines and castanets and cymbals. But when they came
> to a certain threshing-floor, the oxen stumbled, and Uzzah reached out
> to the Ark of God and took hold of it. The Lord was angry with Uzzah
> and struck him down there for his rash act. So he died there beside the
> Ark of God (2 Sam. 6:3–7).

To sum up, Yahweh manifests himself as the absolute Lord, pointing
out the line that separates what man is in charge of (i.e., the profane)
from what dominates man (i.e., the sacred). In the latter realm the
only attitude that holds good is obedience to ritual order; even good
intentions cannot save man from the terrible wrath of the divinity.

II God as Moral Providence

The prophets and the book of Deuteronomy express strong criticism
of ritualistic religion:

> I hate, I spurn your pilgrim-feasts;
> I will not delight in your sacred ceremonies.
> When you present your sacrifices and offerings
> I will not accept them,
> Nor look on the buffaloes of your shared-offerings.
> Spare me the sound of your songs;
> I cannot endure the music of your lutes.
> Let justice roll on like a river
> And righteousness like an ever-flowing stream.
> Did you bring me sacrifices and gifts
> You people of Israel, those forty years in
>   the wilderness? (Amos 5:21–25)

The same contrast between ritual cult and righteousness in social relationships shows up in Deutero-Isaiah, even though it comes from a later
era:

> Shout aloud without restraint;
> Lift up your voice like a trumpet.
> Call my people to account for their transgression

And the house of Jacob for their sins,
Although they ask counsel of me day by day
And say they delight in knowing my ways,
Although, like nations which have acted rightly
And not forsaken the just laws of their gods,
They ask me for righteous laws
And say they delight in approaching God.
Why do we fast, if thou dost not seek it?
Why mortify ourselves, if thou payest no heed?
Since you serve your own interest on your fast-day
And make all your men work the harder,
Since your fasting leads only to wrangling and strife
And dealing vicious blows with the fist,
On such a day you are keeping no fast
That will carry your cry to heaven.
Is it a fast like this that I require,
A day of mortification such as this,
That a man should bow his head like a bulrush
And make his bed on sackcloth and ashes?
Is this what you call a fast,
A day acceptable to the Lord?
Is not this what I require of you as a fast:
To loose the fetters of injustice,
To untie the knots of the yoke,
To snap every yoke
And set free those who have been crushed? (Isa. 58:1–6)

But this religious transformation would not be viable if it were not based on a maturing of the reciprocal relationship between the Israelite nation and Yahweh. Between the people and God there exists a mutual choice:

"But if it does not please you to worship the Lord, choose here and now whom you will worship: the gods whom your forefathers worshipped beside the Euphrates, or the gods of the Amorites in whose land you are living. But I and my family, we will worship the Lord." The people answered, "God forbid that we should forsake the Lord to worship other gods, for it was the Lord our God who brought us and our fathers up from Egypt, that land of slavery; it was he who displayed those great signs before our eyes and guarded us on all our wanderings among the many peoples through whose lands we passed. The Lord drove out before us the Amorites and all the peoples who lived in that country. We too will worship the Lord; he is our God." Joshua answered the people, "You cannot worship the Lord. He is a holy god, a jealous god, and he will not forgive your rebellion and your sins. If you forsake the Lord and worship foreign gods, he will turn and bring adversity upon you and, although he once brought you prosperity, he will make an end of you." The people said to Joshua, "No; we will worship the Lord." He said to them, "You are witnesses against yourselves that you have chosen the Lord and will worship him" "Yes," they answered, "we are witnesses" (Josh. 24:15–22).

If God still appears as a jealous god here, it is because a particularistic notion of God still prevails. Yahweh is the one and only God of Israel indeed, but that does not mean that other divine or celestial powers do not exist beside him in the minds of those people:

> They then sent envoys to the king of Edom asking him to grant them passage through his country, but the king of Edom would not hear of it. They sent also to the king of Moab. . . . The Lord the God of Israel drove out the Amorites for the benefit of his people Israel. And do you now propose to take their place? It is for you to possess whatever Kemosh your god gives you; and all that the Lord our God gave us as we advanced is ours (Judg. 11:17–24).

Hence the covenant is grounded on mutual fidelity. And Israel's task is the fulfillment of the moral law: i.e., worship of the one God and social justice. That is how they conceive the decalogue which relates to that particular epoch:

> Moses summoned all Israel and said to them: Listen, O Israel, to the statutes and the laws which I proclaim in your hearing today. Learn them and be careful to observe them. The Lord our God made a covenant with us at Horeb. It was not with our forefathers that the Lord made this covenant, but with us, all of us who are alive and are here this day. The Lord spoke with you face to face on the mountain out of the fire. I stood between the Lord and you at that time to report the words of the Lord; for you were afraid of the fire and did not go up the mountain, and the Lord said:
>
> I am the Lord your God who brought you out of Egypt, out of the land of slavery.
> You shall have no other god to set against me. . .
> Honour your father and your mother, as the Lord your God commanded you, so that you may live long, and that it may be well with you in the land which the Lord your God is giving you.
> You shall not commit murder.
> You shall not commit adultery.
> You shall not steal.
> You shall not give false evidence against your neighbour.
> You shall not covet your neighbour's wife; you shall not set your heart on your neighbour's house, his land, his slave, his slave-girl, his ox, his ass, or on anything that belongs to him (Deut. 5:1–7, 16–21).

Yahweh's role as a participant in this covenant is to concern himself with the historical success of his faithful people:

> Be strong, be resolute; it is you who are to put this people in possession of the land which I swore to give to their fathers. Only be strong and resolute; observe diligently all the law which my servant Moses has given you. You must not turn from it to right or left, if you would prosper wherever you go. This book of the law must ever be on your lips; you must keep it in mind day and night so that you may diligently observe all that is written in it. Then you will prosper and be successful in all that you do. This is my

command: be strong, be resolute; do not be fearful or dismayed, for the Lord your God is with you wherever you go (Josh. 1:6–9).

This fidelity is engraved on the heart of Yahweh, as it were, even when the Israelites prove to be faithless:

"Go and cry for help to the gods you have chosen, and let them save you in the day of your distress." But the Israelites said to the Lord, "We have sinned. Deal with us as thou wilt; only save us this day, we implore thee." They banished the foreign gods and worshipped the Lord; and he could endure no longer to see the plight of Israel (Judg. 10:14–16).

Thus the image of matrimonial union is used to depict Yahweh restoring ties of fidelity each time that his spouse, Israel, proves to be unfaithful:

I will ravage the vines and the fig-trees, which she says are the fee with which her lovers have hired her, and turn them into jungle where wild beasts shall feed. I will put a stop to her merrymaking, her pilgrimages and new moons, her sabbaths and festivals. I will punish her for the holy days when she burnt sacrifices to the Baalim, when she decked herself with earrings and necklaces, ran after her lovers and forgot me. This is the very word of the Lord. But now listen, I will woo her, I will go with her into the wilderness and comfort her; there I will restore her vineyards, turning the Vale of Trouble into the Gate of Hope, and there she will answer as in her youth, when she came up out of Egypt. On that day she shall call me "My husband" and shall no more call me "My Baal"; and I will wipe from her lips the very names of the Baalim; never again shall their names be heard. . . . Then I will make a covenant on behalf of Israel with the wild beasts, the birds of the air, and the things that creep on the earth, and I will break bow and sword and weapon of war and sweep them off the earth, so that all living creatures may lie down without fear (Hos. 2:12–18).

So we can see that before the idea of God's universality (i.e., of monotheism) had been purified. Yahweh's claims to universality are dependent on the success of his one and only people:

Joshua said, "Alas, O Lord God, why didst thou bring this people across the Jordan only to hand us over to the Amorites to be destroyed? If only we had we had been content to settle on the other side of the Jordan! I beseech thee, O Lord; what can I say, now that Israel has been routed by the enemy? When the Canaanites and all the natives of the country hear of this, they will come swarming around us and wipe us off the face of the earth. What wilt thou do then for the honour of thy great name?" (Josh. 7:7–9).

So Israel is the sole collaborator of Yahweh in history. And this signifies several things:

I. **History is susceptible of interpretation.** When something shows up that appears to go beyond the normal course of events, some intention of Yahweh must be at work. The Philistines operate on this hypothesis when they have captured the Ark and are suffering misfortunes:

When the Ark of the Lord had been in their territory for seven months, the Philistines summoned the priests and soothsayers and asked, "What shall we do with the Ark of the Lord? Tell us how we ought to send it back to its own place." They answered . . . "Why should you be stubborn like Pharoah and the Egyptians? Remember how this god made sport of them until they let Israel go . . . Then take the Ark of the Lord . . . and let it go where it will. Watch it: if it goes up towards its own territory to Beth-shemesh, then it is the Lord who has done us this great injury; but if not, then we shall know that his hand has not touched us, but we have been the victims of chance" (1 Sam. 6:1–9).

Everything falls under this interpretation, even the abnormal stubbornness of Yahweh's adversaries:

It was the Lord's purpose that they should offer an obstinate resistance to the Israelites in battle, and that they should be annihilated without mercy and utterly destroyed, as the Lord had commanded Moses (Josh. 11:20).

"If a man sins against another man, God will intervene; but if a man sins against the Lord, who can intercede for him?" For all this, they did not listen to their father's rebuke, for the Lord meant that they should die (1 Sam. 2:25).

The same event (e.g., occupation of the promised land) is susceptible of radically opposed interpretations, depending on whether it is seen as a victory or a partial defeat:

Thus the Lord gave Israel all the land which he had sworn to give to their forefathers; they occupied it and settled in it. The Lord gave them security on every side as he had sworn to their forefathers. Of all their enemies not a man could withstand them; the Lord delivered all their enemies into their hands. Not a word of the Lord's promises went unfulfilled; they all came true (Josh. 21:43–45).

The angel of the Lord came up from Gilgal to Bokim and said, "I brought you up out of Egypt and into the country which I vowed I would give to your forefathers. I said, I will never break my covenant with you, and you in turn must make no covenant with the inhabitants of the country; you must pull down their altars. But you did not obey me, and look what you have done! So I said, I will not drive them out before you; they will decoy you, and their gods will shut you fast in the trap." . . . They gave up none of their evil practices and their wilful ways. And the Lord was angry with Israel and said, "This nation has broken the covenant which I laid upon their forefathers and has not obeyed me, and now, of all the nations which Joshua left at his death, I will not drive out to make room for them one single man. By their means I will test Israel, to see whether or not they will keep strictly to the way of the Lord as their forefathers did." So the Lord left those nations alone and made no haste to drive them out or give them into Joshua's hands (Judg. 2:1–3, 19–23).

2. This interpretation of history is based on the fact that Yahweh is making use of Israel to conquer his enemies and thus establish

his glory. Thus Israel has both a divine right and a divine duty to conquer and even to exterminate those nations that put up real resistance to this divine plan:

> When the Lord your God brings you into the land which you are entering to occupy and drives out many nations before you—Hittites, Girgashites, Amorites, Canaanites, Perizzites, Hivites, and Jebusites, seven nations more numerous and powerful than you—when the Lord your God delivers them into your power and you defeat them, you must put them to death. You must not make a treaty with them or spare them. You must not intermarry with them, neither giving your daughters to their sons nor taking their daughters for your sons; if you do, they will draw your sons away from the Lord and make them worship other gods. Then the Lord will be angry with you and will quickly destroy you . . . for you are a people holy to the Lord your God; the Lord your God chose you out of all nations on earth to be his special possession. . . . You shall devour all the nations which the Lord your God is giving over to you. Spare none of them, and do not worship their gods; that is the snare which awaits you (Dent. 7:1–4, 6, 16).

3. In the eyes of the prophets the fundamental sin against the covenant, so conceived, is to forget that Israel's duty is to be morally faithful to Yahweh while Yahweh's role is to concern himself with Israel's historical success. To work for the latter goal with purely human means is to forget the divine import of history:

> On that day you looked to the weapons stored in the House of the Forest; you filled all the many pools in the City of David, collecting water from the Lower Pool. Then you surveyed the houses in Jerusalem, tearing some down to make the wall inaccessible, and between the two walls you made a cistern for the Waters of the Old Pool; but you did not look to the Maker of it all or consider him who fashioned it long ago. On that day the Lord, the Lord of Hosts, called for weeping and beating the breast, for shaving the head and putting on sackcloth; but instead there was joy and merry-making, slaughtering of cattle and killing of sheep, eating of meat and drinking of wine, as you thought, Let us eat and drink; for tomorrow we die. The Lord of Hosts has revealed himself to me; in my hearing he swore: Your wickedness shall never be purged until you die. This is the word of the Lord, the Lord of Hosts (Isa. 22:9–14).

> Foreigners fed on his strength, but he was unaware; even his grey hairs turned white, but he was unaware. So Israel's arrogance cries out against them; but they do not return to the Lord their God nor seek him, in spite of it all. Ephraim is a silly senseless pigeon, now calling upon Egypt, now turning to Assyria for help (Hos. 7:9–11).

To sum up, Yahweh manifests himself as a provident force on Israel's side. But that presumes moral conduct of the right sort on the part of the whole nation and its individual members. Thus history takes on meaning, but as yet the interest and involvement of God in history is conceived along narrow lines. It is too readily identified with the interests of Israel.

III God as Transcendent Creator

This whole pattern confronts a crisis when the nation is exiled to Babylon, a great empire ruled by different monarchs and deities. Real consolation—that is, real hope of liberation—can only come from a deepened idea of Yahweh. Deutero-Isaiah stresses four attributes of Yahweh:

1. He is the one and only creator of everything that exists:

Thus says the Lord, your ransomer, who fashioned you from birth: I am the Lord who made all things, by myself I stretched out the skies, alone hammered out the floor of the earth. I frustrate false prophets and their signs and make fools of diviners; I reverse what wise men say and make nonsense of their wisdom. I make my servants' prophecies come true and give effect to my messengers' designs. I say of Jerusalem, "She shall be inhabited once more," and of the cities of Judah, "They shall be rebuilt; all their ruins I will restore." I say to the deep waters, "Be dried up; I will make your streams run dry." I say to Cyrus, "You shall be my shepherd to carry out all my purpose, so that Jerusalem may be rebuilt and the foundations of the temple may be laid" (Isa. 44:24–28).

2. He is the one and only God of the universe:

Thus says the Lord, Israel's King, the Lord of Hosts, his ransomer: I am the first and I am the last, and there is no god but me. Who is like me? Let him stand up, let him declare himself and speak and show me his evidence, let him announce beforehand things to come, let him declare what is yet to happen. Take heart, do not be afraid. Did I not foretell this long ago? I declared it, and you are my witnesses. Is there any god beside me, or any creator, even one that I do not know? (Isa. 44:6–8).

3. The things that are compared or set up in opposition to him are mere images fabricated by man:

The woodworker draws his line taut and marks out a figure with a scriber; he planes the wood and measures it with callipers, and he carves it to the shape of a man comely as the human form, to be set up presently in a house. A man plants a cedar and the rain makes it grow, so that later on he will have cedars to cut down; or he chooses an ilex or an oak to raise a stout tree for himself in the forest. It becomes fuel for his fire: some of it he takes and warms himself, some he kindles and bakes bread on it, and some he makes into a god and prostrates himself, shaping it into an idol and bowing down before it. The one half of it he burns in the fire and on this he roasts meat, so that he may eat his roast and be satisfied; he also warms himself at it and he says, "Good! I can feel the heat, I am growing warm." Then what is left of the wood he makes into a god by carving it into shape; he bows down to it and prostrates himself and prays to it, saying, "Save me; for thou art my God" (Isa. 44:13–17).

4. God the creator is also providence in its totality:

I am the Lord, there is no other; there is no god beside me. I will strenghten you though you have not known me, so that men from the rising and the setting sun may know that there is none but I: I am the Lord, there is no other; I make the light, I create the darkness, author alike of prosperity and trouble. I, the Lord, do all these things (Isa. 45:5–7).

In the face of a God so conceived, religion moves from being a relationship between the Israelite and the god of his nation to being every creature's ("all flesh" in the language of the Bible) relationship of adoration to the Creator-God who transcends human power, human righteousness, and human comprehension:

> For, as the new heavens and the earth which I am making shall endure in my sight, says the Lord, so shall your race and your name endure; and month by month at the new moon, week by week on the sabbath, all mankind (i.e., "all flesh") shall come to bow down before me, says the Lord; and they shall come out and see the dead bodies of those who have rebelled against me; their worm shall not die nor their fire be quenched, and they shall be abhorred by all mankind ("all flesh") (Isa. 66:22–24).

Thus the destiny of Israel is viewed in terms of a new universality which she has among the nations of the earth. This is the gist of the following text, which is probably a text from Deutero-Isaiah worked into the text of the original Isaiah:

> The Lord will make himself known to the Egyptians; on that day they shall acknowledge the Lord and do him service with sacrifice and grain-offering, make vows to him and pay them. The Lord will strike down Egypt, healing as he strikes; then they will turn back to him and he will hear their prayers and heal them. When that day comes there shall be a highway between Egypt and Assyria; Assyrians shall come to Egypt and Egyptians to Assyria; then Egyptians shall worship with Assyrians. When that day comes Israel shall rank with Egypt and Assyria, those three, and shall be a blessing in the centre of the world. So the Lord of Hosts will bless them: A blessing be upon Egypt my people, upon Assyria the work of my hands, and upon Israel my possession (Isa. 19:21–25).

Israel, to be sure, will continue to have a privileged destiny. But rather than seeing it as a two-sided election and a bilateral contract, the writers of this era tend to see it as pure gratuitousness on Yahweh's part. So we find variations in Hosea's classic image of Yahweh and Israel as mutual, jealous lovers:

> Can a woman forget the infant at her breast, or a loving mother the child of her womb? Even these forget, yet I will not forget you. Your walls are always before my eyes, I have engraved them on the palms of my hands (Isa. 49:15–16).

The fact is that a bilateral sort of contract could exist only if the creature could balance off his side of the scale with his moral righteousness and goodness. But this he cannot do. In the face of his Maker, the creature is always impure and sinful:

> Plunderers have swarmed across the high bare places in the wilderness, a sword of the Lord devouring the land from end to end; no creature can find peace (Jer. 12:12).

Gradually, then, a crisis develops around the older idea of the covenant whereby the Israelites thought they could comprehend the meaning

of historical events. In a previous epoch Isaiah presents the older notion
in terms of the individual:

> Happy the righteous man! all goes well with him, for such men enjoy the
> fruit of their actions. Woe betide the wicked! with him all goes ill, for he
> reaps the reward that he has earned (Isa. 3:10–11).

The same sentiment finds expression in Psalm 1:

> Happy is the man who does not take the wicked for his guide nor walk the road
> that sinners tread nor take his seat among the scornful; the law of the Lord is
> his delight, the law his meditation night and day. He is like a tree planted be-
> side a watercourse, which yields its fruit in season and its leaf never withers;
> in all that he does he prospers (Ps. 1:1–3).

The fulfillment of this equation between moral conduct and success
is a proof of God's presence within the events of history:

> And men shall say, "There is after all a reward for the righteous; after
> all, there is a God that judges on earth" (Ps. 58:12).

But reality seems to belie this optimism. In the following period, the
period of Hellenic conquest, we get a clear example that fidelity to
Yahweh is not associated with success:

> At that time many who wanted to maintain their religion and law went
> down to the wilds to live there. They took their sons, their wives, and their
> cattle with them, for their miseries were more than they could bear. . . .A
> large body of men quickly after them, came up with them, and occupied
> positions opposite. . They prepared to attack them on the sabbath. . . Without
> more ado the attack was launched; but the Israelites did nothing in reply;
> they neither hurled stones, nor barricaded their caves . . . So they were
> attacked and massacred on the sabbath, men, women, and children, up to
> a thousand in all, and their cattle with them (1 Macc. 2:29–38).

It is the Book of Job that draws the ultimate conclusions from such
experiences, where history seems to go beyond the religious interpretation one would like to make of it. Job is a just man who suffers misfortune
and complains about it. His friends, hearkening back to the older notion,
presume that these great sufferings must be the consequence of serious
sins. In the midst of his dialogue with them and his protestations of
righteousness, Job exclaims:

> But it is all one; therefore I say,
> "He destroys blameless and wicked alike."
> When a sudden flood brings death, he
> mocks the plight of the innocent (Job 9:22–23).

When God intervenes at the end of the book, he affirms Job's thesis
that his sufferings have no relation to his conduct. But he reproves
him for trying to interpret the sense of events. He alone, the Creator,
is in charge:

> Then the Lord answered Job out of the tempest: Who is this whose ignorant
> words cloud my design in darkness? Brace yourself and stand up like a

man; I will ask questions, and you shall answer. Where were you when I laid the earth's foundations? Tell me, if you know and understand. Who settled its dimensions? Surely you should know (Job 38:1–5).

To sum up, the God who appeared so close to human history in a prior epoch now manifests his full transcendence—not only in creation, of which he is the sole author, but also in the providence with which he guides historical events. The creature now discovers God's universality; but at the same time the creature loses the comprehension of historical events it believed it had. That which belongs to history is separated from that which belongs to religion. Religion is man's response of adoration and selfless moral conduct to the transcendent God.

IV God as Legislator and Moral Judge

At this point God, who once seemed so close to human history and man, has moved away from it and cut the tie between the notions of moral rectitude and success in life. He ways are now mysterious. Hellenic influence will step in at this point to give impetus to a new approach to man by God. Instead of attributing success or failure in history to Yahweh, people will now come to realize that God is the creator of only the good that exists in the universe. This is the new point of departure:

For God did not make death, and takes no pleasure in the destruction of any living thing; he created all things that they might have being. The creative forces of the world make for life; there is no deadly poison in them. Death is not king on earth, for justice is immortal (Wis. 1:13–14).

Thus things are good in themselves and destined for life. Sorrow, evil, and death have been introduced into creation by man's bad use of them (under the prompting of the evil spirit):

Do not stray from the path of life and so court death; do not draw disaster on yourselves by your own actions (Wis. 1:12).

Let us now go one step further. The order created by God for life should be superior to the sorrow and death created by man. What is done within the framework of God's order should conquer death. Since it comes from God, "justice is immortal" (Wis. 1:15).

But man cannot experience or prove this. He must play out his life for or against justice, for or against the victory of death. In terms of this radical wager, the wicked devote their lives to the triumph of death over justice and righteousness:

But godless men by their words and deeds have asked death for his company. Thinking him their friend, they have made a pact with him because they are fit members of his party; and so they have wasted away (Wis. 1:15–16).

They structure their lives accordingly:

They said to themselves in their deluded way: "Our life is short and full of trouble, and when a man comes to his end there is no remedy; no man was ever known to return from the grave. By mere chance were we born, and afterwards we shall be as though we had never been, for the breath in our nostrils is but a wisp of smoke; our reason is a mere spark kept alive by the beating of our hearts, and when that goes out, our body will turn to ashes and the breath of our life disperse like empty air. Our names will be forgotten with the passing of time, and no one will remember anything we did. Our life will blow over like the last vestige of a cloud; and as a mist is chased away by the sun's rays and overborne by its heat, so will it too be dispersed. A passing shadow—such is our life, and there is no postponement of our end; man's fate is sealed, and none returns. Come then, let us enjoy the good things while we can, and make full use of the creation, with all the eagerness of youth. Let us have costly wines and perfumes to our heart's content, and let no flower of spring escape us. Let us crown ourselves with rosebuds before they can wither. Let none of us miss his share of the good things that are ours; who cares what traces our revelry leaves behind? This is the life for us; it is our birthright. Down with the poor and honest man! Let us tread him under foot; let us show no mercy to the widow and no reverence to the grey hairs of old age. For us let might be right! Weakness is proved to be good for nothing" (Wis. 2:1–11).

The wicked man specializes, so to speak, in temporal success no matter what the price may be in moral terms. The just man, by contrast, stakes his life on the other end of the wager:

But the souls of the just are in God's hands, and torment shall not touch them. In the eyes of foolish men they seemed to be dead; their departure was reckoned as defeat, and their going from us as disaster. But they are at peace, for though in the sight of men they may be punished, they have a sure hope of immortality; and after a little chastisement they will receive great blessings, because God has tested them and found them worthy to be his (Wis. 3:1–5).

The life of the just man consists in considering temporal values and realities as a test and patiently putting up with the detachment that moral behavior demands. But there will be a judgment after death:

Then the just man shall take his stand, full of assurance, to confront those who oppressed him and made light of all his sufferings; at the sight of him there will be terror and confusion, and they will be beside themselves to see him so unexpectedly safe home. Filled with remorse, groaning and gasping for breath, they will say among themselves: "Was not this the man who was once our butt, a target for our contempt? Fools that we were, we held his way of life to be madness and his end dishonourable. To think that he is now counted one of the sons of God and assigned a place of his own among God's people! How far we strayed from the road of truth! The lamp of justice never gave us light, the sun never rose upon us" (Wis. 5:1–7).

Thus each person will win the object of his wager. All value will be lost to the wicked man, while the just man will win the full measure of justice and life which he purchased through his sufferings:

"What good has our pride done us? What can we show for all our wealth and arrogance? All those things have passed by like a shadow, like a messenger galloping by; like a ship that runs through the surging sea, and when she has passed, not a trace is to be found, no track of her keel among the waves; or as when a bird flies through the air, there is no sign of her passing, but with the stroke of her pinions she lashes the insubstantial breeze and parts it with the whirr and the rush of her beating wings, and so she passes through it, and thereafter it bears no mark of her assault; or as when an arrow is shot at a target, the air is parted and instantly closes up again and no one can tell where it passed through. So we too ceased to be, as soon as we were born; we left no token of virtue behind, and in our wickedness we frittered our lives away."

But the just live for ever; their reward is in the Lord's keeping, and the Most High has them in his care. Therefore royal splendour shall be theirs, and a fair diadem from the Lord himself. He will protect them with his right hand and shield them with his arm (Wis. 5:8–16).

To sum up: after manifesting his infinite transcendence, God sheds light on man's existence and liberty here. He shows that man, by carrying out a law that is in things, can go beyond death and arrive at an existence where moral virtue and success will at last coincide. Man's time here shows up as a time of testing and hope, a time when man's liberty of choice plays out its game.

Bedazzled by the proximity of this stage to the message and even the language of Jesus, we frequently forget that this is not the "good news" or Christianity. It is the last stretch of road which makes clear and comprehensible what we have tried to trace out in the chapters of this volume: i.e., the Christian idea of God.

Springboard Questions

Here we should like to repeat what we said in the first volume of this series. There we noted that we found it absolutely necessary to prepare questions for the discussion periods which were an integral part of our seminars. Only in this way were the participants able to engage in probing discussions that took a direct look at accustomed images and concepts.

The questions were not meant to encourage passivity on the part of the participants. Their purpose was not to get the participants merely to "recall" or "review" what had been said in lectures or texts. They were meant to broaden the outlook of the participants by getting them to think out the logic of what they had heard in terms of real-life situations and problems. In short, they were meant to produce a confrontation between real life and what the participants beleived they knew.

We felt that our readers might like to see the type of question we proposed and the rationale behind it. So here we offer some of the questions we proposed in connection with each chapter topic, together with an explanation accounting for our choice of these questions.

Chapter One

QUESTIONS

We are wont to say that the central aim of Christian living is to achieve a personal relationship with Christ. On the other hand, Saint Augustine tells us that our Lord does not want to hold us back but to see us move ahead. Do you see an opposition between these two notions? If no, then how do they tie together? If yes, then what are the consequences of the first position?

EXPLANATION

The aim here is to point toward an authentic relationship with Christ. Such a relationship is not one of emotion and fantasy directed toward the past of the gospel. It consists in becoming sensitively aware of the Spirit and of the capacity for creativity that he develops in us in the face of unforeseen historical circumstances.

QUESTIONS

Do you think that forgetting the activity of Christ's Spirit can have, or even does have, important consequences in the life of the Church and in the political commitment of Christians? What are these consequences?

EXPLANATION

This is a more direct way of asking the first question above, emphasizing the social and ecclesial aspect. It is meant to help people detect noncreative tendencies that seek security in the past and in familiar responses. The reference to political commitment may help people to see how fear of the unknown and reliance on readymade answers weigh heavily upon the Christian mind and stifle inspired response to politics. It thus paves the way for the discussion in Chapter IV.

QUESTION

What is the importance today of God's revelation in the Old Testament?

EXPLANATION

This question is a bit more subtle than the previous ones, but it is important at a time when reading of the Bible is spreading among all Christians. If what we said in the text of the chapter is true and certain, then every individaul and every generation must repeat the process of being educated to confront history. The Christian message about the history of salvation (or the salvation of history—CLARIFICATION II) is only comprehensible in the light of its previous stages. These stages cannot be omitted in educating people to the faith, no matter how obvious they may sometimes seem to someone who has a fair understanding of the specific and distinctive note of the Christian message.

Chapter Two

QUESTION

Could you specify concretely why we say that man is made in the image and likeness of God?

EXPLANATION

This question alludes obviously to the social aspect as something that is not accidental but rather goes to make up the very essence of God and man. It thus leads the respondent to spell out a fundamental element of the Christian conception of man, one which has important consequences (cf. GS 12, 24, 33). In the typical responses to this question, people tend to place the likeness in qualities that are part of God's nature: intellect, will, etc. But in all these areas one cannot point out a likeness without being forced to affirm an even greater difference.

QUESTION

Is democracy the type of society (or social authority) that is best related to the Christian idea of God?

EXPLANATION

The question is meant to suggest the ever-growing complexity involved in fashioning a society where creative possibilities are afforded to all men. It is centered around the variable content of the word "democracy," and it should lead the respondent to spell out all the dimensions that the reality should have—at least in theory. This will keep people from automatically associating a shibboleth with the Christian message.

QUESTION

In terms of the present American scene what human factor, or characteristic, or attitude would allow for a fuller proclamation of the Christian God?

EXPLANATION

This question spells out the previous question in more concrete detail. And it summons the respondent to think for himself. Our text concentrates on the Latin American scene, affording a concrete example of such analysis. The Medellín Conference, for example, highlighted the fact that a liberator-God can only be grasped within a real process of liberation. This, in turn, calls for a process of *conscientization* whereby man ceases to be a mere object and slowly becomes an active subject of his own society and his own history. The North American reader must try to explore his own reality in terms of similarities and differences to the Latin American scene.

Chapter Three

QUESTIONS

Atheists "are sometimes men of great breadth of mind, impatient with the mediocrity and self-seeking that infect so much of modern society." What ideology lies behind this statement? Do you agree or disagree with it? Why?

EXPLANATION

This is a statement which Paul VI made in his encyclical *Ecclesiam Suam* (n. 104). It can serve as a useful check to see whether the respondent has grasped the intimate connection between one type of bourgeois life and a falsified (hence unacceptable) conception of God. The reference to ideology is important because people often attribute such a statement to a Marxist or materialistic line of thought.

QUESTION

Does what we have considered in this chapter change the way we would ordinarily have tackled the problem of evil? In what way?

EXPLANATION

To clarify this question we can allude once again to the statement of Teilhard de Chardin cited in this chapter, particularly in CLARIFICATION IV. This point is whether we have managed to replace the older outlook ("Why does God will or permit this to happen?") with the conviction that evil is part of our own responsibility from which God cannot release us. The question will also tell whether we have moved from a distinction between moral evil (the product of human liberty) and physical pain and evil (proceeding from God's providence) to a conception in which all physical evil ends up as a moral responsibility.

QUESTION

What traits of (modern) "Modalism" do you find in the present-day life of the Church?

EXPLANATION

The thrust of the question is obvious. It seeks to extend our reflections in the chapter to every area of life: education, politics, attitudes toward authority, etc.

Chapter Four

QUESTIONS

It is possible to have fruitful dialogue between believers and nonbelievers so long as truths of faith do not enter the picture. When they do, however, the dialogue breaks off of necessity. Do you agree that this is what happens? Do you agree that this must happen?

EXPLANATION

These questions points toward the foundation on which a Christian bases and defends the solutions which he sees as most suitable for the problems raised by history. It suggests that the truths of faith are not automatically the bases for choosing a given solution. Thus they should not appear explicitly as the decisive factor in preferring one solution over another. Does that mean that this factor lies concealed in our choice? This further question brings another problem into the discussion: In what way is the language of faith to be applied to involvement in the world?

QUESTIONS

"Strange as it may seem, the Christian religion is essentially a lay, anticlerical religion" (R. Escarpit, *École Laïque, école du peuple*). This is a statement by a nonbeliever. Is it true, partially true, or false? If partially true, in what way is it true?

EXPLANATION

These questions go to the bottom of the previous question. Does the ecclesial community have a separate finality of its own? If no, whence come the solutions tht Christians find for man's problems? From the hierarchy (i.e., the clerical sector)? Do the options made by Christians have some line of verifiction (in their dialogue with others) other than that enjoyed by the arguments which people in general (Gr. *laos;* adj. *laika;* whence our word "lay") use?

QUESTION

What traces of (modern) Arianism do you find in the present-day life of the Church?

EXPLANATION

Like the third question of Chapter III, this question seeks to stimulate a rapid survey of "a-historical" religious tendencies in the life of the Church: e.g., the educational and political realms, spiritual life, liturgy, magisterium, etc.